roast

a very British cookbook

Marcus Verberne

roast

a very British cookbook

A.

First published in Great Britain
in 2013 by Absolute Press,
an imprint of
Bloomsbury Publishing Plc

Absolute Press
Scarborough House
29 James Street West
Bath BA1 2BT
Phone 44 (0) 1225 316013
Fax 44 (0) 1225 445836
E-mail info@absolutepress.co.uk
Website www.absolutepress.co.uk

Publisher
Jon Croft
Commissioning Editor
Meg Avent
Art Director
Matt Inwood
Project Editor
Alice Gibbs
Editor
Imogen Fortes
Photographer
Lara Holmes
Props Styling
Matt Inwood and Lara Holmes
Food Styling
Marcus Verberne
Indexer
Zoe Ross

A catalogue record of this book is available
from the British Library

ISBN: 9781408193464

Printed in China.

A note about the text
This book was set using Century. The first
Century typeface was cut in 1894. In 1975
an updated family of Century typefaces
was designed by Tony Stan for ITC.

———————————————————

Bloomsbury Publishing Plc
50 Bedford Square, London WC1B 3DP
www.bloomsbury.com

contents

Introduction by Iqbal Wahhab OBE Founder, Roast

British food. Difficult, isn't it? When I was embarking upon 'Project Roast', I told one of my teenage nephews that I was going to create a British restaurant and he asked whether this would involve serving chicken tikka masala, my most detested dish. After all, what's more British than that?

It was 2003, where conventional wisdom would more naturally place me – in The Cinnamon Club – when I first started thinking what today sounds slightly absurd. That Britain needed a first-class British restaurant.

Let me give you a simple challenge: if you were in Paris, might you ask your hotel concierge to recommend a decent French restaurant in the city; or in New York, a good American place you might visit? Now imagine you are a visitor to London and you ask your concierge to get you a table in one of London's best restaurants. On his Rolodex he'll probably have: The Square (French), Zuma (Japanese), Hakkasan (Chinese) and Benares (Indian). He would get you into one of these and get himself a hefty tip when you returned. Yet a decade ago, he wouldn't have risked his reward by suggesting a British restaurant – primarily on the grounds there were hardly any to speak of, let alone any worth recommending.

The rediscovery of our love of British food has many complex layers but let me explain my own journey into it. My family arrived in Britain in 1964 from what was then East Pakistan, now Bangladesh. I was an eight-month-old baby; my brother was five and my sister was seven. The rest of my family had only ever eaten Bengali food. As a child I didn't take to spice in the way my family had done (they had had no choice), so strange as it sounds, as a child growing up in south London I really looked forward to school dinners to as an alternative to what was served at home. Mum used to have to make separate meals for me but as she had a busy day job, this would involve compromises. While the rest of family ate rice and fish curry, I would have rice and fish fingers. There was a part of our freezer that was just for me – Bird's Eye beef burgers and chips being a staple. However, as Mum's career took off (she was the first non-Christian head of a Church of England school), it was too much to expect her to make a separate meal for me, so at the age of 11 I made my first shepherd's pie.

As a teenager often in trouble (I ran a small but profitable gang in south London), much of my time was spent away from home in caffs, pie and mash shops, then Wimpy outlets, and finally pubs. I suppose part of my rebellion towards my family involved rebellion to their food. This was the age of assimilation – the precursor to integration and multiculturalism. In those days social policy wonks decreed that what was for the best was for everyone to adopt British ways. My parents were encouraged only to speak English to me, whereas we now know that multilingual children fare much better. To this day my spoken Bengali is laughable and my read- and writeable Bengali non-existent. That remains a gap in my cultural identity – not being entirely English and not being much cop as a Bangladeshi either. The overall umbrella of Britishness forgives a lot.

This desert which I inhabited had many unpredictable food consequences. At the age of 15 I became a curry convert and with all the zealotry that a convert is equipped with, every Saturday I would make a blisteringly hot mutton or oxtail curry for the family as a sort of penance for my weekday misdemeanours. A good curry forgives a lot too.

During the 1970s huge social changes were taking place, often driven by food. The advent of McDonalds, Kentucky Fried Chicken and the Chinese take-away, soon followed by the Indian and the pizza joints, meant that kids were eating away from home for the first time and in due course families that weren't eating together weren't staying together. In the context of the exotic allure of food from other countries, traditional British offerings represented the past – bygone days, brilliantly captured by the satirical TV show Spitting Image with its image of dull Prime Minister John Major proving just how dull he was by portraying him in grey, eating grey chips and peas. That pretty much was a kiss of death for British food for quite a while.

Let's fast-forward to 1994: my food PR company and one my clients, Cobra beer, launched the first ever trade magazine for Indian restaurants, called Tandoori. As the Sun sagely put it at the time, Britain had become jalfrezi crazy and the curry industry was booming. In order to stoke this media frenzy, I initiated a number of what I later called 'curry myths' and the mischief-maker in me still gets a thrill when some of them get quoted back to me as gospel truth. I issued a press release to launch the magazine with the assertion that chicken tikka masala was now more popular than roast beef. This was an unverifiable claim but journalists being inherently lazy wanted to believe it to get their story in so didn't bother to check its veracity and it is now widely believed to be true.

While I had made this up to prove the strength of the curry industry, it was taken in a way I had never expected. In a nutshell, the overwhelming response was that this was a good thing because British food was so dull. In spite of Spitting Image and the fact that my English school and university friends had been to more Indian restaurants than I had, I was genuinely taken aback to find Britain was so disparaging of its own food. I didn't challenge this at the time – that would have been antithetical to my then commercial cause – but I recalled my mother's recollection of my obsession with Cow & Gate baby food, my shepherd's pie, jam roly poly at school, my brother in law's beef stew and dumplings and the beloved chippie and wondered what on earth they were saying. After a day's work in the offices at Tandoori, I would often go home to roast a chicken and invite friends round, who barely concealed their disappointment that they weren't having curry.

Having gone on to create The Cinnamon Club, where with the exceptionally talented chef Vivek Singh, we challenged conventional curry combinations and significantly raised the bar for Indian food, lifting it away from the high street experience to that of a world class cuisine, these old and unresolved dilemmas came back to mind. Having achieved what I wanted for Indian cuisine, my thoughts returned to why the British public was not celebrating what was on its own doorstep in the way the French, the Indians, the Americans and the Italians did with their culinary heritages. It wasn't always so, I found out. Centuries ago the royal courts of Europe played the ultimate sophistication card by hiring British chefs. Yet as time and fads wore on, the opposite became the case. So much so that in 2005, just before we launched Roast, the then French President, Jacques Chirac, threw us a challenge by saying to Russian and German leaders of Britain: 'One cannot trust people whose cuisine is so bad.' This flew in the face of Tony Blair's growing vision of Cool Britannia, from David Beckham, through to Tracey Emin and Oasis. Blair made a point of surrounding himself at Number 10 with these cultural icons, though sadly never saw fit to extricate himself from Italian and French restaurants and their chefs. He famously took President Clinton to a French restaurant on the Thames and brokered his power deal with Gordon Brown in an Italian restaurant in Islington.

The invitation I issued to Chirac to come and dine at Roast when it opened so that he could re-configure his warped thinking about British food should really have come from Number 10 where they should have served him beef Wellington.

I started telling people about my plans to open Roast. There was an almost collective gasp of dismay that I hadn't chosen to do the sensible thing and open more Cinnamon Clubs. This was soon followed by the question: 'British food – why?' This in turn was followed by the most challenging one, one that would remain for years the most common, evoking many different reactions from different quarters: 'Why you?' It's a subject I shall return to later.

Ever since Auguste Escoffier arrived at The Ritz at the end of the nineteenth century, Britain has been in the grip of French cuisine as its highest, most sophisticated form. The very vocabulary we use for food is French – cuisine, chef, sous-chef, sous-vide and so on. Until about a decade ago, the Michelin Guide could have been more accurately called the 'Michelin Guide to French Restaurants'. Britain's biggest kitchen talents, such as Marco Pierre White and Gordon Ramsay, earned their deserved acclaim not by cooking their own food but by cooking French food as well as (if not better than) their French counterparts. And any British chef showing talent would be encouraged to follow the same path.

So as I went about starting to build my second dream restaurant, I encountered an unexpected problem – that British chefs don't want to or often even know how to cook British food. Part of this was driven by the subliminal thought that Britain was no longer ruler of the waves but more directly by the belief that in order to gain success and fame, their cooking had to be formed around a more European template – by how well they could copy the French and the Italians or, for a nightmare-ish phase in London dining, how to fuse different national cuisines.

So, just as I had done with The Cinnamon Club, where I had to go to India to sell the idea of raising a new bar for Indian dining to chefs rather than chefs having to sell their skills to me, I was similarly challenged on my home turf to find chefs capable and willing to cook their own national dishes proudly and properly. After months of discussions, I finally persuaded the ebullient Lawrence Keogh to join the team. Lawrence was the head chef of a fashionable West End restaurant and was in no rush to change ship but we had a mutual friend who brokered our discussions and eventually I persuaded him to take the plunge – to take the risk of doing something as bold as offer the London diner traditional British food. And Lawrence did know how to cook it. Cooking was in his blood. As a child he would often assist his mother, who was a domestic cook for an aristocratic family in St James's. Lawrence knew British food inside out from his time working at The Goring hotel near Buckingham Palace; he just wasn't sure it was the right career move for him. I took him to meet Vivek at The Cinnamon Club who had had similar concerns regarding his own career, only in his case it had also meant leaving India. Vivek suggested Lawrence should trust me and he chose to.

The challenge of finding the right location for this mission was one that was relatively easily resolved. Borough Market, just south of London Bridge, had officially been running for 250 years, when an act of Parliament enshrined that the area would only ever be used for the selling of food. Unofficially it had been a place for food vendors for centuries previously, but until the late 1980s, it had been considered a rough spot and was primarily a wholesale market for trade as opposed to a retail one for the public.

When the tragic onslaught of mad cow disease struck the UK in the 1980s, Britain watched with despair as millions of cattle were destroyed in an attempt to control the crisis and they suddenly became aware of the part we had played in bringing about this miserable outcome. If, as consumers, we hadn't demanded ever-cheaper food, supermarkets would not have placed such onerous demands on farmers to keep cutting their costs and they in turn would not have had to resort to feeding their cattle such filth as to eventually destroy them. Partly out of guilt from this realisation, as consumers we decided to re-configure our expectations from our food choices and scrutinise what we were buying and how it was produced far more carefully.

The act of Parliament that protected Borough Market also left its governance to groups of local residents approved by the local council. George Nicholson, a former Greater London Council (GLC) member who worked alongside Ken Livingstone, was the visionary chair of the trustees and he went around the country and encouraged food producers, fishermen and

farmers to come down to the market where they would find customers willing and able to pay the prices their premium produce demanded. Wild boar farmer Peter Gott, mutton specialist Andrew Sharp and fishermen Les Salisbury and Darren Brown, along with cheese expert Randolph Hodgson were among the early traders to take the punt and soon the market was flourishing, with thousands of people making the trek there on Fridays and Saturdays. Borough made the subtle transition from a farmers' market (more random and local in its offerings) to a recognisable food market. George convinced his fellow trustees that following on from the success of the shopping experience the market should also become a dining experience. Architect Ken Greig was appointed to come up with a suitably noteworthy scheme, a task he more than acquitted by finding a disused structure from another market. The Floral Hall in Covent Garden market had been a stunning construction but was ill suited to its purpose. It was largely a glass building held together by a magnificent iron base, which meant that flowers died from all the sunlight pouring in much more quickly than traders were able to sell them. The Covent Garden authorities had soon dismantled it and it was lying flat-packed in a cave in Wales where Greig discovered it and brought its imposing character back to life in Borough.

At the time, I had won a bid to place Roast in a new development ironically enough also in Covent Garden but was having continual battles with the landlords and so when I heard that Borough was inviting bids from restaurant operators for this iconic building, I pulled out of the first possible birthplace for Roast and pushed my efforts into what would undoubtedly be a much more exciting second one. Inevitably there was stiff competition for the space – both the market and the surrounding Southwark district generally had been transformed from no-go areas to fashionable ones. Luckily my proposal for a restaurant and bar celebrating the best of seasonal British produce and applying it to traditional British cooking, resonated more with George and his colleagues than the submissions made by far more successful restaurateurs than me.

Despite the usual panics and traumas that go with restaurant openings, Roast opened in October 2005 and we benefitted from wide media coverage, largely very positive (The Times called me a National Treasure!), but it still niggles at me that my ethnicity was brought into play by some. The sub-text to

some of the disparaging comments about Roast was that it was audacious of a person of Bangladeshi origin to claim to have given Britain back pride in its national dishes. Of course, my ethnicity and my mission caused bemused responses from many and I had anticipated this, but my Bangladeshi origins had never been referred to before. When I opened The Cinnamon Club, they had not been referenced and ironically it was only when creating a British restaurant that I became a Bangladeshi restaurateur. Our customers, unsurprisingly and refreshingly, couldn't care less whether I was from the Cotswolds or the Congo. What they cared about was getting a good meal, served well, in a unique environment. While we weren't without our fair share of mistakes – one being my decision to have a daily changing menu (aspiring restaurateurs reading this: don't do that!) – we really couldn't have been any way near as bad as were occasionally portrayed because, simply, we would not have 30 per cent of our diners being regulars. Steakhouses around Leicester Square make millions of pounds serving substandard food at inflated prices because they know that their tourist customers will not return and they do not need them to. Roast did and still does and we continue to work on that, so much so that from 120 seats we serve between 2500–3000 diners every week.

We took whatever positive lessons we could from the reviews and streamlined and honed our core culinary offering, developing consistency and desirability. We created an award-winning breakfast menu, which we serve to about 100 people a day. In time we became more assured, we grabbed and owned our space and the reviews became ever more positive. Our social media presence is huge and the customer is now the critic. And our customers were on the whole happy with us and helped spread a more positive message about us. We live in an age now where travel or dining website recommendations are as important to us as the Evening Standard. We use the success that we have been lucky enough to enjoy not just to reward ourselves but also to actively engage with the communities around us. That means more than giving to charity, which we do plenty of: we work with schools on healthy food education programmes, we offer work placements and jobs to ex-offenders as well as to the long-term unemployed and returning soldiers. We motivate and reward our team through an 'escalator principle' towards training; the escalator goes all the way to the top of the company and you can get on and off whenever you want. Programmes like these

have earned us the position as the first, and at the point of writing, the only independent restaurant in Britain to have a gold standard in the coveted Investor in People programme.

After five years of hard and loyal service to us, Lawrence moved on to become head chef at The Wolseley, soon rising to become their company's executive chef. It's a source of pride to me for a former head chef at Roast to do so well. Another source of pride for us was that during the five years following the launch of Roast, many others had seen the vast opportunities in adopting seasonal ingredients and traditional native cooking. Dozens of restaurants and smart food pubs have emerged in the light of the Borough market principle and head chefs from many of these establishments were quick to apply for Lawrence's position. I didn't have to interview many before I knew I had my man. Charming and thoughtful, Marcus Verberne began his interview by being asked if he had eaten at Roast recently and he said he had done so the night beforehand, so I enquired as to what he had eaten. We both agreed that the starter he had chosen was excellent but I said there was something not quite right with it and asked what he thought that was and instantly he said it lacked height and dimension – precisely as I had thought. Pretty much after that my mind was made up and the rest of the hour-long interview became more of a chat about food more generally. His provenance was good, having come to us as executive chef of the Brown's Hotel in Mayfair under the tutelage of the great Mark Hix.

Marcus had never formally trained as a chef. A New Zealander, as a young man looking to find a career, Marcus had moved to Wellington where he had bumped into an old school friend who was working in a wood-fired restaurant called The Beacon where they were looking for a dish washer. After his first night in that role, he knew that he was meant to be in kitchens. His head chef there Dean Clure soon took him under his wing and Marcus began working the grill and then the oven. After just over two years made it to sous-chef before moving to Melbourne where he worked in Italian restaurants. In 2001 he decided to come to London. Marcus joined Le Caprice and stayed there five years, leaving as sous-chef to spend time at The Ivy and J Sheekey. His original plan was to stay in London for two, perhaps three years and then return home, but that idea soon got put to the side as he relished his new culinary life here. After a brief foray as head chef of The White Hart Inn in a village in Suffolk called Nayland (near Colchester), where he enjoyed the foraging but missed the energy of the capital, he took up an offer to become the head chef of Mark Hix's restaurant at Brown's and soon rose to be executive chef of the whole hotel. Before offering him the position I naturally had to test whether his dishes matched his words so I took six of my fussiest foodie friends and our stalwart general manager, Sergei Gubars, to have lunch there. Not a single negative came from the table as we devoured as much of the menu as we could.

Marcus took over from Lawrence on New Year's Day 2012. He soon made the menu his own, adopting some of the Hix traditions, such as having a curry on the menu, which to this day I have to tell people was not my idea, but soon let go of the framework of thinking he'd established at his former employer. Roast's menus today retain the best parts of what Lawrence established and what Hix had taught Marcus but they indistinguishably have a Verberne signature. Each month, Sergei, Marcus and I go out visiting other restaurants not just to see what others are doing – a crucial exercise for any successful and busy restaurant – but also for us to take time off-site to talk about food more generally. Marcus engages the whole team with his enthusiasm. When he arranges foraging or farming trips for the staff, not only do chefs sign up, but so do our receptionists, waiters and bar tenders. His appetite for using unusual ingredients will work not just if the dishes taste good but if our serving team can convince diners to try them; they need to know not just what dogfish is, but also why we use it.

But the Roast experience is not just about food. Our bar team, led by Sebastien Guesdon, enthrals our customers with concoctions using seasonal produce as well as with exciting innovations such as pudding cocktails. Sergei doubles up as wine buyer and he collaborates closely with wine makers to make sure our list is constantly refreshed and relevant. Despite the shaky start, Roast has become a proud player in the London dining scene, constantly surprising our customers not just with food, drink and service but also with revolving art and digital installations; by creating our own beers, coffee and wines; and by making every member of the team a star rather than a bit player. And what do I do? I am the conductor of this orchestra. I wave my arms around and Marcus, Sergei and the team create music.

Our combined history, experience and ideas has led to this, the Roast cookbook, which recreates some of the best recipes served at the restaurant for the home cook and celebrates the people that share our mission to create and enjoy delicious British food and drink. Here are our culinary blueprints for all occasions, from breakfasts, brunches and lunches to dinners, puddings, cocktails and wines, in a book that captures the whole ethos of Roast, from the field and the shore to the kitchen and the bar. We invite you to take your feasting to new heights.

Introduction by Marcus Verberne
Head Chef, Roast

Our menu at Roast is a celebration of quality British produce. So when we came up with the concept for our cookbook, it was important that it not only be a showcase of what we do with this produce, but also a tribute to the farmers, fishermen, growers, winemakers and other producers who with hard work, knowledge, skill and passion, inspire us to do their produce justice whether it be on a plate or in a glass. In most cases there are many crucial stages in the journey from field to fork. All of these stages are as important as each other to ensure that the final product reaches its full potential. Beef is an obvious example. The quality of a steak on your plate starts with the breeding and animal husbandry from the farmer, then the baton is passed to the abattoir responsible for the humane despatch of the livestock, then to the butcher for the aging process and quality of butchery, and then finally to the chef to run to the finish line, often taking the glory. Our book focuses not only on the preparation of a final dish but also puts emphasis on the vitally important role of those who provide us with its ingredients. My approach is very simple. Source the best produce on offer and don't interfere with it too much. It's important to me not to overthink a dish. Nature has an uncanny way of providing us with great seasonal pairings. All I have to do is harness what nature provides us with at any certain time of year and construct our menu from there. If I had to describe the food at Roast, I'd say it was simple but well executed.

I have tried to make the recipes as appropriate and accessible to the home cook as possible. Some of the recipes are for basic preparations that you may already cook often. For these so-called 'basics', such as roasting potatoes or poaching eggs, I have included vital tips and rules that I live by in order to achieve perfect results every time. Other recipes are a bit more 'cheffy' and they use techniques that may be more suited to making an impact with your friends during dinner parties.

For the more difficult, unfamiliar preparations such as opening a live scallop or oyster, butchering a duck or rabbit, or for carving large joints, we have provided you not only with step-by-step photographic instructions, but also with QR codes. These are quick-response barcodes that, once scanned using an appropriate device, will link you to websites or information. In this book they link to videos of me guiding you through a certain technique for butchering, filleting, preparing,

carving or cooking. To access the codes, you will need a smartphone, tablet or similar device. Download a QR scanner app from your device app store (there are several free options). Once the app is open, hold the screen over the QR code on the page, positioning the corners of the scanner over the corners of the code. The app will then take you directly to a short film demonstrating what you've been reading about. These films were created both at the restaurant and on location with our suppliers.

I hope the Roast cookbook will be one you reach for often, whether it be to create a full dish or meal or even just for a quick tip. Don't feel you must follow each recipe to the letter. A recipe is a guideline. Play around with ingredients and flavour combinations – so many wonderful culinary discoveries came from experimentation or even accidents!

Being one of seven brothers and sisters, some of my fondest memories come from sitting round the table as a family enjoying our evening meal. For us it was an important time in the day when we were altogether and could enjoy not just the food, but each others' company. I believe that the closeness and strength of our family was built on the foundation of dinner time.

In the hustle and bustle of daily life, make sure you find the time each day, to enjoy good food with the ones closest to you. It is after all one of the simplest pleasures in life.

carving

Carving

*A wise woman once said: 'The uncouth operations of bad
carvers occasion almost as much discomfort to those who
witness, as they do generally of awkwardness and
embarrassment to those who exhibit them.'*
Eliza Acton, 1858

As our home dining culture has changed over the years,
carving has become something of a forgotten art. This section
in particular is for those who still enjoy the traditional family
Sunday roast, and a table creaking under the weight of a
fine spread.

A joint of meat served on the bone at the table can be a
frightening prospect for an inexperienced carver. Hopefully,
with the following tips I've offered and the help of the
step-by-step photography, some of this anxiety will diminish.
If, however, you're still unsure, the QR codes will transport
you to actual video clips of how to carve the various joints.
Good luck!

Your tools and their upkeep

Any job done well requires the correct tools. To carve
efficiently, it's important to have **a few knives of different
dimensions** for different tasks. For example, I'd use a small
knife with a thin blade for easy navigation around bones or
knuckles and also for smaller game birds. A larger knife with
a longer, inflexible blade is best for even slicing. Sharp knives
are, of course, essential. Never use serrated knives unless
required to saw through pork crackling, as the serrations will
tear the meat.

A carving fork can be handy for slicing in particular, but use it
only to steady the joint. There is no need to plunge it in too
deep or your slices will be full of fork marks. At certain stages
of carving though, the fork can be a nuisance. Sometimes
having a free hand is of much greater benefit.

The upkeep of your knives is most important. The knife's
edge should be kept true using a sharpening **whetstone**.
Whetstones usually come double-sided – one side has course
grit, and the other fine. The course grit is for regaining the
sharp edge and the fine grit for finishing. Submerge the stone
in water for 5 minutes to allow water to be absorbed into it.
Secure the whetstone in place by placing a damp cloth
underneath it on your worktop. It's crucial that the blade of the
knife is at the same angle to the stone for each stroke. If you're
a beginner you can buy an angle guide from a good knife shop.

This clips on to the back of the knife to ensure the correct
angle (22 degrees) is maintained. Stroke the blade of the knife
the full length of the stone working from the tip to the heel.
Make the same number of strokes on each side of the blade,
as many as it takes to regain the edge. I find the best way to
test that the edge is true is by slicing a ripe tomato. Once you
have a sharp edge, turn the stone over to the fine grit and finish
at that same 22-degree angle.

Please note that whetstones are for occasional use to regain a
lost edge on a dull knife. If used too often you will eventually
grind the blade down until it's misshapen and useless. Before
each use of your knife, give it a few strokes on a honing steel
(also called a sharpening steel) to hone the edge. Buy a long
steel with a good safety guard between the handle and the steel
itself. For beginners, the easiest way to sharpen is to hold the
steel vertically with the tip resting securely on a cutting board.
Stroke the knife at that same 22-degree angle down the length
of the steel, working from the heel to the tip of the blade.
It should only take a few strokes on each side to hone the
edge. Make sure that after sharpening on stone or steel, the
knife is thoroughly washed and dried before use to remove
any microscopic steel filings.

Carving tips

- Wash your hands.

- Make sure your joint has been properly rested. Remember, the larger the joint, the longer the rest. I would go so far as to rest a whole fore rib of beef for 30 minutes. If the joint hasn't rested sufficiently, your carving board will flood with meat juices and the meat will be dry.

- Carve on a wooden chopping board with a groove cut around the edge to catch any meat juices. Cutting on a hard surface, such as a metal or ceramic, will not do the integrity of your knife any favours.

- Give yourself plenty of room and have a plate to hand for any scraps so that you keep the board clear. It also helps to have a cloth for wiping your hands on if things get messy.

- Choose the correct knife for the job. You wouldn't use the same knife for a fore rib of beef as you would for a grouse!

- Don't apply too much pressure. Your knife should be sharp enough for the task ahead, let it do the work for you. Applying pressure will press the joint out of shape and the resulting slices will be uneven and look careless and untidy. Use the full length of the blade with long even strokes. Avoid sawing through the meat as the slices will be jagged and unsightly.

- To ensure the slices are even, make sure the tip of your knife is in line with the handle to slice straight and true.

- Place the carved meat on to warm plates so the meal stays hotter for longer.

- The general rule of thumb is to carve against the grain of the meat. This will result in the slices being less chewy than if you'd sliced with the grain. Think of the muscle you're carving as a log of wood. A log of wood has an obvious grain running through its length. In order to successfully split a log with an axe you must stand the log on its end and split it with the grain. If you tried to lie the log down and cut across its grain you would not be very successful and the vibration from the axe would not be pleasant. It's the exact same principle with meat. In carving your slices against this grain, the sharp carving knife is doing the work so your teeth and jaw don't have to endure a lengthy chewing process. It can mean the difference between a successful meal and a disaster.

Carving roast chicken and other birds

This method can also be used for ducks, geese, pheasant or guinea fowl.

You could remove the wishbone from the chicken before roasting. However, if you enjoy the fun of going head to head with a family member in a battle over a wish, then leave it in.

Removing the wishbone is the first step in carving your bird. Should it be left in, it would act as a barrier when slicing the breast meat. To remove it, hold the chicken still with your carving fork. Using a small pointed knife, cut down either side of the wishbone using the bone to guide the blade. Slide the blade under the wish bone and twist until each side is freed. Pull the v-shaped bone until it comes away from the bird (**1**) and have some fun with a family member!

The next step is to remove the first leg. Cut away the string tying the legs together and open them. Make a cut on the inside of the right leg (**2**) prising it open to reveal the knuckle attaching it to the carcass. Cut through the knuckle (**3**), remove the leg and place it to one side. Twist back the wing on the same side as the leg you've just removed (**4**) and cut through the joint attaching it to the carcass to remove it. Now you have free access to the right breast (**5**). Carve even slices, about 5mm thick, all the way down to the breastbone and ribcage (**6**).

I always complete one side of the bird before starting on the next as I find the remaining leg helps steady the carcass when carving the first breast.

Remove the leg on the left side repeating the same steps as on the right. Remove the left wing and then slice the breast.

To joint the legs, turn them over so the inside is facing upwards. This positioning allows you to see the joint. Cut through the joint to separate the drumstick and thigh (**7**).

The best is yet to come! If you turn the carcass over, on its underside you will find the oysters (**8**). This is the muscle on the back where the legs join. As the bird roasts, any juices drip through the oysters keeping them moist and succulent. They are easily prised out with a spoon or your thumbs (**9**).

***more* roast**
Scan the QR code to see
Marcus carving chicken.
http://roastcookbook.com/carving-chicken/

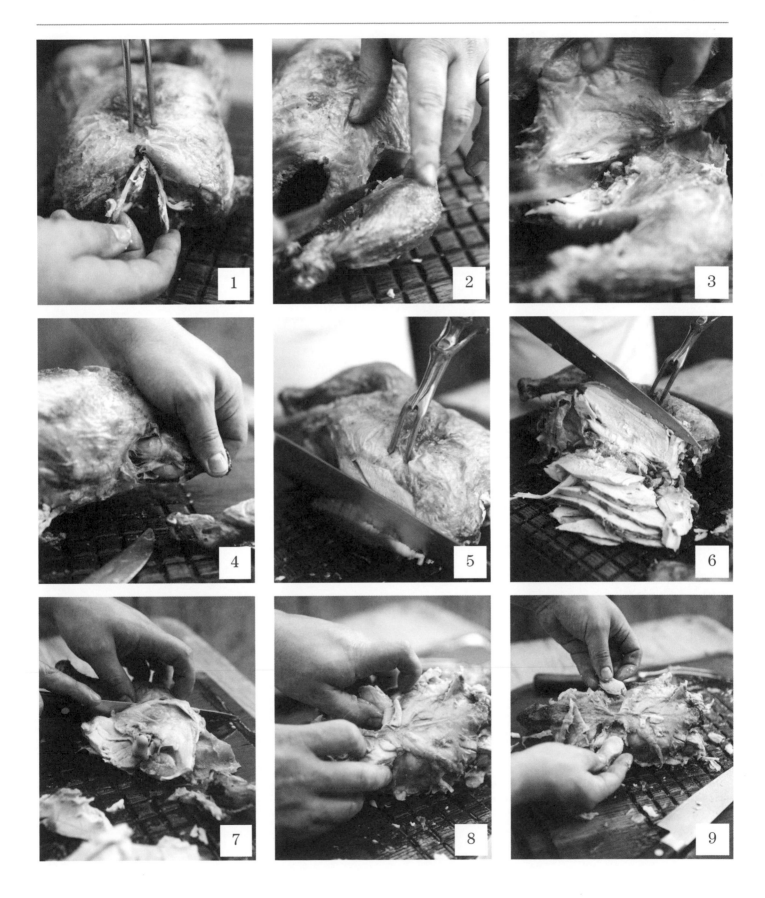

Carving roast fore rib of beef

When presented with a whole fore rib of beef roasted on the bone, the task of carving it and doing the beautiful succulent meat justice seems daunting. It is, however, quite easy when you understand the simple muscle structure of the joint and the bones that frame it. The large prime muscle, the 'rib eye', which runs the length of the fore rib bone, is the most prized meat of the joint. As it is situated against the bone and protected by surrounding muscles and a generous layer of fat, it is helped to retain all its juices while cooking, with the result that it is the least cooked and most succulent part of the roast.

In order to access the rib eye you must first remove the outer layer of fat and the two overlapping muscles that encase it. Rest the fore rib on the flat chine bone with the rib bones pointing upwards. Remove the fat and the first of the overlapping muscles in one piece by locating the muscle's position at the end of the joint and slicing between the two muscles, gently prising them apart as you go (**1**). They will separate easily with a few releasing strokes of your knife (**2**) as there is a thin layer of sinew and fat running between them. Once removed, this outer muscle can be placed to one side and sliced later for guests who prefer their meat well done. The tasty fat should also be sliced later and distributed between the plates.

There is still one outer muscle left to remove. Before this is done there is a thick strip of sinew running between this muscle and the rib eye near the base of the joint that must be sliced free (**3**) and discarded. To remove the second and final overlapping muscle you will need to work from the opposite end of the joint as you did for the first. Repeat the same process as with the first muscle, lifting it and making deft cuts between the sinew and fat (**4**), and then gently lift it off. This muscle may also be sliced for those who prefer their meat well cooked (**5**).

Now that the rib eye has been revealed you must first release it from the flat chine bone. Turn the joint over so it is resting on the rib bones giving you easy access to the chine bone. Being careful not to cut into the rib eye muscle itself, cut carefully between the chine bone and the rib eye using the bone to guide your knife blade (**6**). Release the meat from the chine bone down the full length of the joint. For ease of slicing, the rib eye should now be released from the rib bones (**7**).

This should be done in stages, at 5–8cm intervals. The idea is to free enough of the rib eye from the rib bones to carve a few slices (**8**), then free a bit more, and continue to carve more slices and so on and so on until you have enough slices to fill your guests' plates. When slicing, let the sharp blade do the work. The rib eye is a large tender muscle and if too much pressure is applied while slicing, the meat will bulge making it impossible to carve even slices. The slices should be about 5mm thick. Remember to feel the bone at each stage when releasing the rib eye muscle from the rib bones (**9**), using it to guide your knife, and no meat will be wasted.

***more* roast**
Scan the QR code to see
Marcus carving fore rib of beef.
http://roastcookbook.com/how-to-carve-beef-forerib/

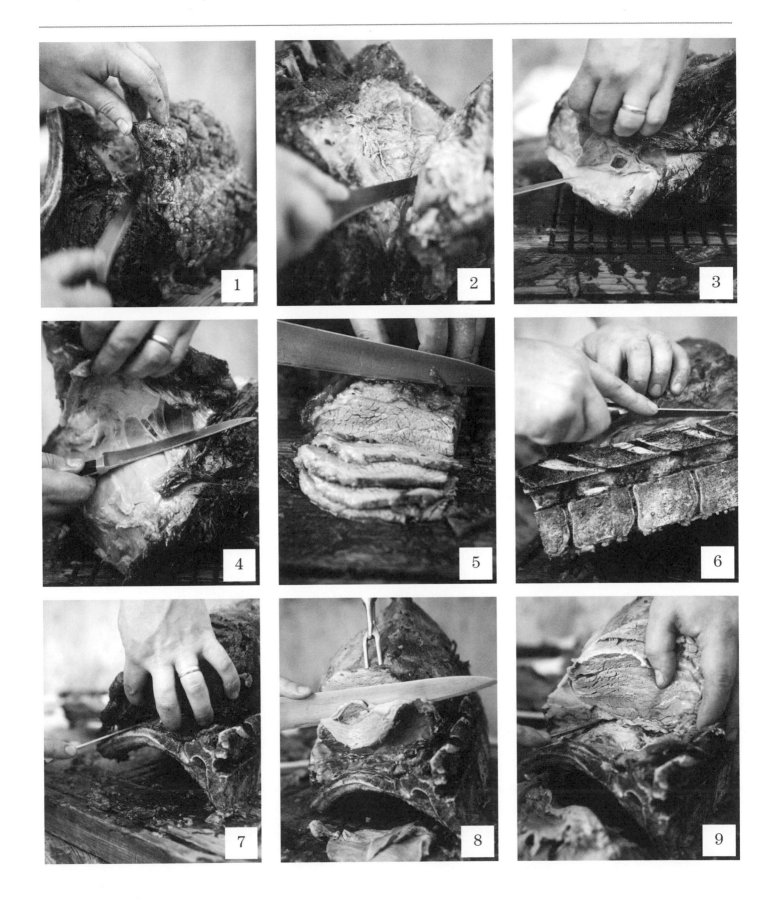

Carving roast leg of lamb or mutton

Carving a leg can be tricky as there are many different muscles involved and bones to negotiate too. The most important rule of thumb is to carve against the grain of the meat, which ensures the resulting slices are more tender. The beauty of carving a leg of lamb is that nature gave you a handle! Ask your butcher to French-trim the shank bone leaving it clean. This gives you a helpful handle, allowing a firm grip, and alleviates the use of a carving fork.

Start carving from the thickest point on the outside of the leg (1). Make your first cut all the way to the bone (2). The first slice should be carved positioning your blade at a slight angle, removing a thin wedge which will give you access for the following slices (3). Continue removing 5mm slices from both sides of the original cut (4). When you hit bone, angle your knife blade slightly to release each slice. Use nature's handle to twist the joint in your favour (5) giving you access to the various muscles. Eventually you will reach the end of the leg and encounter the tricky pelvic bone. Shave the final couple of slices from the pelvic bone (6) and turn the leg over to start on the other side. You may need to carve a few horizontal slices from this side (7), curving your blade as you go to ensure a clean bone (8).

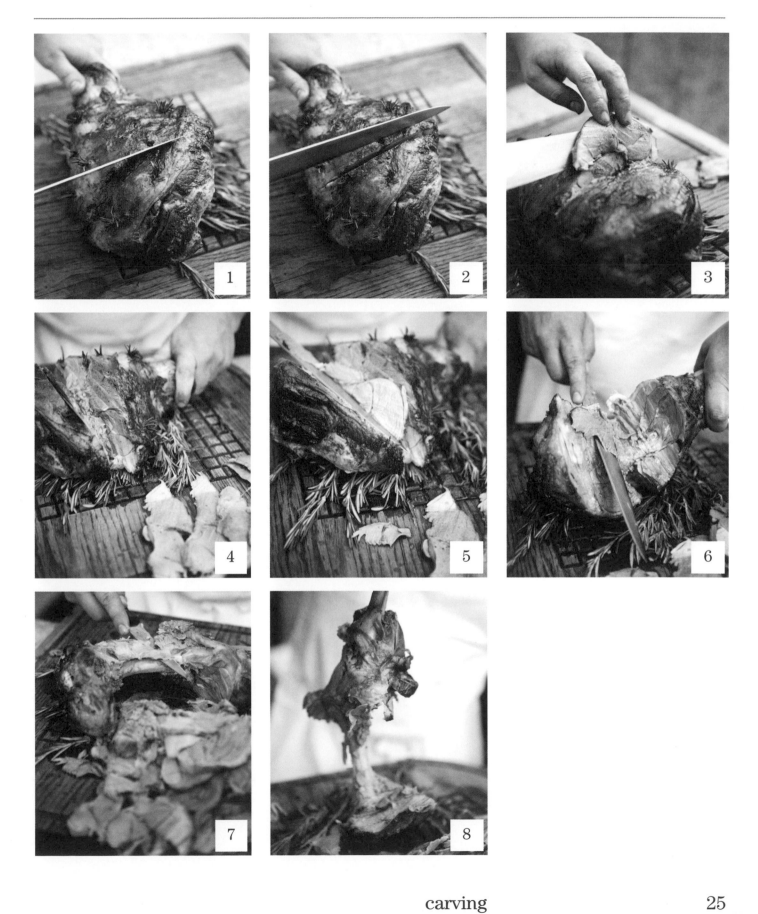

Carving a centre-cut roast saddle of lamb

A saddle of lamb is one of the prime roasting joints. The two loin muscles running down either side of the spinal column that make up the saddle do much less work in comparison to the legs or shoulders. For this reason, they are still very tender when cooked pink. The saddle, however, can be rather tricky to carve as you are having to negotiate your way around the fiddly vertebrae. Hopefully the following instructions will help you along the way. These instructions are for a centre-cut saddle which would comfortably serve six. A full saddle, which has the two rumps and a pelvic bone at one end, would feed 8–10. The carving method is the same, however when you reach the pelvic bone you will have to negotiate it by turning the blade and running it down beside the bone to free the rumps.

There are two methods of carving a saddle of lamb. The first method carves lengthy strips 'with the grain of the loin' while it is still attached to the bone. The second involves removing the loin from the bone altogether before you carve medallions against the grain. I personally prefer the medallions, as they are carved against the natural grain of the meat and therefore easier to chew. However, the two loins running down a saddle of lamb are prime cuts and are tender enough, even if carved with the meat's grain, for this technique still to be successful.

The spinal column of the lamb is shaped like an upside down 'T'. Run your knife down either side of the vertical bone the full length of the joint (**1**) until you hit the vertebrae. Angling your knife slightly, with the point directed towards the central spine, carve out a wedge shaped slice, the full length of the joint (**2**). Remove this (**3**) so that you can gain access as the next step is to release the loin from the horizontal chine bones that form the base of the upside down 'T'. Using the tip of your knife, at one end cut around the vertebrae following its shape until you reach the flat horizontal bones (**4**). Continue this for the full length of the loin and open it up (**5**). Using the flat bones to guide your blade, carve the loin releasing it to the point where the ribs end but still leaving it attached only by the flank. Now you are free to slice strips the full length of the loin that each have a crispy portion of outer fat attached (**6**). Continue until the first loin is carved and then start with the other side.

The second method carves on the opposite side of the joint. This method involves removing the loin in its entirety using the same steps described in the first method. This time however, rather than stopping at the end of the ribs leaving it attached by the flank, carve all the way through, removing the loin totally (**7**). Once the loin is removed carve small slices against the grain, about 5mm thick, along its full length (**8**).

***more* roast**
Scan the QR code to see
Marcus carving a saddle of lamb.
http://roastcookbook.com/carving-lamb/

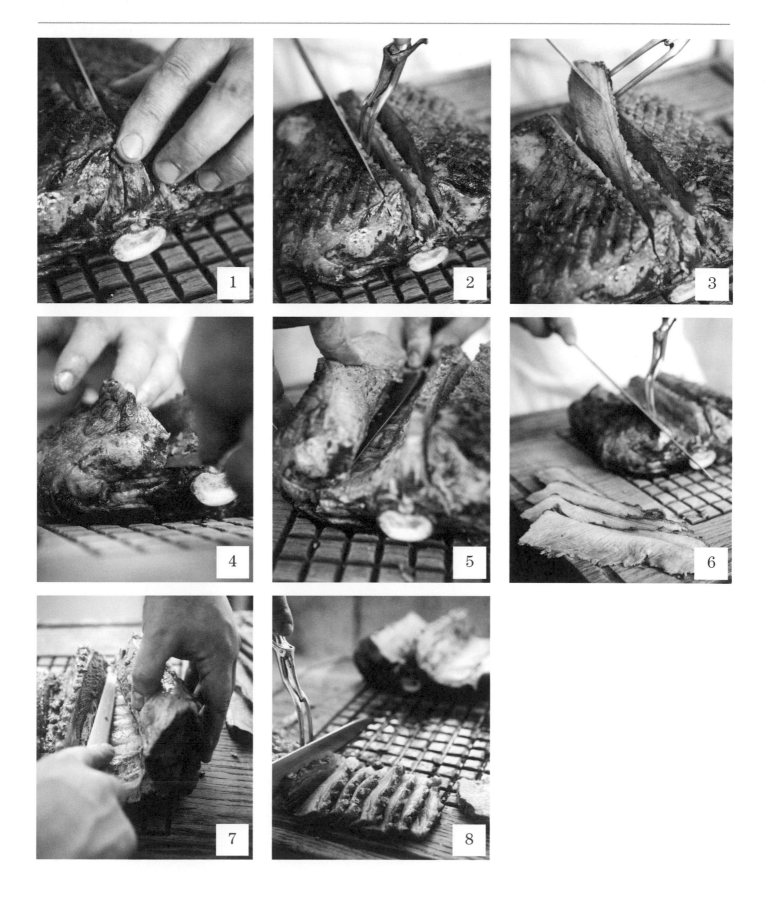

Carving roast loin of pork

The loin is a fabulous cut for roasting as the layer of fat and skin surrounding the outside of the joint, if roasted correctly, will transform into the most divine golden crackling. Follow the same technique for the slow-roasted pork belly on page 151, but cut the cooking time in half or it will dry out. For ease of carving ask your butcher for a loin of pork on the bone, but with the chine bone removed. This means you only have the rib bones to contend with.

The first step is to remove the beautiful golden crackling and hide it from would-be thieves! If you run a narrow-bladed knife under the crispy skin (1) lifting it carefully as you go (2), the whole layer of crackling should lift off in one piece (3). Place the crackling in a low oven to keep it warm and where it is out of sight and out of tempted mind. There is a thick layer of fat between the crackling and the loin (depending on the breed this can be very thick). Middlewhite pork is one of my favourite breeds for roasting as its crackling is sublime – however, there is a very thick layer of fat lying underneath the crackling. Remove most of this fat, shaving it horizontally with your carving knife (4) but leaving a 5mm layer still attached to the loin.

To remove the loin from the bone, sit the joint on your carving board with the ribs pointing upwards. Using the rib bones to guide your blade (5), carve the loin releasing it from the ribs all the way down the length of the joint (6).

Now your loin has been freed from the bone, carve it into slices along its length, about 5mm thick (7), distributing them between warm plates as you go. Remove the crackling from the oven and using a serrated knife (this is the only time I would condone using a serrated knife when carving) saw through the crackling giving (8) a generous portion to each person.

***more* roast**
Scan the QR code to see
Marcus preparing and carving pork loin.
http://roastcookbook.com/preparing-and-carving-pork-loin/

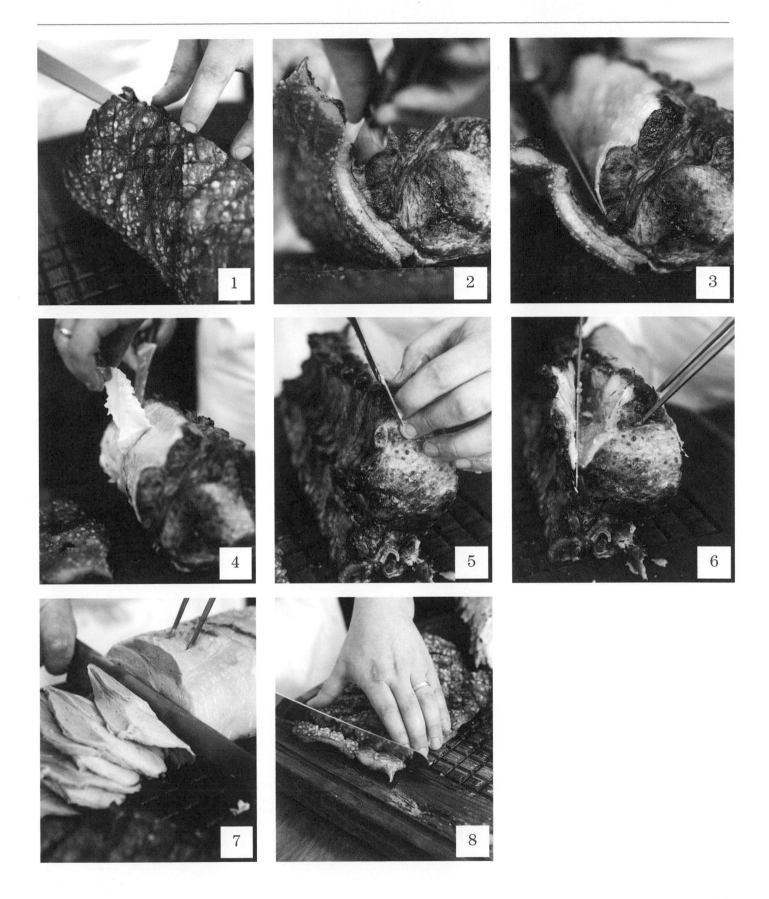

breakfast

Eggs Benedict
serves 4

A wise woman once said: 'Break some new-laid eggs into separate cups, and do this with care, that the yolks may not be injured.' *Eliza Acton, 1853*

Eggs Benedict is quite possibly the perfect brunch dish. One of the questions I get asked most often is, 'how do you make perfect poached eggs?' First of all, the eggs must be very fresh. If the eggs are older the white won't hold together to encase the yolk. For a tear-shaped egg you need a deep pan of boiling water with about 100ml of white wine vinegar. The vinegar acts to set the white around the yolk. A good tip is to crack your eggs into cups and tip them gently, one by one, into the water. As they drop to the bottom of the pan the white will set on the outside creating the desired tear shape. At Roast we do a few variations on the traditional Eggs Benedict. For Eggs Florentine, we substitute spinach for the ham. For Eggs Royal we replace the ham with smoked sea trout from Loch Etive in Scotland. And even more popular is our Lobster Benedict with the addition of a native lobster claw!

100ml white wine vinegar
8 fresh eggs, at room temperature
8 slices of lightly smoked ham
4 English muffins, halved
sea salt and freshly milled black pepper

For the hollandaise sauce
100ml white wine vinegar
2 small shallots, chopped
a few sprigs of tarragon
8 black peppercorns
500g unsalted butter
5 egg yolks
50ml warm water

For the hollandaise, place the vinegar, shallots, tarragon and peppercorns in a saucepan over a medium heat and bubble until reduced to about 2 tablespoons. Strain and set aside.

Melt the butter in a saucepan and simmer it on a low heat for about 5–10 minutes until it separates. Remove from the heat and allow to cool for a few minutes. The whey will settle on the bottom leaving the clarified butter on top. Pour off the warm clarified butter and discard the whey.

Put the egg yolks into a rounded bowl with half the vinegar reduction. Place over a pan of barely simmering water, making sure the base of the bowl does not touch the water, and whisk until the mixture becomes light and fluffy. Be careful not to heat the mixture too much at this vital stage as this will cause the eggs to scramble – remove the pan from the heat if necessary. Slowly drizzle the warm clarified butter into the eggs, whisking continuously over the heat to form an emulsion. As the sauce thickens you may need to add a little of the warm water if it becomes too thick, before continuing with the butter. Season with salt and pepper, and taste to see if more vinegar reduction is needed for your liking. Keep warm until required.

To serve, preheat your grill to high. Add the vinegar to a deep pan of boiling water, and poach the eggs as described above – they should take about 2–3 minutes. While the eggs are poaching, grill the ham until crispy, and toast the muffins on both sides. Place two muffin halves on each plate, followed by the sliced ham and the poached eggs. Finish with a generous spoonful of hollandaise sauce over each egg.

Clockwise from top-left: Eggs Benedict, Eggs Florentine, Lobster Benedict and Eggs Royal.

Fried duck's egg with baby squid, chorizo and wild garlic serves 4

This is actually a Spanish tapas-style dish, but it is also great for brunch or breakfast. There are now British producers making fantastic chorizo allowing us to use this very versatile ingredient on our menu at Roast. Tim French and Matthew Chiles from 'The Bath Pig' make the best one I've tried!

Wild garlic is one of the ingredients I most look forward to at the beginning of spring. I always get excited when I see the first daffodils in bloom as the wild garlic arrives at the same time.
You should be able to get it from your local farmers' market, or why not pick it yourself; it grows along the banks of some rivers or streams.

There is nothing worse than a crispy fried egg. When frying eggs, always use butter. They are less likely to stick to the pan in comparison to oil. Rule number one though is make sure your pan isn't too hot. I'm always saying to my chefs, 'If you can hear the egg sizzling and spattering, it's screaming to be turned down!'

50g butter
4 duck eggs, at room temperature
2 tbsp rapeseed oil
80g cooking chorizo, sliced into 1cm
  discs
120g baby squid (whole)
6 wild garlic leaves, roughly chopped
sea salt and freshly milled black pepper

Heat half the butter in a frying pan over a low-medium heat until it is just starting to bubble. Crack the eggs into the pan, being careful not to break the rich yolks, and season them with sea salt and pepper. Make sure the pan is not too hot. I always tell my chefs that if they can hear the egg over the noise of the kitchen their pan is too hot. If the egg is sizzling and bubbles are forming around the edge of the white, then reduce the heat or your egg will become crispy on the bottom and around the edges. You will achieve better results if you cook the eggs with more control over a lower heat spooning the hot butter over the yolk and raw white to slightly cook the top of the egg.

At the same time, place the rapeseed oil and chorizo in a separate pan over a medium-high heat and fry the chorizo, rendering out all the beautiful orange fat. When the chorizo starts to crisp slightly, add the baby squid. The squid will cook very quickly and only wants to be in the pan for about a minute. Remove the pan from the heat and toss with the remaining butter and wild garlic. Scatter the mixture over the eggs to serve.

The 'Mighty' full Borough serves 4

Our Full Borough is a vast plate of food and not for the faint-hearted. It will easily keep you going until dinner, so don't make any plans for lunch! We carefully source all the ingredients to ensure our customers are having the best full English breakfast Britain has to offer.

In conjunction with Wicks Manor Farm in Essex (see page 162) we have developed our own unique sausage recipe based on an original Victorian recipe. It's a blend of pepper and nutmeg and a hint of coriander and earthy thyme. The sausages are made with quality pork shoulder, filled in natural casing and have no added fat. Wicks Manor also supply our smoked streaky bacon. The black pudding we use is from Ramsay of Carluke in Scotland. Ramsay also provide us with haggis and their famous Lorne sausage, which we use in our Full Scottish.

As for eggs, the freshest free-range eggs are a must. Most good supermarkets stock Clarence Court's Burford Brown eggs. They have a rich deep orange yolk and taste divine cooked in any style. I have provided instructions for scrambling eggs here; poaching is explained on page 32 and frying on page 35.

vegetable oil, for frying
100g plain flour
4 portions of Bubble 'n' Squeak
  (see page 41)
4 tomatoes, halved
4 field mushrooms
softened butter
8 'Roast Recipe' sausages (or sausages
  of your choice)
4 thick slices of black pudding
16 rashers of rindless smoked streaky
  bacon

2 very thick slices of white bread
8 free range eggs, at room temperature
40ml double cream (optional)
sea salt and freshly milled black pepper

Preheat your oven to 180°C/Gas Mark 4.

Heat a large frying pan over a medium-high heat and add a little vegetable oil. Sprinkle the flour on to a plate and press both flat sides of each bubble 'n' squeak gently into the flour. Shake off any excess flour and add the bubble 'n' squeak to the pan. Brown both sides, then transfer to a large baking tray. Place the tomatoes, cut-side up, on the baking tray.

Remove the stem from the mushrooms and smear the gills with softened butter. Place them on the same tray, with their gills facing upwards. Season the tomatoes and mushrooms with salt and pepper and place the tray in the oven for about 20 minutes.

While the tomatoes, mushrooms and bubble 'n' squeak are cooking, heat a large frying over a medium heat and add a little oil. Fry the sausages until they are well browned all over. Make sure the pan doesn't get too hot or the sausages will burst. Remove them from the pan and place them in the oven on a separate tray for about 8 minutes.

Place the slices of black pudding in the pan and fry them lightly for about 1 minute on each side. Place them in the oven with the sausages. They will need about 6 minutes to cook through.

Put half the bacon rashers into the frying pan and fry them for about a minute on each side. Place them in the oven with

the sausages and black pudding. They will crisp further in the oven. Repeat the process with the remaining bacon.

Place your pan back on the heat and add a good knob of butter. Fry the bread in the butter until crispy on both sides. Remove the fried bread from the pan and cut each slice in half diagonally. Place in the oven briefly while preparing the eggs.

Crack the eggs into a bowl and whisk until well beaten, then season with salt and pepper. Wipe your frying pan clean and place it back over a low heat.

By this stage, everything in the oven should be cooked. Divide it all up between four warm plates before scrambling the eggs. The eggs won't take long and will need your full attention.

Melt approximately 50g of butter in the pan and add the beaten eggs. Allow the eggs to sit for a few seconds before stirring gently with a wooden spoon. Allow them to sit for a few more seconds and stir again. The eggs should cook slightly on the bottom of the pan before being folded back through the raw egg. Scrambled eggs are a slow gradual process that you need complete control over. If you feel the eggs are cooking too quickly, remove the pan from the heat for a minute or so, to regain control. Cook the eggs until they're done, but still soft and loose. If you'd like to add a little cream, now is the time, just before they're plated. Check the eggs for seasoning and adjust if required. Spoon the scrambled eggs on to the plates, loosen your belt a few holes, and prepare for belly expansion.

Drop scones with yoghurt cream and summer berries

Makes about 20 drop scones

I used to make these at home as a kid with my mother. In New Zealand we call them pikelets. Our recipe was from the Edmonds Cookery Book, which is New Zealand's cookery gospel and on the shelf in most homes. I've tweaked the recipe slightly, using self-raising flour instead of plain flour to make them a little lighter. They're a cheap and easy breakfast, and fun to prepare on the weekends with your kids.

225g self-raising flour
1 tsp baking powder
50g caster sugar
2 eggs
250ml milk
about 50g butter, for frying
icing sugar, for dusting
selection of fresh summer berries,
*   to serve*
Yoghurt Cream (see page 265), to serve

Sift the flour and baking powder into a large mixing bowl. Add the caster sugar and make a well in the middle of the dry ingredients. Crack the eggs into the well and add 200ml of the milk. Mix thoroughly with a whisk to form a thick smooth batter that reluctantly 'drops' off the end of a spoon. You may need to add a little more of the milk to reach this consistency.

Heat a large non-stick frying pan over a medium heat and grease it with a little butter. Drop the mixture into the pan in spoonfuls allowing enough room between each one for them to spread a little. Let the scones cook for 2–3 minutes, until bubbles start to form on top. As the first of the bubbles start to burst, flip the scones over and cook for another 2–3 minutes on the other side. Keep warm in a low oven while you cook the remainder.

Dust the drop scones with icing sugar and serve warm with a selection of summer berries and the yoghurt cream.

Black pudding hash with a fried egg and girolles serves 6

I find a waxy potato works particularly well for hash, but leftover roasties will also do the trick. Remember, your hash will only be as good as the quality of black pudding that goes into it. You can make this hash with all manner of ingredients. It's also great with salt beef or even duck confit.

500g Charlotte potatoes (or a similar
* waxy variety, such as Roseval)*
120g butter
2 onions, peeled and sliced
1 garlic clove, peeled and finely chopped
1 tsp chopped thyme leaves
500g good-quality black pudding,
* roughly chopped*
3 tbsp vegetable oil
50g flour
250g girolles, brushed clean
a handful of chopped flat-leaf parsley
6 eggs, at room temperature
sea salt and freshly milled black pepper

Roast the Charlotte potatoes following the method on page 282 then allow them to cool.

Place a saucepan over a medium-high heat, add a third of the butter then the onions, garlic and thyme. Cook the onions for 10 minutes or so, allowing them to caramelise a little. Remove from the heat and leave to cool down, then place in a large mixing bowl. Add the black pudding and roasted potatoes, and use your hands to mix them all together, crushing the potatoes as you go to form a mixture that binds well. Taste the mixture and season with salt and pepper, according to your taste.

Form the mixture into six even-sized cakes.

Preheat your oven to 200°C/Gas Mark 6.

Heat a large frying pan over a medium-high heat and add the vegetable oil. Sprinkle some flour on to a plate and press both flat sides of each cake gently into the flour. Shake off any excess flour and place the cakes into the pan. Brown both sides of each hash then transfer them to a baking tray and place in the oven. Cook for 15–20 minutes until they're hot in the centre. Before serving, test their core temperature with the tip of a small pointed knife – they should feel piping hot.

If you make a larger batch, you can form any extra hash mixture into cakes and freeze them. Take them out of the freezer the night before you want to cook them and defrost in the fridge for breakfast the following morning.

When the cakes are almost cooked, clean out the frying pan and place it back over a medium heat. Fry the girolles gently in another third of the butter. Season with salt and pepper and cook until tender. Finish the mushrooms with the parsley and set to one side to keep warm.

Fry the eggs to your liking (see page 35 for how best to fry an egg) in the remaining third of butter.

To serve, place each hash into the middle of a warm plate and sit a fried egg on top. Scatter the mushrooms over the egg and around the plate.

Bubble 'n' Squeak serves 6

This breakfast favourite is one I have every Boxing Day without fail.
The vegetables listed in the recipe are those I'd have left over from Christmas dinner, but should be treated as a guideline. In spring or summer for example, I'd substitute the green vegetables for seasonal ones such as peas, asparagus, broad beans and spring onions. The roast potatoes are a must though, crushed up to bind all the other ingredients together.

Bubble 'n' squeak doesn't have to be restricted to the breakfast table; it makes a great accompaniment for grilled lamb or pork chops, or even a few bangers.

400g cold roast potatoes, roughly chopped into small dice
100g cold roast parsnips, roughly chopped into small dice
100g cold boiled carrots, roughly chopped into small dice
300g cold boiled Brussels sprouts, roughly chopped into small dice
100g cooked Savoy cabbage, roughly chopped into small pieces
1 tbsp Worcestershire sauce
3 tbsp vegetable oil
plain flour, for dusting
celery salt and freshly milled black pepper

Preheat your oven to 200°C/Gas Mark 6.

Place all the vegetables in a large mixing bowl, then use your hands to mix them thoroughly, crushing them with your hands as you go to form a mixture that is bound well by the crushed potatoes. Add the Worcestershire sauce, mixing it in with a fork. Taste the mixture, then season according to your taste with the celery salt and pepper. It's important to taste the mixture first as the vegetables were probably already seasoned for the meal the night before. Form the mixture into six even-sized cakes.

Preheat a large frying pan over a medium-high heat and add the vegetable oil. Sprinkle some flour on to a plate and press both flat sides of each cake gently into the flour. Shake off any excess and place each bubble 'n' squeak into the pan. Brown both sides of each cake, then transfer them to a baking tray and place in the oven. Cook for 15–20 minutes, until they're hot in the centre. Before serving, test their core temperature with the tip of a small pointed knife – it should feel piping hot.

If you make a larger batch, form any extra mixture into cakes and freeze them. Pull them out of the freezer the night before and defrost them in the fridge for breakfast the following morning.

Porridge serves 4

Porridge is hailed as a superfood. It's packed full of complex carbohydrates that take time for the body to digest, therefore releasing energy slowly over sustained periods, keeping you feeling fuller for longer. It is also thought to lower cholesterol. Milk or water? This is the big question. I suppose it's a matter of what you've been brought up on. For me there is no question, it has to be milk! And everyone has their favourite topping; mine is chopped banana and brown sugar (lots of it!).

A couple of tips for cooking porridge; it needs cooking for longer than you'd think if the starch is to be cooked out properly. Add the salt at the end. If introduced too early it can toughen the oats.

150g rolled oats
350ml milk or water, or a mixture
  of both
table salt

Bring the milk or water to the boil over a medium heat, then add the oats. Turn the heat down to low and cook the oats for 7–8 minutes, stirring regularly to keep them from catching on the bottom of the pan. Add more water or milk, if required, to gain the consistency you like and then season the porridge with salt.

Smoked haddock kedgeree serves 4

Kedgeree is thought to have evolved from a rice dish called khichri, which was brought back to the United Kingdom in Victorian times by British colonials on their return from India. Anglo-Indian cuisine was very fashionable in the Victorian era and over the years dishes such as kedgeree have evolved into what we know today. Smoked fish in different forms has traditionally been eaten for breakfast, so kedgeree naturally fell into this category of meal.

200g long grain rice
400g undyed smoked haddock fillet,
  with skin
50g ghee or clarified butter
1 large onion, peeled and finely diced
1 tbsp finely chopped fresh root ginger
1 tsp mustard seeds
1 tsp ground turmeric
$\frac{1}{2}$ tsp ground cumin
$\frac{1}{2}$ tsp ground fenugreek
1 tsp curry powder
4 green cardamom pods
15 curry leaves
280ml boiling water, for cooking
  the rice
2 eggs, at room temperature
juice of $\frac{1}{2}$ lemon
1 tbsp roughly chopped coriander
sea salt

Place the rice into a large sieve and run it under cold water for about 4 minutes, moving it around as you go, until the water runs clear. It's very important to wash the starch out of the rice to achieve separated, fluffy grains. Place the washed rice to one side to drain well.

Place the smoked haddock fillet in a large saucepan and cover with cold water. Bring the water to the boil, then remove from the heat. Allow the haddock to stand in the water for 2 minutes, then strain. Once the haddock is cool enough to handle, remove the skin and any bones, flake the fish and place to one side.

Preheat a large saucepan to over a medium heat. Add the ghee and cook the chopped onion and ginger for about 4–5 minutes, until the onion is soft and translucent. Add the mustard seeds, turmeric, cumin, fenugreek, curry powder, cardamom pods and curry leaves. Cook the spices for 3 minutes, then add the washed rice. Season the rice with salt, stir it into the spices and add the boiling water. Cover the pan with a tight-fitting lid and reduce to a low heat to simmer. Cook for 12–15 minutes, until the rice is tender and the water has been completely absorbed.

While the rice is cooking, place the eggs in a pan of boiling water and boil for 7 minutes. Run them under cold water so they can be handled, then peel them while they're still warm.

Once the rice is cooked, remove the lid and fold in the lemon juice and flaked haddock. Cut the warm boiled eggs into quarters and gently mix them into the kedgeree. Transfer to a serving dish, sprinkle the chopped coriander over the top and serve.

Grilled kippers with lemon butter
serves 2

Kippered herrings (kippers) have made a bit of a comeback in recent times. This is partly due to the British food revival but also due to their low cost and health benefits. Herring are an oily fish high in Omega 3. To kipper them, they are split down the back and splayed open. They are then heavily cured in strong brine before being cold smoked for up to 16 hours, traditionally over oak chips.

2 kippers, opened out
50g softened butter
juice of 1/2 lemon
1 tbsp chopped chives
freshly milled black pepper
brown toast, to serve

Open all the windows in your kitchen unless you want the smell to linger for most of the day.

Preheat your grill to a medium heat.

Smear half the butter over the opened side of your kippers. Melt the remaining butter in a large ovenproof frying pan over a medium heat and lay the kippers into the pan skin-side down. Place the pan under the grill and warm the kippers through for about 4 minutes or so.

Remove the kippers from under the grill and place back on the hob. Squeeze in the lemon juice and sprinkle over the chives. Baste the kippers with the lemon butter and serve with brown toast.

Eggy bread with crispy bacon and roast bananas in golden syrup serves 4

I first tried this dish in the 1990s back home in Dunedin, New Zealand, at a café called Fuel where a few of my friends worked. It's basically what many people know as 'French toast'.

New Zealand and France have a chequered political history because of the stance the New Zealand government took on nuclear testing in the Pacific. On the menu at Fuel they named the dish 'Mururoa' toast as a jibe at the French for their extensive nuclear testing at Mururoa Atoll in the South Pacific. They served it with this garnish and it eats like a dream!

4 large thick slices of white crusty
   bread
4 eggs, beaten
12 rashers of smoked streaky bacon
50g butter
4 bananas, peeled, each cut into 3
100ml golden syrup
150g caster sugar mixed with 1 tsp
   ground cinnamon

Preheat the oven grill to high. Soak the slices of bread in the beaten eggs until the egg is well absorbed.

Lay the bacon rashers out flat on a tray and place them under the grill. Grill for about 8–10 minutes, turning halfway, until crispy and golden. Then turn off the grill and leave inside to keep warm.

Heat a large frying pan over a medium heat, add half the butter and cook the egg-soaked bread until lightly browned on both sides. Remove the eggy bread from the pan, place on a baking tray and keep it warm in the oven underneath the tray of bacon.

Place the frying pan back on a medium heat. Add the bananas and golden syrup to the pan, with a teaspoon more of butter and fry them, turning the bananas regularly so they caramelise evenly. After about 3 minutes the bananas should be soft and golden in colour. If the pan becomes too hot, lift it off the heat from time to time so the golden syrup doesn't burn. Add the rest of the butter and boil to form an emulsion with the golden syrup to create your sauce.

Remove the bacon from the oven. Dust the eggy bread generously with the cinnamon sugar and serve with the bacon, roasted bananas and the caramel sauce drizzled on top.

Toasted crumpets with poached eggs, Bath Pig chorizo and sweetcorn

serves 4

I love a bit of crumpet for breakfast. Crumpets are so versatile, working well with sweet or savoury toppings. My favourite preparation is simply spread with butter and clear honey. The crumpet acts as a vessel soaking up the melted butter and honey like honeycomb. However, this savoury version is also very good. The bright orange fat from the chorizo soaks straight into the crumpet so every mouthful is packed with flavour. I've offered a really simple recipe on page 50 to make your own crumpets, but shop-bought crumpets are equally good.

4 crumpets (see page 50 for home-made), toasted
1 ear of sweetcorn, husk removed
30g butter
250g cooking chorizo, sliced into small rounds
1 tbsp chopped flat-leaf parsley
4 poached eggs (see page 32 for how to poach your eggs)

Bring a small saucepan of lightly salted water to the boil. Stand the corn ear on one end, holding it at the other, and run a sharp knife down the cob, slicing off the kernels. Work your way around, removing all the kernels. Blanch the corn kernels for about 2 minutes in the boiling water, then drain and place to one side.

Heat a frying pan over a medium heat. Add the butter and cook the chorizo, rendering out that lovely orange fat. Add the cooked sweetcorn to warm through. There should be no need to season as the chorizo should be seasoned enough. Add the chopped parsley.

To serve, place the hot crumpets on four serving plates and top each with a poached egg. Scatter the corn and chorizo over and around so the fat and butter is soaked into the absorbent crumpet.

Crumpets makes 8–10

I grew up on crumpets as a kid but never thought about making my own. I became curious, found a few recipes, and after tweaking them here and there came up with this recipe of my own. Crumpets are relatively simple to make and so delicious and fresh.

10g fresh yeast
300ml warm water
225g self-raising flour
1½ tsp salt
40g butter, plus extra for greasing

You will also need: 4–5 crumpet rings

In a large mixing bowl, mix the fresh yeast with the warm water until dissolved. Sift the flour and salt into the bowl and mix with a whisk until smooth. Leave the thick batter in a warm place for 40–60 minutes or so to allow the yeast to activate. After this time the batter will have risen and be bubbling.

To cook the crumpets, heat a large frying pan over a low-medium heat. Grease the inside of your crumpet rings with butter and place them into the pan. Add a small knob of the butter to the pan and then spoon the crumpet batter into the rings to a depth of about 1cm. As the crumpets cook, large bubbles will rise to the top. Once all of the bubbles have burst, remove the rings and carefully turn the crumpets over.

Cook the crumpets for 1–2 minutes only on this side, just long enough to seal. Allow the cooked crumpets to cool on a cooling rack before toasting until crispy. The crumpets can be stored in the fridge for a couple of days before toasting or you could even freeze them. They will keep for a couple of months in the freezer.

Baked beans serves 4–6

At Roast we make our own baked beans. It's so simple and there is so much room for playing around with the recipe to suit your own tastes. Try a Southern American approach with the addition of a little smoky bacon or salt pork. If you don't have much time on your hands, you can use tinned beans. Cannellini beans are slightly larger than the haricot we use, and are readily available in cans. Cooking your own is much tastier.

200g dried haricot beans, soaked in
    cold water for 24 hours (see below)
10 good-quality ripe tomatoes, halved,
    eye removed
2 tbsp soft light brown sugar
50ml extra virgin rapeseed oil
1 onion, diced
1 tbsp tomato purée
2 tsp Worcestershire sauce
sea salt and freshly milled black pepper

Make sure you cover the haricot beans with three times the amount of water as there are beans because they will swell substantially and need to stay submerged.

The next day, preheat your oven to 200°C/Gas Mark 6. Drain the beans in a colander and give them a rinse under cold water. Place the beans in a saucepan and cover with cold lightly salted water. Bring the beans to the boil, then reduce the heat to a simmer. Cook the beans for 45 minutes or so until soft, topping up the water as required to keep the beans covered. Check the beans from time to time as the cooking time may vary from product to product. Once they're cooked, drain in a colander and place to one side.

Put the tomatoes into a roasting tin, cut-side up and sprinkle them with the brown sugar. Roast for about 15 minutes, until soft and well caramelised.

While the tomatoes are roasting, preheat a saucepan over a medium heat. Add the oil and cook the onion for 5–7 minutes, until they're soft and translucent. Stir in the tomato purée and cook for a further minute. Add the roasted tomatoes and the Worcestershire sauce. Season with salt and pepper and cook for 3–4 minutes, stirring regularly, until the tomatoes have disintegrated.

Place the tomato sauce in a blender and blend until very smooth. Be careful not to overload the blender or the hot sauce may end up spraying all over the kitchen when you switch the blender on. It pays to drape a tea towel over the lid of the blender just in case.

Place the smooth sauce back into the pan and add enough of the cooked beans as the sauce will allow. Heat the beans through over a medium heat and taste them. Add a little more Worcestershire sauce, brown sugar and salt and pepper if you feel it's required to balance the flavour of the beans to your liking. Any leftover beans will keep for a week in the fridge.

from the sea

Salt-baked wild sea bass
serves 4

This is one of my favourite techniques for cooking fish and perfect for a summer dinner party. The fish bakes in a thick salt crust retaining all its moisture and goodness.

You will need to ask your fishmonger to scale and bone the fish from the underside, but leave the two fillets attached, head on, and remove the central pin bones running down the centre of the fillets. In the industry this is known as canoe filleting, as the resulting fish resembles a canoe. You will be left with a whole fish, completely boneless, with a large pocket between the two fillets, perfect for stuffing with lemons and herbs.

Firmer-fleshed species are more suited to this cooking technique: sea bream, snapper or even grouper would be more than adequate as alternatives to sea bass.

Serve with a light fresh salad and some new potatoes. The Crisp Summer Vegetable Salad with Caerphilly on page 232 is perfect (but served with the fish, I would omit the cheese).

350g coarse sea salt
350g table salt
4 egg whites
1 lemon, sliced crossways
a few sprigs of dill and parsley,
*   with stalks*
one 1½ kg wild sea bass, prepared
*   as above*

Mix the two salts together with the egg whites and about 150ml of cold water. Leave to stand for a couple of hours in a covered bowl.

Preheat your oven to 180°C/Gas Mark 4.

Place the lemon discs and herbs evenly between the two fillets and lay the fish on to a buttered baking tray. Drain the excess liquid from the salt mixture and mould it over and around the fish packing it down tightly as you go. Bake the fish for 25–30 minutes. As the fish bakes, the egg whites set, acting as cement to create a hard dry crust encasing the fish. To test if the fish is cooked, insert a metal skewer or sharp knife into the fattest part of the fish; if it is hot to touch, the fish is ready. Leave to rest at room temperature for 5 minutes.

To serve at the table, break the salt crust with the back of a heavy knife and pull the large slabs away from the fish. Remove the head and divide the fish into four portions.

Preparing and filleting brill

See page 58 for
instructions

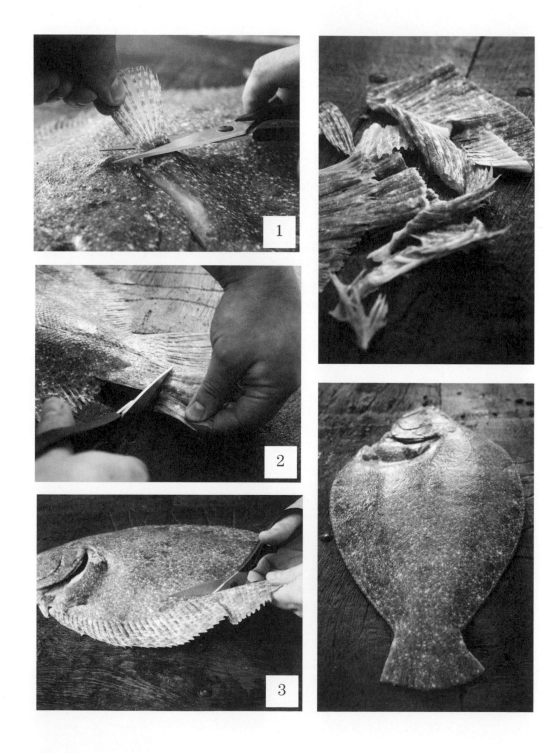

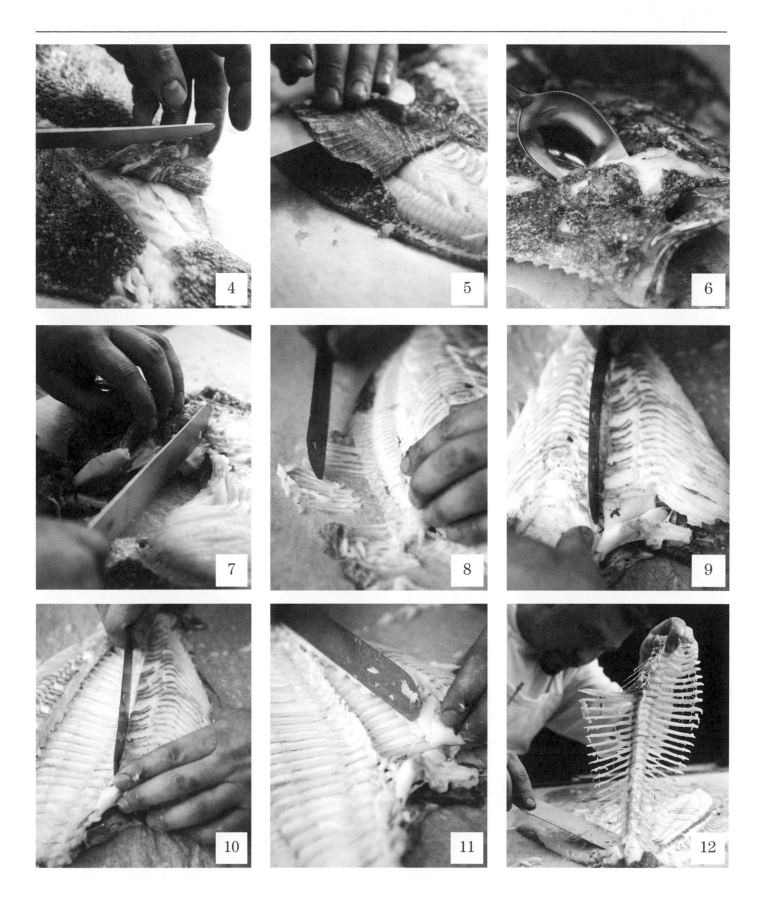

Roasted brill with brown shrimps and capers serves 2–3

A wise woman once said, when cleaning a fish: 'Let this be always done with the most scrupulous nicety, for nothing can more effectually destroy the appetite, or disgrace the cook, than fish sent to table imperfectly cleaned.' *Eliza Acton, 1853*

Brill, in many opinions, is considered an inferior fish to turbot. I beg to differ. Traditionally turbot has always been held high on a pedestal but I much prefer the slightly lighter, more delicate brill. The two species are very similar in appearance and are very closely related (so close in fact that they have been known to interbreed).

Brill is in season and at its best from October–March. During the late spring and summer months brill are spawning and should be avoided so they can get on and procreate. Besides, the mature female fish at this time will be carrying a large roe and much of her energy will be put into producing the eggs, which leaves the flesh of inferior quality in comparison to the seasonal months.

When purchasing any whole fish use your senses. Make sure the eyes are bright and clear and check that the gills are clean and pink-red in colour. The gill fronds should be clearly separated and free from mucus. Smell the fish. It should smell of the sea, not fishy.

Ask your fishmonger where their brill is caught. If it's from the North Sea, don't buy it, as it's likely to be an immature by-catch from the controversial beam trawlers that destroy everything in their path as their heavy nets are indiscriminately dragged across the sea bed.

This brown butter sauce is one of the simplest and tastiest accompaniments for all flat fish, including skate or ray.

one 1.2kg brill
50ml vegetable oil
150g softened butter
100g peeled brown shrimps (most good
*   supermarkets will stock these, but if*
*   not, you can make the sauce without*
*   them and it's still very good)*
100g capers
juice of 1/2 lemon
a good handful of chopped flat-leaf
*   parsley*
sea salt and freshly milled black pepper

Preparing a flat fish to be cooked whole
(See also the photographs on page 56.)
If the fish hasn't been scaled and you don't have a descaler, use a blunt knife. In the kitchen sink, remove the scales by scraping the fish from tail to head, against the natural line of the scales. Flat fish scales are small in comparison to round fish and a little easier to manage. If you're buying a round fish, such as sea bass or sea bream, ask your fishmonger to do the dirty work or you'll be finding scales days later, in the strangest of places!

To gut the fish, feel around for the soft cavity just below the pectoral fin. Make a cut around the edge of the cavity and pull out the innards. Rinse out the cavity thoroughly under cold water.

Using a sturdy pair of scissors, cut off the pectoral fins (**1**) and trim the tail (**2**) and the skirt from around the edge of the fish (**3**). Don't skin the fish. Although brill skin isn't the best for eating, it protects the fish and keeps it moist while cooking. Dry the fish well with kitchen paper before cooking.

Cooking your brill
Preheat your oven to 180°C/Gas Mark 6.

Heat a large non-stick frying pan over a medium-high heat and add the vegetable oil. Rub the dark skin on the upper side of the brill with a little of the soft butter and season liberally with salt and pepper. The butter gives the salt flakes something to stick to rather than just bouncing off the skin. Lay the fish gently into the hot pan, dark-skin-side down, working away from yourself, so as not to be splashed by the hot oil. Season the underside and after a couple of minutes, once the dark skin is crispy, carefully turn the fish over.

With a little more of the soft butter, grease a large baking tray and lay the brill on it, dark-skin-side up. Rub a little more of the butter over the skin, being careful not to tear it. The butter will melt over the fish keeping it moist as it cooks. Roast in the oven for 10-12 minutes, basting with the melted butter every so often. To check the brill is cooked press gently on the fattest part of the fillet near the head. You should feel the fillet slipping gently from the bone. Rest the fish for a couple of minutes before serving.

While the fish is resting, make your sauce. Place the remaining butter in a cold frying pan and turn on to the highest heat. This butter sauce cooks very quickly, so be sure to have the shrimps, capers, lemon and chopped parsley to hand.

continued on page 60

continued from page 58

Season the butter with salt and pepper. Move the pan around regularly so it cooks evenly. It will go through a series of stages. As it gets hot it will start to foam creating large sizzling bubbles; the bubbles will gradually become smaller and the sizzling will quieten. At this stage the milk solids in the butter will have changed colour to a nutty brown. At this moment, squeeze or pour the freshly squeezed lemon juice into the pan using your free hand to catch the pips.
The lemon juice will instantly stop the cooking of the butter so it doesn't burn. Add the brown shrimps, capers and chopped parsley. Check if the seasoning is to your liking, then pour over the whole fish.

Filleting a cooked flat fish

(See also the photographs on page 57.)
You will need a fish slice, fork, spoon and waste bowl to perform the filleting. Firstly, push the capers and shrimps to one end of the tray. If you don't wish to eat the skin, peel it back carefully (**4**) from tail to head (**5**) and discard in the waste bowl. Scoop out the cheek muscle from the head just between the eye and the gill flap with a spoon (**6**). This is your prize for filleting. Cut off the head with the heel of your knife (**7**) and discard. The next step is to scrape away the skirt bones running down each edge using the fish slice and fork (**8**), placing the bones in the waste bowl as you go. Run the fish slice down the spine separating the two fillets (**9**). Gently slide each fillet off the bone, one at a time, working from the spine to the edge (**10**). If the fish is cooked properly, they should come away easily. With the larger top fillets removed and the skeleton now exposed (**11**) gently lift the bones out in one piece, working from head to tail (**12**). The bottom fillets will slide straight off the under skin when serving. Divide the fillets, shrimps and capers between each plate taking into account that the top fillets are much larger than the underfillets.

***more* roast**
Scan the QR code to see
Marcus filleting flat fish.
http://roastcookbook.com/how-to-fillet-a-flat-fish/

Herb-crusted fillet of pollack with seashore vegetables and oyster cream
serves 4

A large variety of edible seashore vegetables grow abundantly on the shoreline surrounding the British Isles. They are a perfect healthy accompaniment to all fish and shellfish, being packed full of iron and other valuable nutrients. Next time you go to the seaside, take a pair of scissors and a plastic bag and forage. You'll be surprised at what you can collect for free. Sea purslane and sea beet are at their best during the summer months but still grow all year round. Samphire and sea aster, however, only grow during the summer. You will find them on the tide line in estuaries and on muddy flats. The fact that they spend some of their time submerged in sea water when the tide is full, gives them a natural saltiness, so be careful when seasoning.

18 rock oysters
40g butter
1 large shallot, finely diced
150ml dry white wine
500ml good-quality fish stock
300ml double cream
4 thick portions of pollack fillet, skinned
200g selection of wild seashore vegetables (samphire, sea aster, sea beet, sea purslane)
50ml Lemon and Rapeseed Oil Dressing (see page 292)
sea salt and freshly milled black pepper

For the herb crust
1/2 loaf of sliced white bread, crusts removed
1/4 bunch parsley, chopped
1/4 bunch chervil, chopped
1/4 bunch chives, chopped
1/4 bunch dill, chopped
125g softened butter
1 tbsp Dijon mustard
75g Cheddar, grated

Start by preparing the herb crust. Tear the slices of bread into large pieces and process to coarse crumbs in a food processor along with all the chopped herbs. Add the softened butter, mustard and cheese, and blend until well incorporated. Season with salt and pepper. The mixture should have taken on a bright green colour from the herbs.

Lay a large sheet of baking parchment on your work surface and tip the crust out on to it. Lay a second sheet of baking parchment over the top of the mixture and roll it out with a rolling pin to a thickness of about 1cm. Slide the herb crust, still between the two sheets of baking parchment, off the work surface on to a flat tray and place in the freezer for an hour to set.

Once frozen, cut the crust into squares the same size as the portions of pollack it must cover. Store in a sealed container in the freezer until ready to use. Make sure you place a small piece of baking parchment between each portion of crust to stop them from sticking together. (If you have any leftover herb crust it will keep in the freezer for up to 3 months).

Shuck the oysters from their shells (see pages 94–95 for instructions), reserving the oysters and any juices.

To prepare the sauce, place half the butter in a saucepan over a low heat and cook the shallot gently until they're soft – this will take about 7–8 minutes. Add the wine to the pan and increase the heat to bubble and reduce. Once the wine has reduced by half, add the fish stock and oyster juices. Continue to boil until the fish stock has reduced down to approximately 100ml, then add the cream. Bring the sauce back to the boil and reduce further until a light sauce consistency has been reached. Add six of the oysters and poach them for 1 minute, until just cooked. Transfer the sauce to a blender and blend until smooth, then pass it through a fine-meshed sieve. Cool quickly, and refrigerate until ready to use.

Preheat your oven to 200°C/Gas Mark 6. Lightly grease a baking tray with butter.

Season the pollack with salt and pepper and heat a non-stick frying pan. Fry the fish in a little butter until just sealed on the outside. Remove the pollack from the pan and place on the prepared baking tray. Place a frozen portion of herb crust on to each fillet. Bake the pollack on the top shelf of the oven until the fish is cooked – this will be about 8 minutes for a thick fillet. Finish the fish under the grill to crisp the crust if necessary.

While the fish is cooking, bring a saucepan of salted water to the boil for blanching the vegetables. Bring the cream sauce gently to the boil in a saucepan. Add the remaining dozen oysters and cook for 1 minute. Blanch the seashore vegetables for about 30 seconds and drain well in a colander.

To serve, place a pile of seashore vegetables in the middle of each of four large bowls, pour the oyster cream around the vegetables and place the crusted pollack on top. Drizzle a few drops of the lemon and rapeseed oil dressing into the sauce to give the dish a slight acidity and cut through the richness.

Leaving the port of Oban on route to the Isle of Mull, home to The Ethical Shellfish Company (see pages 76–79).

Gin-cured salmon
with soused cucumber
serves up to 15 as a starter

If you're reading this recipe and thinking to yourself, 'what a waste of precious gin; I'd much prefer it with a bit of tonic and a twist of lime', think again! This is the perfect accompaniment to your beloved G & T, while relaxing in the garden on a hot summer's day, stoking up the barbecue.

The salmon takes about five or six days to cure so you need to plan ahead if it's for an upcoming event. The beauty of it, however, is that once properly cured, it will keep in the fridge for 3–4 weeks.

2 sides of salmon from a 3kg fish,
*   with skin, trimmed and pin-boned*
680g demerara sugar
520g rock or sea salt
1 teaspoon coarsely ground black pepper
juice and grated zest of 4 limes
15 juniper berries, chopped
50g wholegrain mustard
400ml gin

For the soused cucumber
1 cucumber, peeled
150ml cider vinegar
2 tsp black mustard seeds
75g caster or white granulated sugar
a few sprigs of dill, roughly chopped
sea salt

Lay the sides of salmon skin-side down in a deep tray or roasting tin. Mix all the other ingredients together in a large bowl and pour over the fish, covering completely. Leave at room temperature for the first hour to kickstart the curing process and then refrigerate for 5–6 days turning the fish and re-mixing the cure daily.

When ready, wash off the curing mixture with cold water, dry well and store in the fridge until required. When slicing, always start from the tail end working your way to where the head would be. Because the fillet tapers at one end, the tail will take less time to cure. If you're feeling impatient you may want to sample the tail end a couple of days earlier.

The soused cucumber needs to be made at least 6 hours before you want to serve the salmon. Slice the cucumber into disks about 2–3mm thick and salt liberally, allowing it to drain in a colander for 20 minutes. The salt draws water out of the cucumber, making it limp and seasoning it for pickling.

Meanwhile, place the vinegar, mustard seeds and sugar in a small saucepan and bring to the boil, then remove from heat. Taste the pickling liquor and make sure the sweet-sour balance is to your liking. Set to one side to cool.

Rinse the cucumber under cold running water for a few minutes to reduce the saltiness. Drain and dry the cucumber on kitchen paper before submerging it in the cold pickling liquor. Allow to pickle for 6 hours before adding the chopped dill and serving with the sliced salmon. You want to add the dill just before serving otherwise it will discolour.

Pan-fried gurnard fillet with clams in cider and wild boar pancetta serves 4

When I first got my job at Roast I started thinking about ways in which we could use our location in the market to offer something unique. I came up with the 'Market Forage', which is where this dish was born.

I put together a menu using ingredients available in the market and split a group of guests into two teams, giving them a budget and a shopping list to go and hunt for their lunch. For this dish they went off to Furness Fish and Game for the fish and clams; to Peter Gott's Sillfield Farm stall for the wild boar pancetta; and to the New Forest stall for the cider. When they return with the fruits of their labour, we prepare the meal and they sit down to a relaxing lunch in the window looking out over the market. It's a fun day out for all.

One-pan cooking like this doesn't just alleviate the washing-up; the right combination of ingredients results in a well balanced amalgamation of flavours.

four 180g gurnard fillets, with skin,
  pin-boned (hake or line-caught cod
  are good alternatives)
100g plain flour
2 tbsp vegetable oil
100g thinly sliced wild boar pancetta
  (if you can't find wild boar pancetta
  a quality standard pancetta will
  suffice), roughly chopped
100ml good-quality dry-medium cider
20 clams
100g chilled butter
1 tbsp chopped flat-leaf parsley
sea salt and freshly milled black pepper

This dish should only take about 5 minutes to cook from start to finish, so you need to make sure you're well organised and have everything to hand before you start.

Season and lightly flour the skin side of the gurnard fillets. Heat a large non-stick frying pan over a medium heat. Add the vegetable oil and place the gurnard fillets in the pan, skin-side down, along with the pancetta. As the pancetta cooks, the tasty fat renders giving the gurnard additional seasoning and flavour. When the skin of the fish is golden and crispy, turn the fillets over and add the clams. After about a minute, carefully remove the gurnard and set to one side. Pour in the cider, cover the pan with a lid and turn up the heat to steam open the clams. Once the clams are open, after about 1 minute, add the butter, stirring continuously to emulsify it with the cider and clam juices into a glossy sauce. Season the sauce to taste. You won't need much salt, if any, as the bacon and clams should contain enough. Carefully return the fish fillets to the pan so they are hot for serving.

more **roast**
Scan the QR code to see Marcus cooking a variation of this recipe.
http://roastcookbook.com/gurnard-dish/

Baked razor clams with a chorizo crust serves 4 as a starter

Most of the razor clams collected in the UK sadly end up being exported to Europe. The Spanish and French take the majority. However, if you speak with your local fishmonger, you may be able to pre-order a bundle or two. Another option would be to collect them yourself, which can make for a fun weekend excursion. They are found on tidal flats all around the British coastline, but the most prized come from the cold clean waters of Scotland. The idea is to fool the clams (that bury themselves in the sand when the tide recedes) into thinking the tide has come back in. Simply pour neat salt down the clam's spout hole. At the salty taste of the incoming tide it will poke out its siphon. Pull it from the base, easing it out gently.

Razor clams need to be cooked very quickly until the shells are just open. Overcooked, I'd liken them to the texture of a Wellington boot! They work particularly well with chorizo or other cured meats because the salt content balances with the clam's shellfish sweetness.

8 large live razor clams
200ml white wine
8 slices of fresh white sandwich bread,
  crusts removed
50ml vegetable oil
100g cooking chorizo, peeled and cut
  into very small dice
1/2 onion, finely chopped
120g butter
2 garlic cloves, roughly chopped
2 tablespoons chopped flat-leaf parsley
sea salt and freshly milled black pepper

Preheat your oven-grill to 200°C/ Gas Mark 6.

To open the clams you will need a large saucepan with a lid. The pan must be scorching hot so when the clams and wine are added, the wine boils on contact creating the intense steam required to open the shells. Place the lid on tightly and allow 20–30 seconds for the clams to open. When all the clams are open (discard any that haven't), transfer them to a bowl and cool them quickly in the fridge, along with any remaining liquor left in the pan.

For the chorizo crust, process the bread slices in a food processor into crumbs.

Put the vegetable oil into a saucepan over a medium heat and cook the chorizo, rendering out all the tasty orange fat. Add the onion and approximately 80g of the butter. Cook the onion slowly until soft and translucent before mixing in the breadcrumbs. Once the breadcrumbs have absorbed the butter and chorizo fat, season the mixture with salt and pepper. Try not to overwork the mixture, as you want the breadcrumbs to stay fluffy and not form a ball of dough. Add the chopped parsley and transfer to a tray to cool quickly.

Remove the chilled clams from each shell. They should pop out quite easily once cooked. Wash the shells in cold water to free them from any sand or grit, and lay them out 'inside-up', on a large oven tray. Strain the cooking liquor through a fine-meshed sieve into a saucepan, add the remaining butter, bring to the boil and then turn off the heat.

To clean the clams, remove and discard the large brown waste sack from the middle of the clam, rinsing it under cold water to ensure no grit is left behind. Cut each clam into three pieces and add to the hot liquor to warm through gently. Divide the clam meat and liquor evenly between the shells and then top with the chorizo crust. Bake in the oven for 4–5 minutes and then switch the oven to grill so a crust forms. Serve immediately.

Monkfish curry with crispy spiced shallots serves 4

In the melting pot of multicultural Britain we are exposed to foods from countless different ethnicities. One cuisine, which has been embraced with open arms and permanently adopted, is Indian. At Roast we regularly feature a curry on the menu and this is a cracker!

I learnt this recipe from a former colleague, Joseph Benny. Benny was an Indian chef working in the private dining kitchen at Brown's Hotel while I was there, and he cooked the most phenomenal Indian food. Cheers Benny.

Monkfish lends itself well to this dish as it is a meaty fish ideal for braising and it has only one large spinal bone running between each juicy fillet rather than lots of tiny bones that can be difficult to eat.

Being quite a complex dish involving a lot of ingredients and preparation, I have broken this recipe down into steps so it's easier to follow. Don't be put off, it's a dish I have prepared at home on a few occasions for guests and once the prep is done, it's actually quite simple to put together and the feedback is very positive.

four 350g skinned monkfish tails on
    the bone, each cut into 3 pieces
30ml vegetable oil
200g shallots, peeled and finely diced
250g ripe tomatoes, diced
2 tsp ground turmeric
2 tsp garam masala
2 tsp ground cumin
1 tsp chilli powder
1 tsp ground coriander
1 tsp ground fenugreek
3 tbsp chopped coriander leaves
lemon juice (optional)
sea salt
steamed basmati rice, to serve

For the marinade
juice of ½ lemon
3 tbsp vegetable oil
1 tsp chilli powder
1 tsp ground turmeric
1 tsp sea salt

For the tamarind and coconut purée
50g tamarind pulp
100ml warm water
20g fresh root ginger, peeled and
    roughly chopped
2 garlic cloves, roughly chopped
2 green chillies, deseeded
700ml coconut milk

For the crispy spiced shallots
vegetable oil, for deep-frying
1 tbsp ground turmeric
1 tbsp garam masala
1 tbsp ground cumin
1 tbsp ground coriander
500g gluten-free flour
300ml milk
3 banana shallots, peeled, halved and
    sliced lengthways about 3mm thick
20 fresh curry leaves
table salt

For the tempering
75ml vegetable oil
2 tsp black mustard seeds
1 tsp of fenugreek seeds
15 curry leaves
1 shallot, finely chopped
1 garlic clove, chopped

Start by marinating the fish. Mix all the marinade ingredients, coat the monkfish well then cover and leave to marinate in the fridge for 2 hours.

While the fish is marinating, prepare the tamarind and coconut purée and the crispy spiced shallots. For the purée,

place the tamarind paste in the warm water and mix thoroughly before pushing through a sieve to separate the hard seeds and pod from the pulp. Reserve the pulp and discard what couldn't be passed through the sieve. Blend the remaining ingredients in a blender with the tamarind pulp until smooth. Set aside.

Set your deep-fat fryer to 180°C. If you don't have a fryer, place the oil into a large, deep saucepan, but only fill it half full: when you add the shallots they will boil fiercely and the oil level will rise dramatically. Place the oil over a high heat but be very careful that it doesn't get too hot – you will need a cooking thermometer so that you can regulate the temperature.

Sift the spices and flour into a shallow bowl and mix well to combine. Place the milk in a second bowl. Coat the shallots in the spiced flour then dip in the milk. Put the shallots back into the spiced flour for a second coating, then lift out with your fingers shaking off any excess flour. Carefully deep-fry the shallots until golden and crispy. Just before the shallots are done, add the curry leaves for the final 10 seconds. Using a slotted spoon carefully lift the shallots and curry leaves out of the oil and drain well on kitchen paper. Season with table salt. Set aside until you're ready to flash them through a hot oven just before serving. Heat a non-stick frying pan and when hot seal the marinated monkfish on all sides then remove from the pan and set the fish to one side.

continued on page 70

continued from page 69

In a large saucepan, heat the vegetable oil over a medium-high heat and cook the shallot, stirring frequently until lightly caramelised. Add all the spices and cook for a further 2 minutes, stirring constantly to toast the spices and develop their flavour.

Add the tomatoes and cook for a further minute or so using the juice from the tomato to loosen any shallots or spices that may have caught on the bottom of the pan. Add the tamarind and coconut purée and bring up to a gentle simmer stirring regularly so it doesn't catch. Season with sea salt and simmer for 10 minutes or so.

While the sauce is cooking, prepare the ingredients for tempering the curry. In a small saucepan heat the vegetable oil almost to smoking point. With a lid to hand, add the mustard and fenugreek seeds and cover immediately. When the seeds have stopped popping, carefully add the curry leaves, standing back as these will also pop in the hot oil. To cool the oil and arrest the toasting of the spices, add the shallot and garlic. Cook for a few seconds making sure the garlic doesn't brown and then add the mixture to the curry sauce. This tempering process adds a lovely toasted savoury flavour to the sauce balancing it and bringing all the flavours together.

Season the curry sauce with sea salt, to taste. When tasting the sauce, check for a balance of acidity and if you think it's required, add a little lemon juice. Finally, add the sealed monkfish to the sauce, cover with a lid and simmer gently for about 3–4 minutes until the fish is just cooked through. Flash the crispy shallots quickly through the oven to heat them through, and just before serving add the chopped coriander to the curry. Serve topped with the crispy spiced shallots and steamed basmati rice.

Opening live scallops

Your live scallops should either be tightly closed or close quickly when given a firm tap. The best knife to use is a standard butter knife. Anything too sharp can be dangerous. If you are right-handed, hold the scallop in your left hand, with the flat shell facing upwards and the hinge away from you. Wiggle your butter knife between the shells, sliding it in about $2\frac{1}{2}$ cm towards the right side of the hinge with the sharp edge going towards the hinge (1). Use the knife to release the tendon, which holds the scallop to the flat shell. Once the tendon is cut, twist the blade of the knife partially prising the scallop open. You will need to hold the shell open with your thumb (2) as the scallop is still live at this point and you will feel it trying to close. Look inside the shell and see where the scallop is attached to the flat shell. Using the flat shell to guide your knife, carefully and slowly detach the scallop from the flat shell discarding the shell and leaving you with the scallop sitting inside the concave shell. The next step is to remove the top skirt by holding it between your thumb and the blade of the knife and lifting it up gently to remove it (3). Then using the same technique, remove the gills (4). Once the gills are removed, still holding the scallop with the hinge away from you and using the sharp edge of the knife, cut the black stomach from the scallop being careful not to pierce it as it contains toxins (5). Now you must remove the bottom skirt using the same technique and you did for the top skirt (6). As you pull it away the stomach and pancreas will all go with it as they are attached to the bottom skirt (7). To remove the intestinal loop, using your thumb, push it out of the bright orange roe or coral to expose it, and holding it between your thumb and the blade of the knife (8), pull it out.

Remove any sand or grit by running the scallop gently under cold water (8).

If you wish to remove the scallop completely from the concave shell I find it easiest to use a dessert spoon as its shape is the same as that of the shell therefore reducing the likelihood of leaving any meat attached to the shell.

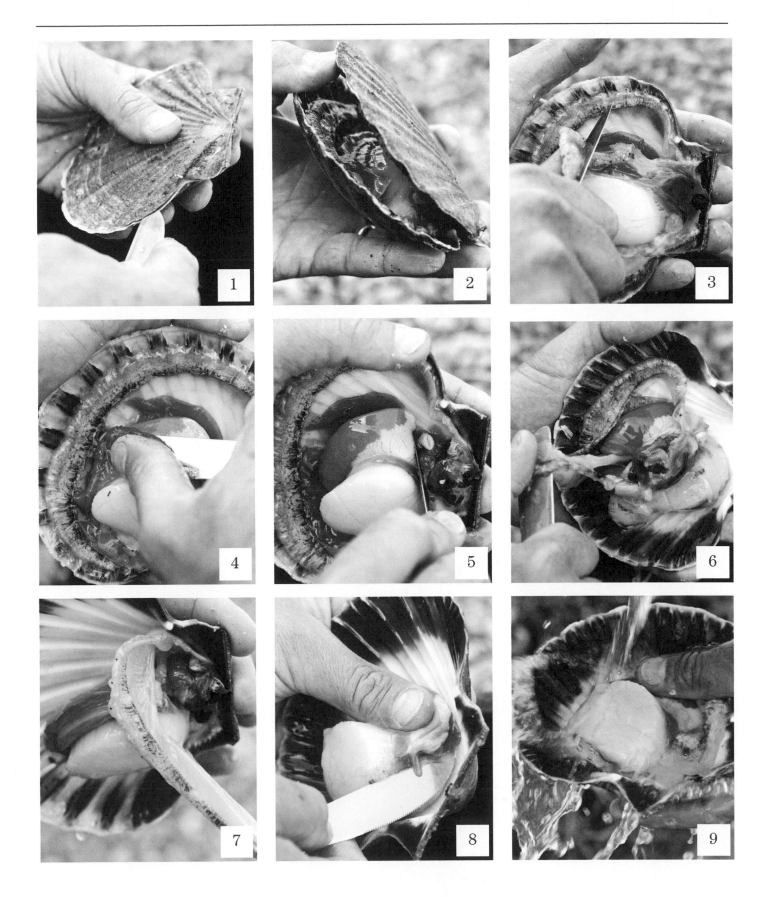

Pan-fried scallops with whipped cauliflower and cobnut butter

serves 4 as a starter

Scallops and cauliflower are one of those perfect combinations in food. The juicy texture and sweetness of the scallop work so well with the velvety smooth creaminess of the whipped cauliflower.

12 live medium scallops
80g shelled fresh cobnuts (if you can't find fresh cobnuts, you could use standard hazelnuts)
3 tbsp vegetable oil
1 small cauliflower, broken into florets and finely chopped
250ml milk
50g butter
a few flat-leaf parsley leaves, chopped
sea salt and freshly milled black pepper
1 lemon, cut into wedges, to serve

Prepare the scallops as described on pages 72–73 and remove them from their shells.

Preheat your oven to 190°C/Gas Mark 5.

On a small baking tray, toast your cobnuts for about 5 minutes in the oven with a little sea salt and a light drizzle of vegetable oil. They should only be toasted lightly, to bring out the oils and flavour. Once cooked, remove them from the oven and when they're cool enough to handle, chop them roughly.
Place the concave scallop shells in the oven, switch it off and leave them in there to keep warm until you need them.

For the whipped cauliflower, place the cauliflower in a small saucepan with the milk, a pinch of salt and a twist of pepper. Over a medium heat, slowly bring the milk to a simmer and cook until the cauliflower is very soft. With a slotted spoon, remove the cauliflower from the pan to a blender and blend until very smooth. You may need to add a touch of the milk to achieve the desired consistency. Return to the pan over a very low heat to keep warm.

Divide the hot scallop shells between four plates.

Heat a large heavy-based frying pan over a high heat. Place the scallops into a bowl and season them with salt and pepper. Add the oil and coat the scallops. It's better to oil the scallops than the pan so you use minimal oil and the scallops sear rather than boil. Carefully place each scallop into the hot pan. Scallops must be cooked quickly so they caramelise but don't overcook. Sear the scallops until caramelised on one side, then turn over. Don't be tempted to shake the pan around, this will only cool it down. After a few seconds, add the butter and cobnuts. Put a tablespoon of warm whipped cauliflower into each shell, followed by a scallop and a spoonful of cobnut butter. Be careful not to over do it with the cobnuts, they are deceivingly strong in flavour. Serve with a wedge of lemon.

The Ethical
Shellfish Company
and the responsible upkeep
of our precious seas

In 2008 Guy and Juliet Grieve embarked on a long sailing journey with their two young children. Living on a boat for a period of 10 months instilled in them a love and respect for the sea and an awareness of the fragile ecosystems that exist within it. On returning from their adventures, Guy, an experienced and passionate outdoorsman, began working as a scallop diver in the waters surrounding the Isle of Mull. During that time he became increasingly disturbed by the damage being done to the marine environment by invasive fishing methods. Not being the kind of man to sit back and accept these goings on, Guy and his wife Juliet established The Ethical Shellfish Company in April 2010. Their company pledges to support fishermen using sustainable methods, and will never sell shellfish that has been fished in a way that is damaging to the marine environment. By proving that it is possible to run a successful business that only deals in ethically sourced shellfish, they hope that they can contribute towards the recovery of our seas.

I have been lucky enough to go out on the boat with Guy on a couple of occasions when he's been diving. The logistics and processes he adheres to in order to manage his local waters in a sustainable fashion are fascinating. Guy likens himself to an 'ocean-going shepherd', and after each dive, hand grades the scallops, putting the small ones to one side. At the end of the day's diving all of these small scallops are carefully redistributed in areas of the seabed, out of reach from the destructive dredge boats. He chooses an area with high tidal flow where he knows they will be well fed and will flourish. The small scallops are left in this ideally chosen habitat to grow to a suitable size. During their stay in these 'chucky patches', as they are known in the trade, the scallops spawn many times before they are finally harvested. In the ebb and flow of the tides, spawn from Guy's chucky patches will be carried for many nautical miles. This method of fishing creates areas of intense fertility, helping to safeguard scallop stocks for the future.

From a chef's perspective, my conscience is put at ease knowing that I'm dealing with a company that puts ethics at the heart of its business. As a result, our customers can feel confident that what they receive on their plate are scallops of the highest quality that have not been harvested at the expense of the environment. After all, it is the responsibility of all of us to ensure that what we enjoy eating today is still available in abundance for future generations to enjoy.

from the sea

Herb-roasted fillet of wild sea trout with a warm spring vegetable salad and crackling serves 4

After the long winter, spring makes such a refreshing change. The number of new ingredients at your fingertips is an exciting prospect: the first of the season's asparagus, new-season Jersey Royals, and early peas and their shoots, to name but a few. In late spring the first of the wild sea trout arrive at the market. Sea trout are very similar in appearance to salmon; however, they start their lives in rivers as trout eggs. When the eggs hatch some of the small trout will stay river-bound while others will venture out to sea. The sea trout, due to their environment and a high-protein diet of crustacea, squid and small fish, grow to be much bigger than the river trout. If you don't manage to find sea trout for this dish it can be substituted with salmon.

one 800g fillet of wild sea trout, with skin, scaled
3 tbsp vegetable oil
200g small Jersey Royal potatoes
8 asparagus spears
500g broad beans, in their pods (will yield about 150g of podded broad beans)
a few sprigs of dill, chopped
a few sprigs of parsley, chopped
a few sprigs of chervil, chopped
400g peas in their pods (will yield about 150g of podded peas)
80ml Lemon and Rapeseed Oil Dressing (see page 292)
a good handful of pea shoots
sea salt and freshly milled black pepper

Lay the trout fillet skin-side down on a well secured chopping board. Remove the pin bones with a clean pair of pliers or tweezers starting from the head end. To skin the fillet, clasp the tip of the tail between your thumb and forefinger and draw a knife down the length of the fillet, slicing between the skin and the flesh with the blade angled slightly towards the chopping board, using it as a guide. Cut the fish into four even portions and store in the fridge; reserve the skin.

For the trout crackling, preheat your oven to 200°C/Gas Mark 6.

Lay the skin flat out on your chopping board and scrape a sharp knife across the skin to remove any remaining flesh. Line a roasting tray with a sheet of greaseproof paper and lay out the skin with the outside facing upwards. Sprinkle the skin with sea salt and drizzle with a little vegetable oil. Place another sheet of greaseproof paper over the skin and another tray on top, sandwiching the skin between the two trays. Bake for 15–20 minutes, until crispy.

Place the Jersey Royals into a saucepan and just cover with cold water. Add a heaped teaspoon of salt and bring them to the boil over a high heat. After they have boiled for about 8 minutes, they should be cooked. Test them with the point of a small knife. Once they're cooked, drain and cut each one in half. Set aside.

Remove the woody end from the asparagus spears and cut each spear into 3.

Blanch the broad beans for 1 minute in boiling water, then refresh in iced water. Once the beans are cold, pop them out of their bitter skins.

Mix all the chopped herbs together and spread them out on a tray. Season the sea trout with salt and pepper then lay the portions in the herbs, turning them to coat both sides.

Bring a saucepan of lightly salted water to the boil. Heat a large non-stick frying pan over a medium-high heat, then add the vegetable oil.

Lay the trout portions gently in the frying pan, and cook for 2 minutes on one side until lightly browned before turning over. Cook for a further 1–2 minutes and remove from the pan to rest while you cook the vegetables. Drop the potatoes, asparagus, peas and broad beans into the boiling water and cook for 2–3 minutes. Drain the vegetables and toss in a bowl with the lemon and rapeseed oil dressing and a touch of seasoning. Divide the vegetables between four serving bowls and flake each portion of trout into large chunks over the top. Crack the crispy trout skin into bite-sized pieces and place a few into each salad. Scatter with pea shoots and serve.

Garfish fingers and chips with tartare sauce serves 4

The first time I tried garfish was in the Algarve in Portugal; I hooked one while I was mackerel fishing. Garfish are often caught with mackerel as they have a similar diet and hunt alongside each other. They're a spectacular fish to catch, leaping high out of the water in a last-ditch struggle for freedom. I was staying in a small fishing village called Alvor. The waterfront at Alvor is lined with open-air seafood restaurants and all the fish is on display for you to choose as you walk past; the chef is right there cooking over hot coals. Their barbecues are made from a 200-litre oil drum, which they cut in half, set a wire rack over the cavity and fill with hot coals. The smell of barbecued sardines wafts through the whole village. This wonderful memory leaves my mouth watering! Once the boat landed, I took my garfish and a few mackerel to one of the restaurants and asked the chef if he could cook the garfish for my lunch in return for the mackerel. When it came to the table, I was unexpectedly shocked to see the bright green bones. The waiter went on to tell me that some folk don't eat garfish as they're worried they're not safe. Well it's their loss, as straight from the charcoal, the fish was delicious.

At Roast we use garfish for fish fingers, either in the restaurant or as a bar snack. The deep-fried skeleton makes a striking garnish. Whiting are a good alternative if your fishmonger doesn't have garfish.

100g plain flour
2 eggs, beaten
200g Japanese panko breadcrumbs
vegetable oil, for deep frying
4 garfish, about 500g each, filleted
sea salt
4 portions of Thrice-cooked Chips
  (see page 283)
200g Tartare Sauce (see page 291)
1 lemon, cut into wedges, to serve

Place the flour in a shallow bowl; the beaten eggs in a second bowl and the breadcrumbs in a third. Set your deep-fat fryer to 190°C. If you don't have a fryer, place the oil into a large, deep saucepan, leaving enough room at the top to allow for rapid boiling when the fish fingers are added. Place the oil over a high heat but be very careful that it doesn't get too hot. If you have a cooking thermometer, use it so you can regulate the temperature. If not, test the heat by dropping a cube of bread into the oil; it should bubble on entry and start to brown after about 15 seconds.

Have to hand some kitchen paper and a slotted spoon to remove the fish fingers from the hot oil. (Don't try to use spring-loaded tongs; this can be very dangerous for obvious reasons.)

Cut down the centre of each fish fillet removing the row of small pin bones that runs down the middle. The fillets from 500g fish should be large enough to enable you to cut fingers from either side of the bones. The fingers should be about 8cm in length but there is no need to be too precise.

Coat the fish fingers in the flour and shake off any excess. Dip the fingers into the egg, a few at a time, and then into the breadcrumbs. If you're not happy with the coating of crumbs, dip them back into the egg, then into the crumbs again for a second coat.

Deep-fry the fish fingers for a couple of minutes, until golden and crispy. You may need to do this in batches. Once ready, drain on the kitchen paper to soak up any oil before seasoning with sea salt. Serve with the thrice-cooked chips, tartare sauce and lemon wedges.

Wild sea bass with Dublin Bay prawns and summer vegetables in a saffron broth serves 4

I came up with this dish a few years before I had even started at Roast, when hunting through Borough Market one Saturday looking for something to cook for friends I had invited for dinner. My first stop was Furness fish and game where I picked up a nice fat side of wild sea bass and a few Dublin Bay prawns. Then it was off to see Tony Booth (now supplying us from Bermondsey) for the vegetables and herbs. I've known Tony for over 10 years now and he is one of the first suppliers I call when I'm changing the menu and want some ideas involving forthcoming British produce. His experience and knowledge are second to none and he has taught me so much over the years.

The vibrant colours of this dish are the epitome of summer and it went down a treat with my friends.

1 small fennel bulb, cored and cut into quarters
1 red pepper
12 medium Dublin Bay prawns
1/2 small onion, roughly chopped
a sprig of thyme
1 small bay leaf
2 tbsp tomato purée
100ml white wine
1 litre water
a pinch of saffron threads
one 800g–1kg piece of boneless wild sea bass fillet, with skin, cut into 4 even portions
1 small courgette, balled using a melon baller
1 large ripe tomato, deseeded and cut into 2½cm dice
50g chilled butter, plus a small knob for cooking the fish
10 basil leaves, torn
olive oil
vegetable oil
sea salt and freshly milled black pepper

Preheat your oven to 200°C/Gas Mark 6.

Place the pieces of fennel and the whole pepper into a small roasting dish, season with salt and pepper and drizzle with olive oil. Cover with foil and bake in the oven for 20–25 minutes until softened and starting to caramelise around the edges.

While the fennel and peppers are cooking prepare the shellfish stock required for the broth. Cut the heads off the prawns and set the tails to one side. Heat a large saucepan with a little olive oil and fry the prawn heads and attached claws over a medium heat for about 3 or 4 minutes, crushing them with a wooden spoon to extract all their flavour as you move them around the pan. Add the onion, thyme and bay leaf and cook for a further 2 minutes, until the onions are starting to soften. Add the tomato purée, wine and water. Bring the stock to the boil then turn down to a gentle simmer. Cook the stock for 30 minutes, skimming every so often with a ladle to remove any residue, then strain through a fine-mesh sieve.

Bring a pan of salted water to the boil and poach the prawn tails for 30 seconds only, then refresh in cold water. Peel the tails and set to one side.

Once the fennel and red peppers are cooked, place the pepper into a small bowl and cover with clingfilm. After about 5 minutes the skin of the pepper will have loosened due to the steam given off and it will be easier to peel. Once the pepper is peeled, remove the core and seeds, slice it into strips and cut the fennel into 2½cm dice.

Now that all the preparation work is done you can cook the fish, make the broth and assemble the dish. Bring 400ml of your prawn stock to the boil along with a pinch of saffron. If you have any remaining stock, it will keep in the freezer for up to 3 months.

Heat a non-stick frying pan with a little vegetable oil over a medium-high heat. It's better to use a non-stick pan, but if you don't have anything non-stick you will need to flour the skin side of the fish first. Season the sea bass portions with salt and pepper and fry the fish, skin-side down. Once the skin of the fish is crispy, add a small knob of butter to the pan and turn each fillet over, lowering the heat to finish cooking the fish gently.

Add the courgettes to the boiling stock and allow to cook for 1 minute before adding the diced tomato, fennel and red pepper. Bring the stock back to the boil and whisk in the chilled butter gently so as not to damage the vegetables. The butter will enrich the broth, creating a light emulsion.

Just before serving, season the broth with salt and pepper and add the prawn tails and torn basil. To serve, ladle the vegetables, prawns and broth into four shallow bowls and place the sea bass on top.

Marinated Manx queenies with lime, peas and dill serves 8–10 as a light starter, or more as part of a canapé selection

The queenies (queen scallops) we use at Roast are pulled out of the water off the Isle of Man one day and with us before midday the next. The fact that they come in so fresh and gleaming gives us the option to serve them raw. This dish is an adaptation of the South American dish ceviche in which fish is marinated in a mixture of lime juice, chilli, herbs and sometimes other aromatics. The fish is served raw, only being 'cooked' a little by the acid in the lime. Ceviche is usually prepared using coriander, but I think the sweet peas and the dill really complement the lime.

24 fresh queenies, in half shells
100ml extra virgin olive oil
juice and zest of 3 limes
1 small green chilli, deseeded and
  finely chopped
½ small red onion, finely diced
100g frozen peas, defrosted and
  roughly chopped
1 tbsp chopped dill
sea salt

Clean your queenies under running water, ensuring they are free from grit and remove from their shells. Reserve the shells for serving.

In a bowl mix together the olive oil, lime juice and zest, chilli and red onion. Allow to stand for 10 minutes for the flavours to infuse.

Add the chopped peas and dill to the bowl followed by the queenies and allow to marinate for 5 minutes. (The reason the peas and dill are added later is because the acid in the lime juice discolours them very quickly.)

Lay out the shells on your serving platter and spoon one queenie into each, topped with the pea marinade.

Preparing crab

See page 88 for instructions.

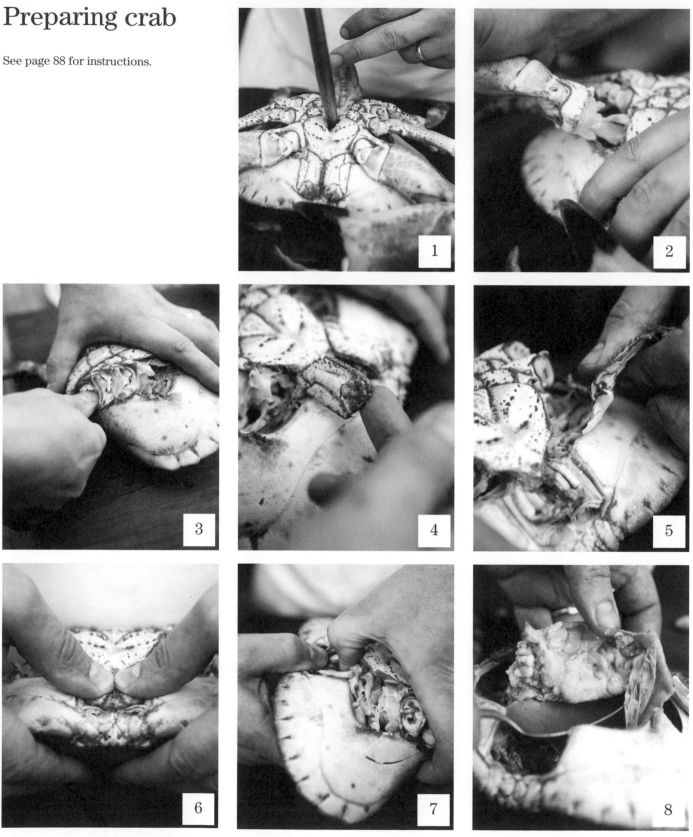

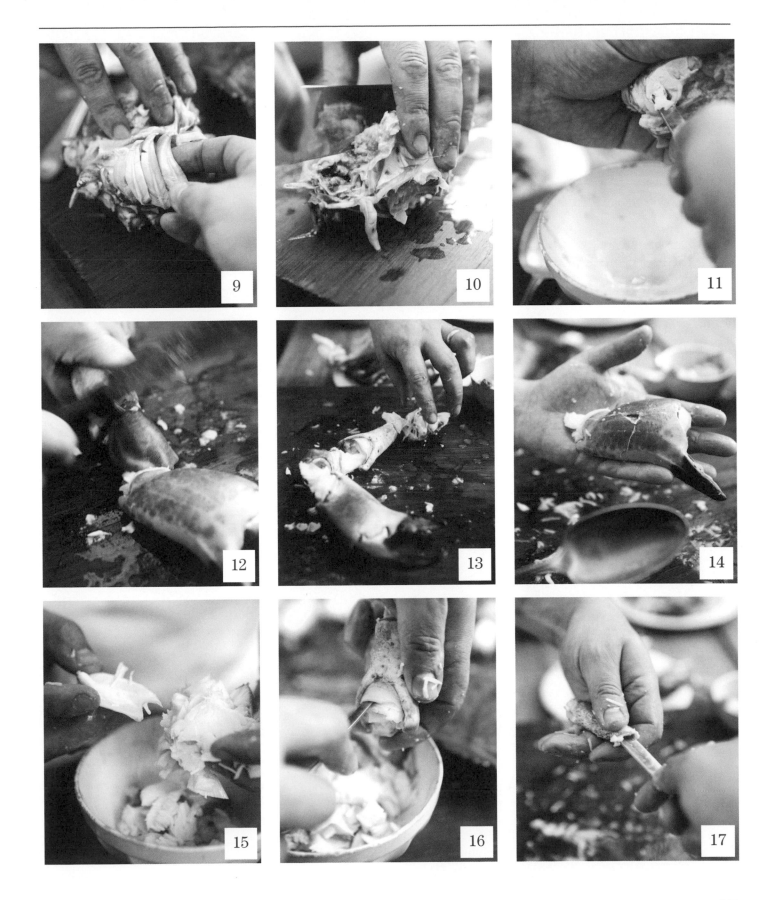

Crab on toast serves 4

Brown crabs patrol the sea floor around the British Isles like armoured military tanks. They are definitely my favourite of all the crustacea pulled from these waters and one of the best eating crabs you will find anywhere. There are healthy stocks of brown crab in most waters around the UK due to carefully managed size restrictions and a ban on the sale of egg-laden females.

2 live cock crabs, about 800g–1kg each
100ml Mayonnaise (see page 290)
a pinch of cayenne pepper
4 thick slices of crusty bread
sea salt
a bunch of watercress, leaves picked
*   and washed, to serve*
1 lemon, cut into wedges, to serve

Preparing your crabs

Bring a large pan of heavily salted water (about 30g salt per litre of water) to a rapid boil. To kill the crabs, turn each one on to its back and lift the triangular tail flap on its underside. Under the flap, directly between the frontmost pair of legs, is a small cone-shaped indentation. Hold the crab steady, avoiding the powerful claws, and push a strong metal skewer or the tip of a pointed sharpening steel into the crab with enough force to break through the undercarriage (1). This will kill the crab instantly. Plunge the crabs straight into the water and once the water comes back to the boil, cook for 12 minutes. Once cooked, allow to cool on a tray for 10 minutes before chilling completely in the fridge.

There are two types of meat in a crab. The sweet, flakey white meat from the claws, legs and body, and the rich, creamy brown meat from inside the shell. To extract the meat, twist off the claws and legs (2, 3) and set to one side. To prise the heavy shell from the body, firstly remove the mouth frame (4, 5), then with both thumbs press firmly on the mouth, just below the eyes, pushing it inside the body (6), and with your thumb still inside the resulting hole, lift the shell from the body detaching it completely (7). With a spoon, scrape the brown meat from inside the shell (8) into a bowl, cover it and store in the fridge.

Remove and discard the gills, or 'dead man's fingers' as they are known, from the body (9). Split the body in half straight down the middle with a heavy knife (10) in order to open all the small compartments of white meat. Using a crab pick or the handle of a teaspoon, remove all the meat from the body into a bowl (11). With the back of a heavy knife break the claws into the four obvious sections at the joints (12, 13). Crack the shell of the claw sections with the back of a heavy spoon (14) and pick out the meat (15), removing the hard cartilage that runs down the middle of the claw. Do the same with the other claw sections (16) and the legs (17). Pick through the white meat carefully, to ensure you haven't missed any fragments of shell. Place all the shell remains in freezerproof bags and freeze for making stock or soup at a later date. They will keep frozen for up to 3 months.

Toast the slices of bread and while they are toasting, mix the brown crab meat with the mayonnaise and season with salt and a pinch of cayenne pepper. Spread the crab mayonnaise liberally onto the hot toast and top with a generous helping of sweet white meat. Serve with a scattering of watercress and a lemon wedge.

Mussel and fennel broth serves 10–12

This rich velvety soup is perfect on a cold winter's day with a torn up loaf of crusty bread spread generously with good butter. It may seem strange to have the addition of chicken stock to a fish-based soup, however, if you were to use only fish stock in this recipe it would be too strong in flavour. Good fresh stocks are readily available these days but you still can't beat home-made.

3kg live mussels
1 tsp fennel seeds
200ml good-quality dry cider
100g butter
3 fennel bulbs, with tops, bulbs cut into
* 1 cm dice and tops roughly chopped*
1 small onion, cut into 1cm dice
100g plain flour
1½ litres Fish Stock (see page 299)
1½ litres Chicken Stock (see page 298)
200ml double cream
juice of ½ lemon
sea salt and freshly milled black pepper
crusty bread and butter, to serve

If your mussels are rope grown they should be free from sand and grit, but if not, run cold water over them for a few minutes. If you come across any mussels that are open, give them a couple of taps on the worktop and if they don't close, discard them. Heat a large lidded saucepan or stockpot over a high heat until very hot. Add the mussels, fennel seeds, and cider and quickly cover with the lid, placing it on tightly, to steam the mussels. Shake the pan from time to time to redistribute them so they all open together. Discard any that do not open. Transfer the mussels quickly to the fridge to chill and strain the liquor through a fine-mesh sieve to remove any grit. This well flavoured stock will be used as a base for the soup. Keep the mussel stock warm over a low heat.

Using the same saucepan set over a low heat, cook the diced fennel and onion in the butter for 3–4 minutes until soft. Add the flour and stir until well amalgamated with the butter, fennel and onions. The flour is used as a thickening agent, giving the soup more body.

Slowly add the hot mussel stock, stirring constantly to avoid lumps. Add the fish and chicken stocks and bring the soup to the boil. Turn the heat down and simmer for 10–15 minutes before adding the cream. Season with salt and pepper.

Meanwhile, remove two thirds of the mussels from their shells, removing the beards as you go (the beard is the small fibrous growth the mussel uses to attach itself to the rock or rope). Remove the beards from the remaining mussels but leave them in their shells to garnish. When you're ready to serve add the chopped fennel tops and the mussels to the hot soup and bring back to the boil. Serve immediately with plenty of crusty bread and butter.

Steamed mussels in cider with smoked bacon and Cox's apple serves 6–8

I have fond childhood memories of collecting sacks of green-lipped mussels straight from the rocks with my father. He used to steam them open and pickle them in jars that would always come out when the All Blacks were playing. The New Zealand green-lipped is a much larger mussel than the varieties available in the UK. As far as flavour goes though, I much prefer the smaller sweeter Blueshell mussels, grown from ropes in the Shetland Isles. For this dish, and any other for that matter, make sure you find a quality dry-medium cider. Don't just settle for the commercial sweet brands that litter the market.

2kg live mussels
50ml rapeseed oil
6 rashers of smoked streaky bacon,
   roughly chopped
250ml good-quality dry-medium cider
2 Cox's apples, grated
50g butter
200ml double cream
a large bunch of flat-leaf parsley,
   roughly chopped
a good pinch of sea salt
crusty bread, to serve

Rinse the mussels under the cold tap. If they're rope grown they should be free from sand and grit, but if not, run cold water over them for a few minutes. Pull the beard out of each mussel. The mussel uses this to attach itself to the rock or rope. If you come across any mussels that are open, give them a couple of taps on the worktop and if they don't close, discard them.

Place a large lidded saucepan or stockpot over a high heat and add the rapeseed oil. When the oil just starts to smoke add the bacon, and moving it constantly with a wooden spoon, fry until crispy. Add the mussels, cider, apple and butter and place the lid on tightly, trapping in the steam so the mussels open quickly. Shake the pan from time to time to redistribute them so they all open together. Discard any mussels that do not open. Spoon the opened mussels into the serving dish and place the pan with the mussel stock back on the heat. Add the cream and parsley, bring it back to the boil and pour the broth over the mussels making sure all the bacon and apple goes with it. Serve with plenty of crusty bread to hand to soak up all the flavoursome broth.

***more* roast**
Scan the QR code to see Marcus cooking a variation of this recipe.
http://roastcookbook.com/mussels-in-cider/

Mum's fish pie serves 4–6

This was one of the dinners I most looked forward to as a child. There's something wonderfully comforting about a rich creamy fish pie on a miserable rainy day. The fish species can be varied in accordance with season, availability, sustainability and value. However you should always include something smoked for depth of flavour. Mussels are also a welcome addition. To make it more luxurious, why not add some prawns or even some lobster meat.

1½ onions
300g white fish fillet (haddock or
    pollack are ideal)
100g undyed smoked haddock
300g salmon fillet
2 tbsp chopped flat-leaf parsley leaves
    (reserve the stalks)
1 bay leaf
500ml milk
50g butter
40g plain flour
1 tbsp Worcestershire sauce
2 tbsp anchovy sauce (Watkins is a
    good brand)
1½ tbsp English mustard
3 hard-boiled eggs, cut into quarters
juice of ½ lemon

For the topping
700g floury potatoes (Maris Piper are
    ideal), peeled and halved
80g softened butter
100ml warm whole milk
80g fresh white breadcrumbs (not
    dried)
80g grated Cheddar

Preheat your oven to 180°C/Gas Mark 4.

Slice the half onion and place in a large saucepan along with the three types of fish, the parsley stalks, and the bay leaf. Cover with the milk, bring to the boil, then remove from the heat and rest for 1 minute or until the fish is almost cooked.

Strain through a sieve, reserving the milk, and flake the fish into 3–4cm pieces. Cut the remaining onion into small dice, place in a large saucepan with the butter and cook over a low heat until soft. Add the flour and stir constantly for about 1 minute, before adding the warm reserved milk a little at a time, stirring continuously to avoid lumps. Cook the sauce for 3–4 minutes, stirring regularly until you can no longer taste the flour. Remove from the heat and add the Worcestershire sauce, anchovy sauce, mustard and chopped parsley.

Lay out the flaked fish evenly in a baking dish. Place the egg quarters among the fish. Finally, pour the sauce over the fish and eggs to cover and allow enough room for the topping. Place in the fridge to cool and set.

For the topping, place the potatoes in lightly salted cold water and bring to the boil. Cook for about 15–20 minutes, until well cooked, then drain and allow them to release some steam for a couple of minutes. Mash the potatoes using a masher or even better, a potato ricer. Gently fold the warm milk and butter into the mash until smooth.

Spread an even layer of mash over the pie and drag the prongs of a fork across the top creating grooves, which will help to form a crust when baked. Bake in the oven for 25–30 minutes until hot through. Mix the breadcrumbs and grated Cheddar in a bowl, then sprinkle over the top of the pie. Bake for a further 5 minutes until the topping is golden and crispy. Finish under the grill if necessary.

shucking oysters

For safety reasons, only shuck oysters using an oyster knife –
they are sometimes sold by fishmongers; if not try a kitchen
equipment shop. I remember buying some oysters from the
dockside in Bari while backpacking in Italy. All I had on me to
open them was a Swiss Army knife. Don't try this at home; the
knife ended up snapping shut on my thumb and I had to find a
hospital to get it stitched up.

To shuck the oysters, fold an old tea towel so that you have
three layers of cloth and place it on your work surface.
Sit the oyster in the middle of the towel with the flat shell, or
'lid', facing upwards, and the hinge pointing towards the right.
(These instructions are for right-handers. Lefties, please
reverse.) With your left hand, hold the oyster still by folding it
inside the towel, but still leaving access to the hinge. The
folded towel will give your left hand some protection should
you slip with the sharp oyster knife.

Hold the oyster knife firmly in your right hand with the butt of
the handle resting comfortably in your palm. Push the point of
the oyster knife firmly into the hinge, wiggling it as you go (1).
Once you're about 1cm inside the oyster, twist the knife to pop
the hinge (2). When the hinge is popped, to release the lid
you'll have to cut through the muscle the oyster uses to open
and close its shell (3). If you were holding the oyster with the
hinge facing towards you, the muscle is situated on the right-
hand side of the shell. Slide the sharp edge of the knife blade
along the inside of the right-hand side of the oyster's lid, keep
the knife hard up against the roof of the lid to ensure you don't
cut into the precious oyster inside. Once you've cut through
the muscle, the lid will lift off revealing the juicy oyster (4).

Discard the lid and slide your knife underneath the oyster
releasing it from the bottom shell (5). Enjoy your oysters! (6)

more **roast**
Scan the QR code to see
Marcus shucking an oyster
http://roastcookbook.com/how-to-shuck-an-oyster/

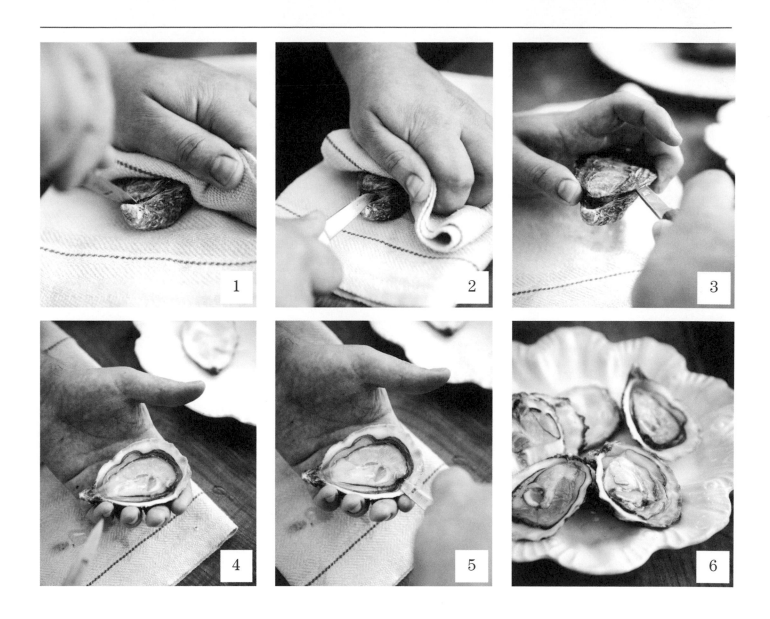

Scrumpy-battered rock oysters with sweet apple and shallot vinegar
serves 6 as a starter

The sweet apple vinegar we use in this recipe is from Scrubby Oak Fine Foods in Norfolk and can be purchased online from their website. It's a great product and well worth having a bottle in your pantry. We also use it in any coleslaws containing apple to stop the apple from browning and to boost the flavour.

Like the Scrumpy-battered Onion Rings on page 175, if you stick to using gluten-free flour for dusting the oysters, they remain a gluten-free dish.

1 quantity of Scrumpy Batter
*   (see page 175)*
18 rock oysters
100g Doves Farm gluten- and wheat-
*   free self-raising flour*
80ml Scrubby Oak Farm sweet apple
*   vinegar*
2 tbsp finely diced shallots
2 litres vegetable oil, for deep-frying
300g rock salt, to serve

Start by making up the batter as this will need to rest for 30 minutes.

Once the batter has rested, set your deep-fat fryer to 180°C and preheat your oven to 200°C/Gas Mark 6. If you don't have a fryer, place the oil into a large, deep saucepan, leaving enough room at the top to allow for rapid boiling when the oysters are added. Place the oil over a high heat but be very careful that it doesn't get too hot. If you have a cooking thermometer, use it so you can regulate the temperature. If not, test the heat by dropping a cube of bread into the oil; it should bubble on entry and start to brown after about 15 seconds.

Have to hand some absorbent kitchen paper and a slotted spoon to remove the oysters from the hot oil. (Don't try to use spring-loaded tongs; this can be very dangerous for obvious reasons.) Place the apple vinegar into a small dipping bowl and add the chopped shallots to infuse.

Shuck the oysters as described on pages 94–95 and place in a colander to drain. Wash the bowl-shaped shells in cold water and reserve them to serve the oysters in once they've been battered and fried. Choose the platter you'd like to serve the oysters on and fill it with the rock salt. The salt will hold the oyster shells in place.

Coat the oysters with the flour and shake off any excess. Place the oyster shells on to a baking sheet and into the oven for 3 minutes to warm them up. Once the shells are hot, remove them from the oven and sit them on the platter of rock salt.

Drop the oysters into the batter and lift them out one at a time placing them carefully into the fryer with a spoon. Hold the oyster in the spoon, submerged in the oil for a few seconds to allow the batter to set before letting it go. This will stop the oysters from sticking to the bottom of the fryer basket. Only cook six at a time or you'll find they all stick together. Deep-fry the oysters for about 2 minutes, until golden and crispy. Drain on kitchen paper to soak up any oil, before placing them into the shells to serve. There shouldn't be any need to season the oysters as they will be salty from the sea. Serve them with the apple and shallot vinegar for dipping.

poultry

Cock-a-leekie serves 10

This simple rustic Scottish broth is traditionally cooked using stewing beef such as shin or flank. I tried it once at Roast using salted brisket as we had a surplus of stock left over from a batch of boiled salt beef. Since then I have stuck to this recipe as the clear stock produced from salted beef has a magnificent depth of flavour. The addition of prunes may seem a little odd, but the sweet prunes are a good balance with the salted beef. You can choose to leave the chicken thighs on the bone and the brisket in large pieces and serve it as a light stew, or flake the meat down for a soup.

You may need to give your butcher advanced warning before trying to buy the brisket as he will have to brine the beef for about 10 days to cure it.

1kg salted beef brisket, soaked in water
*   overnight*
1 onion, halved with the skin on
1 carrot, split lengthways
2 celery sticks
1 bay leaf
2 sprigs of thyme
8 black peppercorns
12 chicken thighs, on the bone
1 large leek, white part only
40 prunes

Place the soaked brisket in a large stockpot. Add the onion, carrot, celery, bay leaf, thyme and peppercorns and cover well with cold water. The skin of the onion gives the soup a rich golden colour. Bring the beef to the boil then turn it down to a gentle simmer. Simmer very gently for 2 hours, skimming off any scum as it rises and collects on the surface. Do not boil or the broth will become cloudy. Add more cold water to keep the beef covered as the level of broth reduces.

After 2 hours, add the chicken thighs. Bring the broth back up to a simmer for another 45 minutes, skimming regularly. Once the beef is tender and the chicken thighs are falling from the bone, lift both out of the broth to cool. Strain the broth through a fine-mesh sieve into a clean pan.

Split the leek down the middle lengthways with a sharp knife. Remove the central few layers of leek and place them to one side. Lay the rest of the layers of leek opened out on the chopping board and cut them into strips lengthwise, about 1cm wide. Line up all the lengths along with the central layers. Carefully cut across the strips at 1cm intervals to form squares. Wash the chopped leek thoroughly to remove any grit.

Once the meat is cool enough to handle flake the brisket into pieces that would sit comfortably on a soup spoon, and do the same with the chicken, discarding the skin and bones. Bring the broth back up to a simmer and add the leek and prunes. Once the leek is tender, after about 2 minutes, add the flaked beef and chicken back to the broth to warm through. Season with salt and pepper, if required, before serving. Any left over soup will keep in the fridge for about a week, just bring back to the boil before serving.

Roast chicken with sage-roasted squash, smoked bacon and creamed sweetcorn serves 4

You need to be very careful when choosing your chicken. People eat chicken more than any other meat and due to demand, many producers cut costs by pumping their birds full of growth promoters so they reach their slaughter weight in as little as five weeks. Flavour takes time to develop, the way nature intended, so really the birds should have been reared for 8–10 weeks. The difference in flavour is astounding. When I buy a chicken for cooking at home I always buy corn-fed as I find the flavour superior and the meat more succulent and less fibrous. Not to mention the fact that the roasted bird has a beautiful crispy golden skin.

one 1½ kg chicken
1 carrot, peeled and roughly chopped
1 celery stick, roughly chopped
½ leek, roughly chopped
1 onion, peeled and roughly chopped
2 garlic cloves, unpeeled
½ quantity of Sage-roasted Squash with Smoked Bacon (see page 281)
½ quantity of Creamed Sweetcorn (see page 280)
vegetable oil
sea salt and freshly milled black pepper
300ml Gravy for Roast Chicken (see page 295), to serve

Preheat your oven to 200°C/Gas Mark 6.

I always remove the wings before roasting so that they can be scattered around the bird along with the vegetables while it's cooking, and used later for the gravy. If your chicken has a bag of giblets stuffed inside the cavity, these will also add to the quality of the gravy. Using the heel of a heavy cook's knife, remove the wings at the second joint and chop them each into 3 pieces. Scatter the chopped wings, and the giblets, if you have them, into the bottom of your roasting tin. Add the carrot, celery, leek, onion and garlic. Drizzle in a little vegetable oil and toss the vegetables and chicken trimmings to coat them in it lightly. Tie the chicken's ankles together with a piece of string and place the bird on its back, in the middle of the roasting tin among the vegetables and trimmings. Rub the chicken with a little vegetable oil and season it with salt and pepper. Place the bird into the middle of the oven and set the timer for 55 minutes

Prepare the sage-roasted squash and place it in the oven on the shelf below the chicken. (The squash takes about 40 minutes to roast.) While the chicken and squash are roasting, you can prepare the creamed sweetcorn.

You will need to keep an eye on the vegetables and trimmings under the chicken and turn them from time to time so they caramelise evenly. They will only take about 30 minutes to cook before you'll have to remove them from around the chicken and prepare the gravy according to the recipe on page 295.

After 55 minutes, check the chicken. To see if it's cooked, make a small cut down the inside of the thigh and open the leg slightly. If the meat inside is still pink cook it for a few more minutes before checking again. Once the bird is cooked, remove it from the tray to rest for 10 minutes in a warm part of the kitchen. Deglaze the roasting tin with a splash of water and try to scrape up all those tasty caramelised morsels to add to the gravy.

While the bird is resting warm your serving plates in the oven, and make sure the gravy is heated through, before serving the meal.

Chicken, leek and oyster mushroom pie serves 6

For this recipe, you can either choose to prepare individual pies encased in pastry, as we do in the restaurant (I much prefer these as I have a soft spot for pastry and you get more this way); or if you have less time on your hands you could fill a baking dish with your pie filling and lay a large sheet of pastry over the top. If you choose this option though, increase the pastry quantity to 400g and brush a little egg wash on the outside rim of the dish and fold the pastry over the edge sticking it fast with the egg, or the pastry top will shrink.

You can use different varieties of mushroom for this pie, but try to avoid large field or portobello mushrooms as the dark gills will turn the sauce an unsightly grey.

15 chicken thighs, on the bone
50ml vegetable oil
150g butter
1 large onion, sliced
5 sprigs of thyme
1 bay leaf
150g plain flour, plus extra for dusting
200ml good-quality dry white wine
2 litres hot Chicken Stock (see page 298)
150ml double cream
1 tbsp Dijon mustard
200g oyster mushrooms, cut into large chunks
1 large leek, white part only
1kg good-quality puff pastry
6 egg yolks, lightly beaten
sea salt and freshly milled black pepper
1½ quantities of Mashed Potato (see page 281), to serve
buttered peas, to serve

You may also need: 6 individual pie dishes (optional)

Preheat your oven to 200°C/Gas Mark 6.

Season the chicken thighs with salt and pepper. Rub them with vegetable oil and place them into a large roasting tin skin-side up. Roast the thighs for 25 minutes, until the skin is crispy.

Meanwhile, place a large saucepan over a medium heat, add half the butter then the onion, thyme and bay leaf. Cook gently for 4–5 minutes, stirring regularly, until the onions are soft. Add the flour and cook for another minute stirring continuously so it doesn't catch on the bottom of the pan. Stir in the wine a little at a time so lumps don't form. Once all of the wine has been added, pour in the hot stock and bring it to the boil. Taste the sauce and season with salt and pepper accordingly. Reduce to a simmer.

Remove the chicken thighs from the oven and place them into the sauce one by one so that no fat from the roasting tray is added. Gently simmer the thighs for about 30 minutes, stirring regularly, so the sauce doesn't catch on the bottom. Once the meat is falling from the bone lift the thighs out of the sauce with a slotted spoon and place them to one side until they are cool enough to be handled.

While the thighs are cooling, strain the sauce through a fine-mesh sieve into a separate saucepan. Bring to a simmer over a medium heat, then add the cream and stir in the mustard. Simmer the sauce gently, continuing to stir regularly, until it reaches the consistency of a thick gravy that would coat the back of a spoon. The sauce must be the right consistency. If it is too thin the pastry on the sides and bottom of the pie will not cook sufficiently, and if too thick, the pie will be dry and stodgy.

Once the chicken thighs are cool enough to handle, carefully flake the meat from the bones to ensure any gristle and skin is discarded along with the bones. Add the thigh meat to the sauce and remove the pan from the heat.

Place the remaining butter in a large frying pan over a medium-high heat and fry the mushrooms for a minute or two, until soft. Season with salt and pepper, then add them to the sauce.

Bring a saucepan of water to the boil and add a little salt. Split the leek down the middle lengthways with a sharp knife. Remove the central few layers of leek and place them to one side. Lay the rest of the layers of leek opened out on the chopping board and cut them into strips lengthwise, about 1cm wide. Line up all the lengths along with the central layers. Carefully cut across the strips at 1cm intervals to form squares. Wash the chopped leek thoroughly to remove any grit. Blanch the leek in the boiling water for a couple of minutes, until tender, then drain well. Fold the leek into the pie mix and allow the mix to cool completely before assembling the pies.

If making individual pies, divide the pastry into six even slabs. From each slab cut away one quarter of the pastry to be used for each pastry lid. Dust your work surface and rolling pin liberally with flour and roll the pastry lids first. They will need to be about ½ cm thick and the perfect size to fit just inside the rim of each pie dish, so use the rim of the pie dish itself as a stencil, trimming around it with a small pointed knife.

Using a small round cookie cutter, cut a 2cm hole into the centre of each lid, so that as the pies cook, they can release a little steam. Dust the lids lightly with flour and place them to one side.

Lightly grease your pie dishes with butter. Place a piece of baking parchment in the base of each pie dish, so that once cooked the pies can be easily turned out. Roll the pastry cases out one at a time, making sure they're large enough to line your pie dishes with 1cm overhang. Lay the rolled pastry sheets into each of the pie dishes trimming the edges of the pastry so they are only overlapping the sides by 1cm.

Fill each pie base almost to the top with the cooled filling, then cover with a lid. Using a pastry brush, lightly brush a little egg yolk around the edge of each lid and fold over the overlapping pastry, pinching it all the way around to seal the pie. Brush the top of each pie with egg yolk and rest in the fridge until ready to bake. The pies can be prepared a few hours in advance.

Preheat your oven to 200°C/Gas Mark 6.

Bake the pies on the middle shelf for 30 minutes until the pastry is golden brown. Rest the pies for a couple of minutes before attempting to turn them out. Carefully run a small knife around the sides of the pie dish to make sure they aren't stuck, then turn out and serve with the mashed potato and buttered peas.

Johnson & Swarbrick Poultry Farm, poultry supplier to the chefs

Brothers Reg Johnson and Bud Swarbrick have been producing excellent British poultry for the past 30 years. It all began at Swainson House Farm, situated on the edge of the Ribble Valley near the picturesque village of Goosnargh in Lancashire. They started out on a relatively small scale with a market stall, but made their break into the restaurant trade when they were approached by the chef and restaurateur Paul Heathcote, who asked if they could produce an English corn-fed chicken. No one in the UK was rearing corn-fed birds at that time; they were being imported from France at a premium. Reg and Bud began producing a slow-grown chicken, fed on a natural diet without any growth promoters, antibiotics or other additives. Through trial and error and working closely with chefs, they have developed a range of bespoke natural feeds. Over the years they have expanded, rearing not only chickens, but ducks, geese, turkeys and guinea fowl.

Their birds are not free-range. Having tried free-range in the past, they became rather sceptical about the process of rearing birds exposed to the elements. Reg explained to me that for three months of the year, the birds are cold, wet and miserable. And with six to eight weeks of frost, they don't have enough access to the water they need. Not to mention the stress the birds suffer, caused by the ever-present threat from predators. Reg knows through his years of experience that his birds are happier and more comfortable in the environment he provides for them. They are reared in large airy, climate-controlled barns, and have the freedom of fifty per cent more space to run around in than government regulations stipulate.

The combination of their comfortable stress-free environment, natural slow maturation and their unique diet, results in a table bird with a far superior flavour and texture.

This page: A small selection of Reg's fantastic poultry.
Opposite: Reg explains to me the unique diet his birds
are fed which is so key to producing poultry
of superior flavour and texture.

poultry

Jointing duck

See page 113 for instructions.

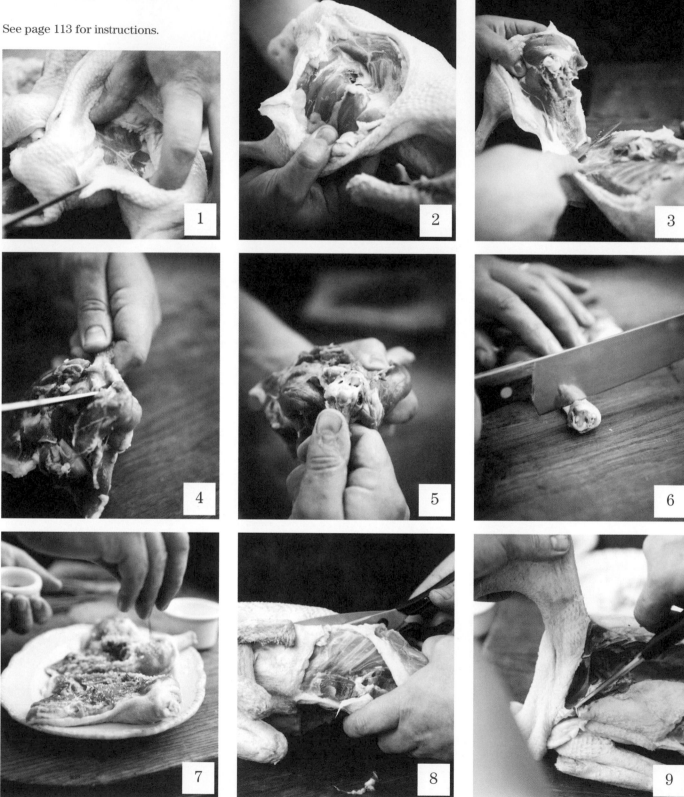

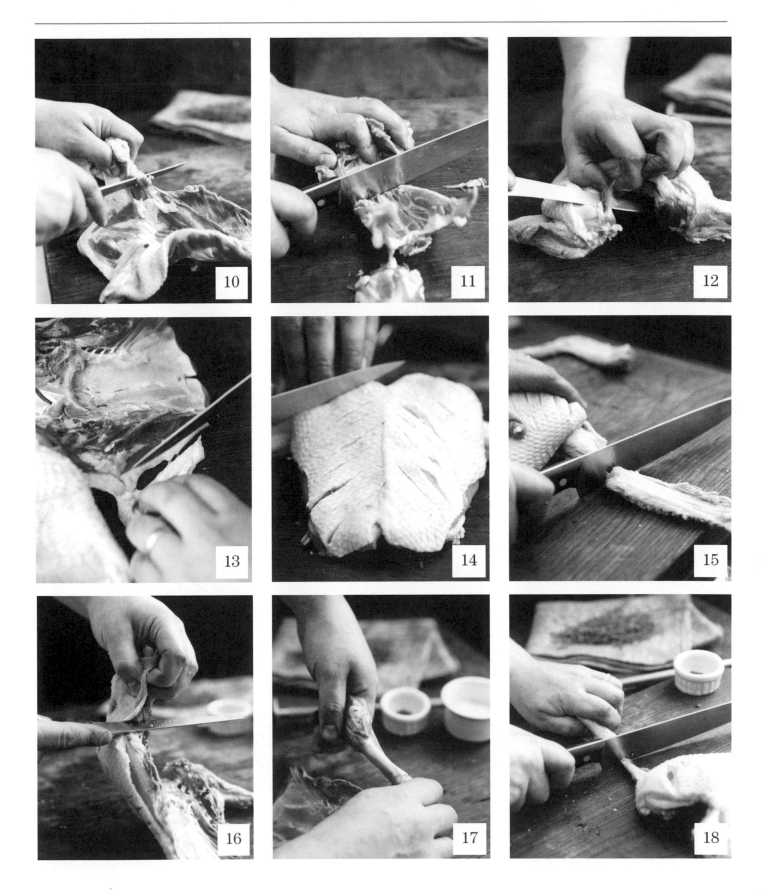

Roasted corn-fed duck with thyme-roasted beetroot and blood orange sauce serves 2–3

If you buy a large duck, you could probably get away with feeding four with this dish. At Roast we serve it on a wooden board for two to share, the legs slowly cooked in the duck fat and the crown cooked medium-rare. We buy the smallest of ducks from our supplier, Reg Johnson. They weigh in at about 1.8kg so are a very substantial meal for two people. His ducks have a great depth of flavour because of his special feed, especially his corn-fed birds. You'll find his ducks on the menus of many top restaurants (see pages 106–109 to learn more).

The intense sweet-and-sour-orange-infused sauce complements the duck perfectly. We often have it on the menu over winter when blood oranges are in season, but if they're not, just substitute regular oranges.

one 1.8kg corn-fed duck
a few sprigs of thyme, leaves only
500g duck or goose fat
200g baby red beetroot, tops removed
200g baby golden beetroot, tops removed
50ml extra virgin rapeseed oil
sea salt and freshly milled black pepper

For the sauce
$1/2$ onion, roughly chopped
1 small carrot, roughly chopped
2 celery sticks, roughly chopped
1 tsp tomato purée
150ml red wine
1 tbsp plain flour
300ml Beef Stock (see page 297)
4 blood oranges
1 tbsp red wine vinegar
1 tbsp caster sugar

Preparing the duck

Remove the duck's legs by opening them out and cutting the skin down the inside of each one with a sharp knife (1). Holding each leg in turn, with your fingers on the outside and your thumbs on the inside of the legs, open the legs further and press firmly with your fingers towards you, twisting your wrists to pop the legs out of the duck's hip sockets (2). Cut between the now open socket and the thigh bone all the way through, removing the legs one at a time (3).

Trim off any excess fat from each leg and reserve the fat. Remove the thigh bone from each leg by slicing down each side of the bone and then underneath it, being careful not to leave too much meat attached to the bone (4). Pop the thigh bone out of its socket (5) and cut through any tendons holding it in place. With the heel of a heavy knife, cut the knuckle from the end of the leg (6) so as the leg cooks, the skin and meat retract from the bone for an attractive presentation. Season the legs with salt on the inside and out, and sprinkle with a few thyme leaves (7). Fold the thigh meat into the inside to wrap the leg into a ball and place in the fridge overnight.

To prepare the crown, using sturdy kitchen scissors, cut through the ribcage along either side of the breast (8). To remove the backbone, continue cutting all the way through the bones just underneath the wing where it joins the carcass (9). Remove any fat and skin from the backbone (10) and reserve it with the rest of the trimmed fat. Chop the backbone into 4 pieces (11) and reserve for the sauce. Remove the wishbone by cutting down either side of it (12) and twisting it out with your fingers. Lay the crown on its skin and remove any excess skin and fat from around the edges of the crown to make it presentable (13). Reserve the fat with that already collected. Turn the crown over and score the skin (14) so as it cooks the fat renders out. Don't score too deep or you'll cut through the flesh of the breast. Using the heel of a heavy knife, remove the wings at the second joint (15) and chop them each into 3 pieces. Place the chopped wings with the rest of the bones reserved for the gravy. Run your knife around the base of the wing bone still attached to the crown (16) and pull the meat back from the bone over the knuckle tip (17). With the heel of a heavy knife, remove the tip of the knuckle, leaving a clean bone for attractive presentation (18).

To render the fat, place all you've collected into a small saucepan. Add about 100ml of cold water and place the pan on a medium-high heat and bring to the boil. Eventually the water will evaporate leaving a pan of crystal-clear liquid fat with a few crispy bits of skin. Strain the fat through a fine-mesh sieve and allow to cool.

You should have two salted legs, a prepared crown, bones for the sauce and a bowl of rendered fat to be added to the 500ml in the ingredients list. The fat will be used to slowly confit the legs.

continued on page 114

continued from page 115

Cooking your duck

Preheat your oven to 180°C/Gas Mark 4.

To make the sauce, place the reserved duck bones and chopped vegetables in a roasting tin and roast them in the oven for 30–40 minutes, stirring from time to time so they are all evenly caramelised.

As the bones and vegetables are cooking, melt all the duck fat in a saucepan and place the legs in a small deep ovenproof dish. Pour the melted fat over the legs to completely submerge, then cover with a lid or foil.

Remove the caramelised bones and vegetables from the roasting tin, draining them of any fat in a colander for a few minutes. You now need to make a basic gravy, which forms the basis of the sauce. Follow the same steps as for the Beef Gravy on page 294, but use the quantities listed here.

Turn the oven down to 150°C/Gas Mark 2 and place the legs inside. Roast for 1½–2 hours and remove from the oven when the meat is tender to the touch. Take the legs out of the fat and place to one side for later.

While the legs are cooking you can also bake the beetroot. Place on the middle of a large sheet of foil. Drizzle over the rapeseed oil and add a few thyme leaves. Season liberally. Lift the sides of the foil into the middle creating a trough, and pour in about 80ml of cold water. Seal the foil at the top, creating a small parcel. Place the parcel in the oven and bake for 1 hour. Test that they are cooked through with a sharp pointed knife, and allow them to cool a little so they can be handled. Once cool, the skins will rub off easily in your hands. Make sure you peel the red beetroot last or the dye on your hands will leave its distinctive mark on the golden ones. Cut the larger beetroot in half down the middle and place to one side.

To prepare the marmalade for the blood orange sauce, zest two of the blood oranges with a zester or a fine grater, and place the zest into a small saucepan. Juice the zested oranges and pour the juice into the pan with the zest. Add the red wine vinegar and the sugar and place on a high heat to reduce to a syrup. Be careful not to reduce it too far and burn it, or it will be ruined. Add this marmalade to your strained gravy and place to one side.

To cook the duck crown, increase your oven to 200°C/Gas Mark 6.

Season the crown and place it fat-side down, in a large, cold, ovenproof frying pan. The reason we start the duck in a cold pan is so the thick coverage of fat slowly renders into the pan as the skin caramelises. Place the pan over a medium heat. As the duck releases its fat, drain the fat off to allow more to be released. Once the skin has caramelised nicely, turn the crown over. Place the beetroot in the pan around the crown with a sprinkling of thyme leaves and season. Place the pan in the oven and cook for 12 minutes.

At the same time, on a separate oven tray, roast the duck legs to crisp up the skin. After the 12 minutes remove the crown from the pan and allow it to rest for 8 minutes. Give the beetroot a toss and place them back into the oven.

Segment the remaining two oranges using a small sharp knife. Cut both ends off each orange down to the bloody flesh. One at a time sit each orange flat, and in a curved motion, cut off the skin all the way down to the flesh, removing all of the bitter white pith. Holding the now peeled orange in the palm of your hand, carefully cut out each segment removing them one at a time and freeing them of any pips.

Bring the gravy to the boil and add the orange segments. Remove the sauce from the heat without boiling the segments or they will disintegrate. Remove the beetroot and crispy legs from the oven and serve.

***more* roast**
*Scan the QR code to see
Marcus butchering duck.*
http://roastcookbook.com/butchering-your-duck/

Guinea fowl braised in sherry with morels and wild garlic serves 4

Reg Johnson, our poultry supplier, started rearing guinea fowl last year. The guinea fowl most commonly available at the market are French corn-fed birds that have the distinct yellow skin and fat coverage. Reg's birds are fed on a diet of wheat, producing a white bird in a more British style. He sent me one for my wife and I to try for Christmas dinner and the flavour, in particular the legs, was memorable. This dish uses the thighs, which lend themselves well to braising lightly. The sherry is fabulous, producing a sauce with a rich balanced sweetness.

If you can get your hands on some St George's mushrooms, these are good too, and also in season during spring at the same time as the wild garlic.

12 guinea fowl thighs
100g plain flour
150g morel mushrooms, brushed clean
50g butter
1 onion, finely diced
4 sprigs of thyme, leaves picked and
   chopped
200ml sweet sherry
   (we use Harvey's Bristol Cream)
1½ litres hot Chicken Stock
   (see page 298)
250ml double cream
12 wild garlic leaves, roughly chopped
vegetable oil, for frying
sea salt and freshly milled black pepper
steamed English asparagus, to serve

Preheat your oven to 150°C/Gas Mark 2.

Season the guinea fowl thighs with salt and pepper and place them into a large plastic bag (without holes). Add the flour to the bag and holding the bag closed at the top, give them a good shake, coating them with the flour. Remove the thighs from the bag and save the rest of the flour for later.

Heat a large saucepan over a medium-high heat and fry the floured thighs in a little vegetable oil on both sides until the skin is crispy and golden. Remove the thighs from the pan and turn the heat down medium. Add the morels, season with salt and pepper and cook for about 2 minutes, until just softened. Remove the mushrooms from the pan, setting them aside for later.

Add the butter, onion and thyme to the pan and allow to cook for about 4–5 minutes, stirring regularly to release any tasty morsels left behind when sealing the guinea fowl. Cook until the onion is soft. Add the reserved flour and cook for another minute or so stirring continuously so it doesn't catch on the bottom of the pan. Stir in the sherry a little at a time so lumps don't form. Once all of the sherry has been added, pour in the hot stock and bring it to the boil.

Season the sauce with sea salt and pepper, before placing the guinea fowl back in the pan. Turn the heat down to a gentle simmer, place a lid on the pan and lightly braise the guinea fowl thighs for about 25 minutes until they're tender. Give the pan a stir from time to time to ensure that nothing is catching on the bottom and the sauce is still covering the thighs. Add more chicken stock if required, to keep the thighs covered. Once the thighs are ready, add the cream and the mushrooms. Taste the sauce to see if the seasoning needs adjusting and add the wild garlic. Serve with some lovely steamed spears of English asparagus.

Roast Christmas turkey
serves 8–10

I have always preferred to remove the legs from the turkey, stuff them and cook them separately from the crown, the day before. It reduces the cooking time drastically and means that most of the preparation can be done the day before, giving you more time to spend with your family.

When buying your turkey, go to a good butcher. Try to find a bronze turkey as their flavour is superior. They are a bit more expensive but as with most things, you get what you pay for. White turkeys can be good if they've been reared slowly and given enough time for their flavour to develop. Never buy a frozen turkey. They take so much time to defrost fully that it can become dangerous to eat them.

It's really important to have a temperature probe when cooking a turkey. If you decide to cook your bird with the legs separate, probe into the thickest part of the breast. If you choose the more traditional approach, place the probe into the inside of the thigh. The temperature should reach 72°C.

one 5kg turkey, with giblets
60g softened butter
1 carrot, roughly chopped
1 celery stick, roughly chopped
½ leek, roughly chopped
1 onion, roughly chopped
2 garlic cloves
vegetable oil
sea salt and freshly milled black pepper

For the stuffing
50g butter
1 small onion, finely chopped
1 tbsp chopped sage
100g fresh white breadcrumbs
100g good-quality sausage meat

Preparing the stuffing
Remove the giblets from inside the cavity of the turkey. Reserve the neck and gizzard for the gravy and roughly chop the heart, liver and kidneys to use in the stuffing.

Heat a saucepan over a medium heat and melt the butter. Add the onion and sage and season with a little salt and pepper. Cook the onion for about 4-5 minutes, until it's soft and translucent. Add the breadcrumbs and mix well before removing from the heat to cool. Once cool, add the sausage meat and the chopped offal and mix thoroughly until all ingredients are combined. Keep covered in the fridge until required.

Preparing the turkey
Remove the turkey's legs by opening them out and cutting the skin with a sharp knife, down the inside of each one. Open the legs further and pop each leg, one at a time, out of the turkey's hip sockets. Cut between the now open socket and the thigh bone all the way through, removing the legs one at a time.

Remove the thigh bone from each leg by slicing down each side of the bone and then underneath it, being careful not to leave too much meat attached to the bone. Pop the thigh bone out of its socket and cut through any tendons holding it in place. With the thigh bone removed, slice down the full length of the inside of the remaining leg bone, all the way to the bone and open it up. Remove the leg bone from each leg by slicing down each side of the bone and then underneath it detaching it at the end knuckle.

The sinews in a turkey's legs are more like little bones. These will all need to be carefully removed using a small knife before stuffing the legs. Pull off the skin from each boneless leg in one piece, and reserve.

Lay a sheet of clingfilm on a solid area of work surface and place the first boneless turkey leg on top with the inside facing upwards. Place another sheet of clingfilm over the leg and using a meat tenderiser or the bottom of a small solid saucepan, give the leg a few solid taps, flattening it out. Don't bash it too hard. Many lighter taps are more effective than a few hard taps, or you risk tearing the meat. Repeat the process with the remaining leg.

Spread the skin of each leg out flat on the worktop with the inside of the skin facing up. Place the flattened legs inside the skin. Season each one. Place a log of stuffing down the middle of each leg and roll the legs inside the skin, wrapping the stuffing inside. Tie the stuffed legs with cooking string to hold them together. Roll the tied legs tightly in many layers of clingfilm, twisting and tying the clingfilm in a tight knot at each end to seal them in. Bring a pan of water to the boil and poach the legs for 20 minutes, until cooked through. Remove from the water and allow to cool, still wrapped in the clingfilm.

To prepare the crown, using sturdy kitchen scissors, cut through the ribcage along either side of the breast. To remove the backbone, continue cutting all the way through the bones just underneath the wing where it joins the carcass. You should be fine cutting the ribcage with scissors, but you may need a cleaver to

continued on page 118

continued from page 116

get through the heavier bones to remove
the backbone. Once removed, chop the
backbone into six pieces and reserve
with the giblets for the gravy.

Using the heel of a heavy knife or a
cleaver, remove the wings at the second
joint and chop them each into three
pieces. Place the chopped wings with
the rest of the bones reserved for
the gravy.

To roast the turkey, remove the crown
from the fridge 2 hours before cooking
to allow it to come to room temperature.
Preheat your oven to 200°C/Gas Mark 6.

Place the crown in a large roasting tray
and rub it with the butter. Season the
skin liberally and cover the tray with foil.
Place the crown in the oven and roast
for 80 minutes, basting regularly.
Place the reserved bones and vegetables
in a separate tray and roast these on
the shelf under the turkey for about

45 minutes turning them from time to
time so they brown evenly. Once
browned, remove the tray and follow the
instructions for making Gravy for
Roast Chicken on page 295.

To prepare the legs, remove the clingfilm
from each one. Heat a frying pan over a
medium heat, and in a little vegetable oil,
fry them on all sides
until the skin is crispy and browned,
then transfer to a roasting tin.

Fifteen minutes before the turkey is due
to be ready, remove the foil and increase
the temperature of the oven to
220°C/Gas Mark 6 to brown the skin.
Before removing the turkey crown from
the oven, make sure its core temperature
has reached 72°C. If not, leave in the
oven until it has, covered with foil if it's
browning too quickly. Once out of the
oven, rest the crown for 20 minutes.
While it's resting turn the oven back
down to 200°C/Gas Mark 6 and roast the
rolled legs for 20 minutes. Serve with all
the trimmings.

Baked goose eggs with chicken livers, bacon and sourdough soldiers serves 4

Livers, bacon and eggs are truly one of life's perfect marriages and it is one of my favourites. Like duck eggs, goose eggs are very rich: one goose egg is roughly the equivalent of two and a half medium hen eggs so they are a meal in themselves.

50g butter
4 goose eggs, at room temperature
60g smoked bacon lardons
4 thick slices of crusty sourdough bread
160g chicken livers, cleaned and
  patted dry
1 tbsp chopped flat-leaf parsley
sea salt and freshly milled black pepper

You will also need: a deep baking dish and four 10cm cocottes or ovenproof ramekins.

Preheat your oven to 150°C/Gas Mark 2.

Use some of the butter to grease the inside of the cocottes or ramekins, then crack an egg into each one and season with salt and pepper. Place the cocottes in the baking dish and pour boiling water around the cocottes to the same level as the egg. This is best done with the tray already in the oven so you don't have to transfer it once filled with boiling water. Bake for 6 minutes, until the white is just set and the large yolk is still runny. Remove from the oven and rest in the water so they keep warm.

In a large frying pan, heat the remaining butter over a medium heat and cook the bacon lardons until they start to crisp. You won't need too much butter as the fat from the bacon will render while it's cooking. At the same time, toast your sourdough, spread with butter and cut into soldiers.

Season your livers with pepper and a little salt, and add them to the pan. Fry the livers quickly for about 30 seconds on each side before finishing with the chopped parsley. Divide the livers and bacon between the cocottes leaving the yolk accessible for dipping your soldiers.

Roast goose with baked Cox's apples stuffed with boozy prunes and walnuts

serves 6

Goose is the fattiest of all poultry. It gives up much of its fat during its long cooking process. However, you can use a turkey baster to syringe off the fat as it collects in the roasting tray and put it to good use. It's delicious when used for roasting your potatoes.

Goose is often traditionally served with Armagnac-soaked prunes. The prune-stuffed baked apples in this recipe are delicious and the perfect accompaniment to cut through the rich fatty goose. I've used cider brandy produced by Julian Temperley in Somerset as a substitute for the Armagnac as it works well with the apples. If you add an additional tablespoon of brown sugar to the prune stuffing the baked apples make a delicious autumnal dessert served with hot custard.

one 4½ kg goose, with giblets
1 carrot, roughly chopped
1 celery stick, roughly chopped
1 leek, white part only, roughly chopped
1 onion, roughly chopped
vegetable oil, for rubbing the goose
2 tbsp plain flour
600ml hot Chicken Stock (see page 298)
1 bay leaf
2 sprigs of thyme
sea salt and freshly milled black pepper

For the baked apples
15 large prunes, soaked overnight in
*   150ml cider brandy*
60g walnuts, toasted and chopped
3 tbsp fresh white breadcrumbs
2 tbsp shredded vegetable suet
1 tbsp soft light brown sugar
6 Cox's apples
60g softened butter
caster sugar, for dusting

Preheat your oven to 190°C/Gas Mark 5.

Prepare the goose for roasting as you would the Roast Chicken on page 102. However, instead of placing the bird directly on to the vegetables and giblets in the roasting tray, it should be suspended over them on a rack so the fat can be easily removed as it drips from the goose. Calculate the cooking time by allowing 15 minutes per 500g of the goose's weight. For example, a 4½ kg bird should be in the oven for 135 minutes.

While the goose is roasting, keep an eye on the vegetables and giblets and remove them after about 40 minutes, once evenly browned. Drain the vegetables and giblets of fat in a colander for 10 minutes before preparing the gravy as you would for the Gravy for Roast Chicken on page 295.

Once the vegetables and giblets have been removed from beneath the goose, add 150ml of water to the roasting tray so that when the fat drips from the goose it doesn't burn on the bottom of the tray. Syringe off all the fat with a turkey baster and allow it to set hard in a bowl in the fridge. Once set pour off any excess water.

To make the prune stuffing for the apples, roughly chop the brandy-soaked prunes and place them in a large mixing bowl with any leftover brandy. Add the walnuts, breadcrumbs, suet and brown sugar and mix all the ingredients thoroughly.

To prepare the apples, remove the core with a corer or melon baller and dig out a small cavity for the stuffing. With a

small sharp knife, score a horizontal line all the way around each apple about three quarters of the way from the top. The score should only just break the skin.

Holding the apples at each end with your index finger and thumb, use a pastry brush to brush each apple with a thin layer of softened butter, then dust them with a generous layer of caster sugar, which will stick to the butter, coating the apple nicely. Place the apples in a baking dish for the last 25 minutes of the goose's cooking time. As the apples bake they will split at the scored line and puff up like a soufflé.

Once the goose is ready, rest it for 10 minutes before carving. Use the carving instructions for roast chicken and other birds on page 20, but split each thigh into two pieces.

lamb, mutton and goat

Anchovy-rubbed, hay-baked leg of mutton with parsley and caper sauce
serves 8–10

A wise woman once said: 'Mutton is not considered by experienced judges to be in perfection until it is nearly or quite five years old; but to avoid the additional expense of feeding the animal so long, it is commonly brought into the market at three years old.' *Eliza Acton, 1858*

There are varying standards of mutton on the market. Make sure you ask your butcher for mutton that meets the exacting standard drawn up by The Mutton Renaissance. These guidelines ensure a consistent quality. The sheep must be over two years old, have had a forage-based diet, have sufficient fat cover, and be matured (hung for at least two weeks). There are certain breeds known for producing delicious mutton, such as Herdwick, Romney, Blackface, and Southdown. We use the latter at Roast.

Ask your butcher to bone the leg, removing the femur but leaving the shank bone in for presentation (it also gives you something to hold on to when carving). They should then butterfly the individual muscles, opening them out sufficiently for the anchovy rub.

At Roast we bake the leg very slowly for 5 hours on 100°C/Gas Mark ¼, which results in the leg being pink all the way through and means there is minimal moisture loss or shrinkage. However, if time isn't on your side, bake it for 3 hours at 140°C/Gas Mark 1.

If you're worried about where you will find the hay, try a pet shop.

16 salted anchovy fillets
2 garlic cloves
3 sprigs of rosemary, leaves only
2 tbsp rapeseed oil
1 leg of mutton, femur removed and butterflied (ask your butcher to do this, see above)
sea salt and freshly milled black pepper

For the sauce
50g butter
1 large onion, sliced
1 bay leaf
2 tbsp plain flour
500ml hot Lamb or Beef stock (see page 298 or 297)
150ml double cream
80g capers
a small bunch of flat-leaf parsley, chopped

You will also need: enough hay to wrap the leg thoroughly

Preheat your oven to 100°C/Gas Mark ¼ (or see above if you want to cook your meat in under 5 hours). Soak the hay in cold water. While it's soaking, start by making the anchovy rub. Place the anchovies, garlic, rosemary and rapeseed oil into a pestle and mortar and grind to a smooth paste. Open out your butterflied mutton leg with the inside facing upwards. Massage all of the anchovy paste into the meat evenly and season with pepper. Roll the leg back up and tie tightly with cooking string at 5cm intervals. Season the outside with salt and pepper.

Heat a large heavy-based pan over a medium heat and seal the meat, rendering out any excess fat from the outside of the leg. Continue this process until you've caramelised the meat all over.

Lay a large length of tin foil down on your work surface and place the wet hay generously inside the foil saving some for the top. Lay the sealed leg gently on to the hay and cover with the hay you have saved. Wrap the leg up tightly in the foil, adding several more layers so that no moisture is released during cooking. Roast the mutton for 5 hours. Remove from the oven and rest the meat for at least 20 minutes before unwrapping to carve.

For the sauce, melt the butter in a small saucepan and cook the onions and bay leaf gently until the onions are soft. Add the flour and cook for a further 2 minutes, stirring often so it doesn't catch on the bottom of the pan. Add the hot stock a little at a time and stir constantly to avoid lumps. Boil and reduce until a gravy consistency is reached before adding the cream and some seasoning. Add the capers and chopped parsley just before serving. At Roast we serve this dish with Bubble 'n' Squeak (see page 41) but it works just as well with Mashed Potato (see page 281) or champ.

Laverstoke Park Farm, leading the way in bio-dynamic agriculture

Jody Sheckter started Laverstoke Park Farm in 1996. His vision was to be self-sufficient and produce the best-tasting, healthiest food, for himself and his family. However, when as a smallholder he realised that whenever he had a cow slaughtered his family would have beef on the table for an eight-week stretch, he decided to expand the operation, making the same food available to the public. And expand he did, in no uncertain terms! The farm, in North Hampshire, has now grown to an impressive, 2,500 acres.

Conventional processes of agricultural systems strip the soil of its nutrients due to the grazing of livestock, or 'intensive' growing of crops year upon year. If these nutrients are not replaced, the soil gradually becomes barren and infertile, leaving it chemically dependant. What many people don't realise is that some of the chemicals needed to produce the fertilisers used to keep this infertile land productive are not sustainable, and will one day be exhausted leaving us with unmanageable land. At Laverstoke Park they work to a strict bio-dynamic ethos:

healthy soil = healthy grass = healthy animals = healthy meat and milk = healthy people.

Everything begins with the quality of the soil, so each year they produce 25,000 tons of organic compost that goes back over the land to regenerate the soil. They give back, to ensure that future generations can enjoy the same quality of produce from the land that they are producing today.

At Roast we are proud to offer Laverstoke Park Farm's Lleyn lamb to our guests. This Welsh breed produces fine-flavoured meat that with the help of careful animal husbandry becomes exceptional. The lambs graze on a 'mixed salad' of 31 different herbs, clovers and grasses, carefully chosen by the team at Laverstoke to recreate a more natural environment. They are also allowed to grow the way nature intended, at their own pace without their diet being supplemented with grain.

As well as lamb, Laverstoke Park Farm also supplies us with fantastic buffalo mozzarella. They produce it right on the farm, from the rich milk provided by their herd of water buffalo. With over 2,500 animals, theirs is the largest herd of naturally reared buffalo in the UK. Mozzarella is at its best very fresh, and this freshness is compromised even by the short distance it has to travel from southern Italy to us in the UK, but we are very fortunate in that we can place an order in the evening and the following morning, Tommaso Valenzano, Laverstoke Park's expert mozzarella maker, will work his magic and the luxurious cheese will be with us that same afternoon. As a chef it's a real privilege to be able to serve this great product at the same level of quality and freshness as you'd find in Italy.

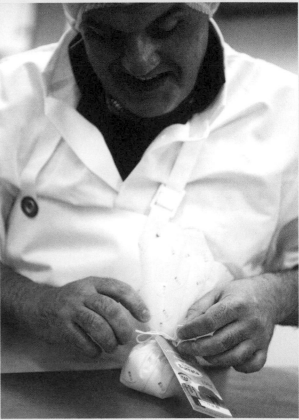

Pan-fried lamb's sweetbreads with smoked bacon and pea shoots serves 4

Don't be turned off by the fact that sweetbreads are a gland. If prepared properly they are delicious, with a luxurious creamy texture. There are two common types of sweetbread. Make sure you ask your butcher for 'heart' sweetbreads as opposed to 'throat'. The heart sweetbreads are more prized. They are spherical in shape and plumper than the long, thin throat sweetbreads.

If you can get your hands on some wild garlic, try using this instead of the pea shoots and mint.

300g lamb's sweetbreads
enough milk to soak the sweetbreads
½ leek, finely sliced
½ small onion, diced
½ carrot, diced
a few sprigs of thyme
1 bay leaf
100g plain flour
1 tbsp vegetable oil
20g butter
100g smoked bacon lardons
150ml good-quality lamb or beef stock
80g peas (frozen are fine)
3 mint leaves, chopped
50ml double cream
100g pea shoots
sea salt and freshly milled black pepper

Soak the sweetbreads in milk overnight to purge them of any excess blood. It's necessary to blanch sweetbreads so they are easy to handle before the second cooking stage: place them in a saucepan with the leek, onion, carrot, thyme and bay leaf and just cover with cold water. Season the water with salt and bring to the boil. Remove from the heat and rest for 1 minute before straining. It is important not to overcook them or they will be tough and will lose that soft, creamy texture.

Once the sweetbreads are cool enough to handle, use a small knife to peel the thin, clear membrane from the outside. Do this while they are still warm as it's much easier. Season the sweetbreads with salt and pepper, then roll them in the flour.

Heat the oil and butter in a frying pan over a medium heat, then fry the floured sweetbreads and bacon until golden and crispy. Add a teaspoon of the flour to the pan (this will thicken the sauce). Pour in the stock. As it hits the hot pan it should boil on contact. Add the peas, mint and cream and bring back to the boil. Adjust the seasoning if necessary and add the pea shoots just before serving so they hold their shape and stay crisp.

Barbecued fillet of lamb neck with a spelt, lemon and herb salad and cucumber yoghurt serves 4

Neck fillet is a very versatile cut of lamb. Its fat content gives it a wonderful flavour and keeps it moist when flame-grilled on the barbecue. It's also good cooked slowly in a hearty Lancashire Hotpot (see page 138).

The salad is a variation of the Lebanese dish tabbouleh, traditionally made with bulgur wheat. At Roast we use an organic spelt grown in Somerset in place of the bulgur wheat. The key is making sure the salad is packed full of fresh herbs and that the acidity from the lemon is balanced with the olive oil and sea salt. Don't prepare it too far in advance as the acid in the lemon juice will cook the herbs and the salad will lose its freshness.

4 lamb neck fillets, about 180g each
50ml vegetable oil
50g rosemary, chopped
sea salt and freshly milled black pepper

For the spelt, lemon and herb salad
500g pearled spelt
200ml extra virgin olive oil
6 small Preserved Lemons
* (see page 288), cut into quarters*
8 ripe tomatoes, deseeded and diced
200g flat-leaf parsley, chopped
100g mint, chopped
juice of 2 lemons

For the cucumber yoghurt
1 cucumber, peeled and halved
* lengthways, seeds scraped, cut into*
* 5mm slices*
1 tbsp sea salt
250g full-fat natural yoghurt

Start by preparing the cucumber yoghurt. Sprinkle the cucumber with the salt and allow to stand in a colander for 20 minutes to drain. The salt draws out some of the water content and slightly wilts the cucumber. Rinse the cucumber under cold water to alleviate the saltiness. Dry thoroughly on kitchen paper before mixing with the yoghurt. Serve at room temperature.

Next, start to prepare the salad. Wash the spelt as you would rice, to remove the excess starch. Bring a pan of well-salted water to the boil and add the spelt. Return to the boil and simmer for 15–20 minutes, until the spelt is cooked but still has some bite. Drain well, place in a large salad bowl and toss with 50ml of the olive oil to keep the grains separated. Allow to cool but do not refrigerate or vital flavour will be lost.

Prepare your barbecue. Rub the lamb with the oil and season with salt and pepper. Spread the chopped rosemary out on a large plate and roll the fillets in it, coating each one thoroughly.

The key to a successful barbecue is the control of the embers once the fire has died down. I'm sure everyone has their own technique and I'd hate to step on the toes of the multitude of proud barbecuers out there (you know who you are!). Mine is quite simple. Build up the embers on one side for sealing and leave the other side for gentler cooking and resting. The lamb should be sealed on a hot section of the barbecue. You want to turn it regularly to caramelise the fat evenly on the outside, then once this is achieved, move it to the gentler heat and continue to turn regularly until cooked to your liking.

Make sure the fillets are rested before serving – 6 minutes should be enough.

While, the lamb is resting, finish the salad. Using a small knife, remove the flesh from the preserved lemon quarters and discard (it's the rind you want to use). Cut the rind into small dice. Mix the lemon and all the remaining ingredients with the cooled spelt and season. Serve immediately, at room temperature (do not refrigerate).

Slow-roasted shoulder of lamb with rosemary root vegetables and Mum's mint relish serves 6

This is one of those dinners you can just put in the oven and forget about. The preparation is very simple and the end result a crowd pleaser. The lamb shoulders we use at Roast are from Jody Sheckter's Laverstoke Park Farm in North Hampshire (see pages 126–129). Their lambs are slow-reared as nature intended, giving them time to develop flavour. They are fed on a mixed salad of wild herbs, clovers and grasses carefully chosen to replicate their natural diet.

This simple dish is very popular on Sundays when the restaurant is filled with families enjoying their traditional Sunday roast. You must try it with my mother's mint relish (see page 290). The feedback we receive for the relish is fantastic!

At Roast we use any leftover lamb shoulder to make Baker's Potatoes (see page 140) but you could always buy a slightly bigger joint and reserve the meat specially if you like.

1 lamb shoulder, about 2½ kg
3 tbsp vegetable oil
4 garlic cloves, peeled and halved
  lengthways
8 sprigs of rosemary
1 onion, peeled and roughly chopped
1 carrot, peeled and roughly chopped
2 celery sticks, roughly chopped
½ leek, white part only, roughly chopped
300ml Gravy for Roast Lamb
  (see page 296)
sea salt and freshly milled black pepper
Mum's Mint Relish (see page 290), to
  serve

For the rosemary root vegetables
3 parsnips, halved lengthways
3 carrots, halved lengthways
½ celeriac, peeled and cut into large
  chunks
½ swede, peeled and cut into large chunks
150ml extra virgin rapeseed oil
1 garlic bulb

Preheat your oven to 180°C/Gas Mark 4.

Heat a large frying pan over a medium-high heat. Season the lamb shoulder thoroughly with salt and pepper. Add the vegetable oil to the pan and sear the shoulder, sealing it until both sides are well caramelised.

Remove the shoulder from the pan and place it on a chopping board with the outside of the shoulder facing upwards. To stud the shoulder with garlic and rosemary, use a small pointed knife to make 16 evenly spaced holes, 2½ cm deep. Stuff the holes with the garlic and just the tips cut from the sprigs of rosemary. Reserve the rest of the rosemary for the root vegetables.

Scatter the onion, carrot and celery onto your roasting tray and place the lamb shoulder on top of the vegetables. Roast in the oven for 3 hours, but after the first hour, once the lamb has developed a good colour, pour about 200ml of water into the bottom of the roasting tray and cover the tray with foil so the lamb doesn't dry out. Turn the oven down to 150°C/Gas Mark 2 for the final 2 hours. Once the lamb is cooked and falling from the bone, remove it from the roasting tray and wrap it in foil to rest. Reserve the vegetables and meat juices from the roasting tray for the gravy and follow the recipe on page 296.

Turn the oven up to 200°C/Gas Mark 6 to roast the root vegetables.

Scatter the vegetables onto your roasting tray and drizzle over the rapeseed oil. Smash the bulb of garlic with the back of a frying pan and scatter the crushed cloves, skin and all, among the vegetables. Add the reserved rosemary sprigs and season well with salt and pepper. Roast the vegetables for about 45–50 minutes, turning them occasionally so they caramelise well.

Once the vegetables are cooked, push them around the sides of the roasting tray, leaving space in the middle for the lamb. Remove the foil from the lamb and place it into the roasting tray and return to the oven for 5–10 minutes to heat it through.

Serve the lamb in the tray surrounded by the vegetables. The slow-cooked meat will pull easily from the bone.

The beautiful grazing grounds at Laverstoke Park Farm

Lancashire hotpot serves 8

There are many different versions of this hearty northern crowd pleaser but they all have the same core ingredients: lamb, onions and potatoes. Some cooks like to add lambs' kidneys but I find their flavour too strong. Some like to seal the meat in a hot pan before braising, and this was the way I preferred until I was lucky enough to try Nigel Haworth's version at The Three Fishes in Ribble Valley, Lancashire. I have since changed my cooking method completely.

A few years ago, I had some family over from New Zealand and I took them to Lavenham, a historic, picturesque little village in Suffolk. Lavenham has a great butcher right on the high street called D M Newman. We went in and bought some lamb neck fillet sourced from a local farm and he threw in the bones for us as well. I took it home and cooked this hotpot for eight of us. My dad still talks about it to this day!

Make sure you ask your butcher for the bones as the fresh stock makes all the difference.

2kg lamb neck fillet, fat trimmed and
   cut into 5cm pieces, and the neck
   bones
100g plain flour
100g butter
3 large onions, peeled and thinly sliced
2 tbsp chopped rosemary leaves
   vegetable oil, for frying
1kg large potatoes (Maris Piper or
   King Edward work well), peeled
   and sliced into 2mm discs
700ml hot Lamb Stock (see page 298)
sea salt and freshly milled black pepper
Pickled Red Cabbage (see page 286),
   to serve

Preheat your oven to 200°C/Gas Mark 6.

Season the lamb neck with salt and pepper and place it into a large plastic bag (without holes). Add the flour to the bag and holding the bag closed at the top, give the lamb a good shake, coating it with the flour. Remove the lamb from the bag and place it into the bottom of a shallow ovenproof dish.

Place half the butter in a large saucepan over a medium heat and cook the onions and rosemary for about 4–5 minutes until soft and translucent but not coloured. Season with salt and pepper, then scatter over the lamb in a layer.

Place the potatoes in a large bowl. Melt the remaining butter in the frying pan and toss it with the potatoes, coating each slice and seasoning with salt as you go. Layer the potatoes over the onions, saving the neatest slices for the top layer. Slowly pour in the hot lamb stock to just below the top layer of potatoes.

Cover the hotpot with foil, place it on the middle shelf of your oven and bake for 45 minutes. After 45 minutes, remove the foil and bake for another 45 minutes or so, until the potatoes are crisp and golden. By this stage the meat will be tender and ready to eat.

Serve with the pickled red cabbage.

Crispy breast of lamb with a minted spring vegetable salad
Serves 6 as a starter

Lamb breast is a very economical, under-utilised cut. It often features on our daily market menu in a variety of different dishes. It needs to be cooked for a long time at a low temperature to render out its high content of fat but as it cooks this fat keeps the meat moist.

Try laying a few salted anchovies inside the breasts before rolling them, but if you choose to do this, adjust your seasoning accordingly. Something else you could try rather than pan-frying the cooked slices of lamb is to breadcrumb them and deep-fry them. They make a great snack with a little caper mayonnaise.

1kg boneless lamb breast
1 tbsp chopped rosemary leaves
2 large garlic cloves, peeled and very
*   finely chopped*
sea salt and freshly milled black pepper
vegetable oil, for frying

For the salad
1 bunch of asparagus
8 radishes, finely sliced into discs, plus
*   the leaves*
80g mangetout, sliced into fine strips
*   lengthways*
50g pea shoots
40g capers
1 tbsp chopped mint
4 tbsp Vinaigrette (see page 292)

Preheat your oven to 160°C/Gas Mark 3.

Lay the lamb breasts skin-side down on your chopping board and trim off any excess fat from the underside. Sprinkle the rosemary and garlic evenly across the breasts. If you can get your hands on some wild garlic leaves, these are a great substitute for the garlic cloves. Season well with salt and pepper and rub the seasoning, garlic and rosemary into the meat. Roll the lamb breasts lengthways into logs with the garlic and rosemary on the inside, and tie them together tightly with cooking string. Each breast should be tied about 5 times at 5cm intervals.

Season the outside of the rolls with more salt and pepper and place them in a large frying pan over a medium heat. Do not preheat the pan as you want the fat to render out slowly rather than caramelise straight away. The pan won't need oil for the same reason. Cook the lamb breasts until well caramelised on all sides. As the fat renders, drain it off so more can be released.

Remove the breasts from the pan and transfer them to a roasting tray. Pour about 150ml of water into the tray with the lamb so that as it roasts slowly it also steams and stays moist. Cover the tray with foil and place in the oven for 2½ hours, until the rolls are tender.

When the lamb breasts are cooked allow them to cool before placing them in the fridge to firm up so they can be easily sliced.

To prepare the salad, remove the woody ends from the asparagus and slice each spear very finely on the diagonal. If the leaves are in good condition, use these in your salad also; they add an intense peppery element. Toss all the salad ingredients except the vinaigrette together in a large bowl. Set aside.

Remove the string from the lamb breast rolls and slice the breasts into discs just over 1cm thick.

Heat a large frying pan over a medium-high heat and fry the lamb discs in a couple of tablespoons of vegetable oil. They should not require any more seasoning if enough was applied before rolling, but it might be an idea to taste one once its been fried to check. Fry the lamb briefly on each side until evenly caramelised and crispy.

To serve, dress the salad, tossing it with the vinaigrette and season with salt and pepper. Place a pile of salad at the top of each plate and lean 3–4 slices of lamb breast against it.

Roasted rack of lamb with buttered turnips and baker's potatoes serves 4

If we have any Slow-roasted Shoulder of Lamb (see page 135) left over from our Sunday roast offering, we often shred the leftover meat from the bone to prepare this hearty accompaniment of baker's potatoes.

The term 'baker's potatoes' comes from the French dish pommes boulangère. Once the French baker or 'boulanger' had finished baking for the day s/he would place this sliced potato dish into the wood-fired oven as it was cooling and come back a few hours later to enjoy the slow-cooked staple for dinner. The sliced potatoes are layered with leftover roasted lamb, onions, garlic and rosemary and baked in the oven with a little lamb stock. The contrast in texture between the slow-cooked shoulder meat and a prime cut, such as rack, is great.

Ask your butcher to French-trim your rack of lamb for you, exposing the rib bones, for an attractive presentation.

2 bunches of baby turnips, with
*   their tops*
30g butter
1 tsp caster sugar
one 8-bone rack of lamb (ask your
*   butcher to French-trim it)*
sea salt and freshly milled black pepper
200ml Gravy for Roast Lamb
*   (see page 296), to serve*

For the baker's potatoes
30g butter
1 large onion, peeled and finely sliced
1 large garlic clove, peeled and finely
*   chopped*
1 tsp chopped rosemary leaves
3 large Maris Piper potatoes, peeled and
*   sliced into 2mm discs*

200g shredded roasted lamb (ideally,
*   use any leftovers from the Slow-roasted*
*   Shoulder of Lamb recipe on page 135)*
150ml Lamb Stock (see page 298)

Preheat your oven to 180°C/Gas Mark 4.

Melt the butter in a saucepan over a medium heat and cook the onion, chopped garlic and rosemary with a little salt and pepper until the onions are soft and translucent.

While the onions are cooking, lay half the potatoes in the bottom of a small baking dish, saving the best slices for the top layer. Season with salt and pepper. Cover the first layer of potatoes with the shredded lamb, then cover the lamb with the cooked onion, garlic and rosemary. Place the rest of the sliced potatoes on top as the final layer and pour over the lamb stock. Cover the dish with foil and bake in the oven for 45 minutes, then remove the foil and continue to cook for a further 20 minutes so the top layer of potatoes forms a crispy crust.

Remove the tops from the turnips leaving a small portion of stem attached for presentation. Wash the turnips and their leaves. Place the turnips into a small saucepan and only just cover with cold water. Season the water with a little salt and add half the butter and the sugar. Place to one side.

To prepare the rack of lamb, score the fat in a criss-cross pattern almost down to the flesh. Season the rack with salt and pepper and place it fat-side down in a cold dry ovenproof frying pan. The reason you start the lamb in a cold pan is so that the fat slowly renders out into the pan as the lamb caramelises.

Place the pan over a medium heat. As the lamb releases its fat, drain it off to allow more to be released. Once the fat has nicely caramelised, seal the rack on each end, then place it fat-side down again and transfer the pan to the oven for 10 minutes.

While the lamb is in the oven bring the turnips to the boil, then reduce the heat and simmer for 7–8 minutes. Test them with the point of a small knife and if cooked through turn off the heat.

Remove the lamb from the oven and leave to rest for a good 6–8 minutes in a warm part of the kitchen before carving.

While the lamb rests, drain the turnips and return them to the saucepan, set over a low heat, with the remaining butter and the turnip tops. Once the turnip tops have wilted, season them with salt and pepper. Meanwhile, heat the gravy in a small saucepan.

To serve, divide the baker's potatoes between four serving plates. When carving the rack, place it on your chopping board fat side down with the bones pointing away from you. Carve carefully between each bone and serve two bones per plate. Serve the buttered turnips and their tops alongside and finish with the gravy.

Crumbed lambs' brains with a broad bean and caper salad serves 4

If you haven't tried lamb brains before, don't be shy, they're delicious! They have a very mild flavour and a lovely creamy texture. Breadcrumbing and shallow-frying them is the ideal way to prepare them, leaving them golden and crispy on the outside with a soft creamy centre.

Like most offal, lamb brains are very good for you, with high levels of protein, enough vitamin B12 in one serving to fulfil your day's requirements, and good levels of phosphorous, iron, copper and zinc. They are, however, very high in cholesterol, so if you're trying to cut down, stick to oats and avoid a serving of these.

Most butchers will be happy to source lamb brains for you, but you may have to pre-order them a day or two in advance.

6 fresh lamb brains
100g plain flour
2 eggs, beaten
100g Japanese panko breadcrumbs
150ml extra virgin rapeseed oil
sea salt and freshly milled black pepper

For the salad
400g broad beans in their pods
  (will yield about 100g of podded
  broad beans)
1 small shallot, peeled
6 radishes, finely sliced into discs,
  plus the leaves
50g broad bean shoots (pea shoots are
  a good substitute)
30g capers
a few small mint leaves
3 tbsp Lemon and Rapeseed Oil
  Dressing (see page 292)

Handle the brains carefully throughout the cooking process, as the tissue is delicate and will easily break up. Before cooking the brains, soak them in a bowl of cold, lightly salted water for 1 hour; this will remove any excess blood.

Drain the brains, then carefully remove as much of the thin membrane coating them as is possible. Cut each brain in half down the middle. Bring a saucepan of lightly salted water to the boil and poach the brains for no longer than 2 minutes. Remove the brains from the water using a slotted spoon and allow them to cool completely so they set and are easier to work with.

Put the flour into a shallow bowl; the beaten eggs in a second and the breadcrumbs in a third. Coat the brain halves with flour and carefully shake off any excess. Dip the floured brains into the egg a few at a time and then into the breadcrumbs. If you're not happy with the coating of crumbs, dip them back into the egg, then into the crumbs again for a second coat.

To prepare the salad, blanch the broad beans in boiling water for 1 minute, then refresh in iced water. Once the beans are cold, pop them out of their bitter skins. Slice the shallot into very thin rings, discarding the smaller central rings. Run the shallot rings under cold water for a couple of minutes to mellow their flavour, then dry them on kitchen paper. If the radish leaves are in good condition, use these in your salad also. They add an intense peppery element. Toss all the salad ingredients except the dressing together in a large bowl.

Heat a large frying pan over a medium-high heat and add the rapeseed oil. Rapeseed oil is great for cooking the brains as it cooks at a high temperature without burning, and has a delicate nutty flavour. To test if the oil is hot enough, toss in a couple of breadcrumbs; they should start to sizzle. Season the brains with salt and pepper, then carefully place them in the oil. Don't crowd the pan. Depending on the size of your pan you may need to fry the brains in two batches. Shallow-fry the brains for a couple of minutes on each side, until they're golden and crispy. Drain on kitchen paper to soak up any excess oil.

Season the salad and toss with the dressing before serving with the crispy brains.

Pan-fried lambs' kidneys with bacon and girolles on a boxty pancake

serves 4 as a starter

Not only does this dish make a great starter, it's also suitable as a hearty breakfast.

Kidneys aren't everyone's cup of tea. They are one of those ingredients people seem to either love or detest as they have a strong flavour, which can be a little off-putting for some. If you've never tried them, have a go at this recipe. Who knows, you may be discovering something very special. Or perhaps the opposite. All I would say is, don't knock it till you've tried it.

To prevent the juggling of frying pans, it would be best to cook your boxty pancakes before the kidneys and keep them warm in a low oven.

*½ quantity of Boxty Pancakes
    (see page 285)
8 lambs' kidneys
100g plain flour
2 tbsp vegetable oil
4 rashers of rindless smoked streaky
    bacon, each cut into 4 pieces
200g girolles, brushed clean
30g butter
1 tbsp chopped flat-leaf parsley
sea salt and freshly milled black pepper*

Preheat your oven to 140°C/Gas Mark 1.

Start by making the boxty pancakes then transfer them to a plate and keep warm in the oven while you finish the dish.

To prepare the kidneys, split each one in half down the middle lengthways with a sharp knife, and peel off the thin membrane covering the outside. Cut out the hard white fat on the inside of each half and discard. Season the kidneys with salt and pepper and place them into a large plastic bag without holes. Add the flour to the bag and holding the bag closed at the top, give them a good shake, coating them with the flour.

Heat a large frying pan over a medium-high heat. The kidneys need to be cooked quickly, and ideally served medium-rare or they will be dry and tough. Add the vegetable oil to the pan and fry the floured kidneys until they're caramelised – they will only need about 1½ minutes on each side. Remove from the pan and put them to one side to rest.

Place the frying pan back on the heat and while the kidneys are resting, fry the bacon pieces until crispy. Turn down the heat to low and add the girolles and the butter. Season the girolles with a little salt and pepper, taking into account that the bacon is already quite salty. Cook the girolles gently for about 2–3 minutes in the butter and bacon fat until soft. Place the kidneys back in the pan with the parsley and give the pan a good toss.

Serve the kidneys sitting on top of the boxty pancakes and spoon the bacon, girolles and butter over the top.

***more* roast**
*Scan the QR code to see Marcus
cooking a variation of this recipe.
http://roastcookbook.com/kidney-dish/*

Goat curry serves 4–6

Due to Iqbal's long history with the Cinnamon Club, I've had the great pleasure in having much contact with Vivek Singh, the Cinnamon Club's executive chef. He has been a great source of inspiration on numerous occasions when I've been trying to come up with interesting curries for the menu at Roast. I wanted to put a goat curry on the menu but was struggling a little in getting the recipe correct. I called on Vivek for some advice and he sent through a couple of recipes he'd done in the past. This is one that we have adapted slightly for Roast. The feedback from customers was fantastic. Many thanks Vivek!

1kg goat shoulder, cut into 2½ cm cubes
100g ghee or clarified butter
1 tbsp cumin seeds
8 green cardamom pods
10 whole cloves
2 bay leaves
750ml Lamb Stock (see page 298)
juice of 1 lemon
2 tbsp chopped coriander
sea salt
steamed rice, to serve

For the marinade
200ml Greek-style yoghurt
2 tsp ground coriander
1 tsp ground turmeric
2 tsp sea salt

For the onion paste
1 large onion, finely chopped
5 garlic cloves, finely chopped
8 green chillies, finely chopped

For the spiced onion yoghurt
1 red onion, finely chopped
1 tsp very finely chopped fresh root ginger

2 green chillies, deseeded and very finely chopped
½ tsp salt
½ tsp caster sugar
5 mint leaves, chopped
100g Greek-style yoghurt

Place the diced goat into a large mixing bowl and add all of the ingredients for the marinade. Cover and place in the fridge for 2–3 hours.

Prepare the onion paste. Place the onion, garlic and green chillies in a food processor, blend to a wet paste and set to one side.

Mix all the spices together in a small bowl. Heat a heavy-based saucepan over a medium heat. Add the ghee and heat almost to smoking point. With a lid to hand, add all of the spices and cover the pan quickly. The spices will pop and crackle violently on contact with the hot ghee. After a few seconds the crackling will calm. Now you must carefully add the marinated goat. This will cool the ghee and stop the spices from burning.

Turn the heat up to high and cook the goat for 10–12 minutes or so until all the moisture has evaporated. Stir regularly at this stage so it doesn't catch on the bottom of the pan.

Once the moisture has evaporated add the onion paste and the bay leaves. Reduce the heat to medium and cook the paste, stirring regularly for 5–8 minutes. At this stage, pour over the lamb stock and bring the curry to the boil. Reduce the heat and simmer for 40 minutes or so until the goat is tender and the stock has reduced to more of a gravy consistency. Stir the curry regularly making sure it doesn't catch.

Meanwhile, prepare the spiced onion yoghurt. Put all the ingredients except the yoghurt in a bowl and mix well. Set aside for 5 minutes to allow the salt and sugar to draw the flavour out of the other ingredients. Slowly fold in the yoghurt. Leave at room temperature until ready to serve.

When the goat is tender, remove the pan from the heat and squeeze in the lemon juice. Taste the curry and adjust the seasoning if need be. Stir in the chopped coriander and serve the curry with steamed rice and the spiced onion yoghurt. Any leftover yoghurt will keep for 2 days covered in the fridge.

pork

Ham hock and girolle pie with pease pudding serves 6

Pease pudding is a classic accompaniment to boiled ham or salt pork. It's a steamed pudding made with dried yellow split peas that have been cooked in a muslin bag in the same pot as the boiling ham. Boiling the dried peas in the flavoursome stock given off by the ham is a clever way to harness more flavour and goodness. This Northern peasant dish has been around for years; I found a recipe almost identical to this one, printed in 1858 by Eliza Acton in her book ironically titled Modern Cookery. Ironic today in any case!

Rather than constructing individual pies, you may like to make one pie for the family to share in a larger pie dish.

For boiling the ham and making the pease pudding

2 green gammon (unsmoked) knuckles, soaked overnight in cold water
1 large carrot, peeled and cut into 4
1 onion, peeled and halved
1 leek, white part only
2 celery sticks
1 bay leaf
5 sprigs of thyme
400g dried yellow split peas, soaked in cold water for 3 hours
60g butter, diced, plus extra for greasing the pudding basins
1 egg, beaten
sea salt and freshly milled black pepper

For the pies

150g butter
250g girolles, brushed clean and halved if large
1 large onion, finely diced
100g plain flour
150ml double cream
1 tbsp wholegrain mustard
3 tbsp chopped flat-leaf parsley
600g good-quality puff pastry
4 egg yolks, beaten

You will also need: 6 individual pudding basins or teacups and 6 individual pie dishes.

Place the soaked ham knuckles into a casserole with the carrot, onion, leek, celery, bay leaf and thyme. Cover with cold water and bring to the boil over a high heat before lowering to a simmer. Simmer for 2 hours topping up with water as required to keep the knuckles covered.

While the ham knuckles are cooking, rinse the soaked peas under cold water and tie them in a muslin bag secured at the top with sturdy string. After the ham knuckles have cooked for 2 hours, carefully place the bag of peas into the pot with the ham knuckles, tying it to the handle so it can be easily retrieved once the peas are cooked. Remove the peas after 1 hour and allow them to drain. Check the ham knuckles; they should be falling from the bone. If so, turn off the heat.

To prepare the puddings, open the muslin bag and tip the soft peas into a large mixing bowl. Fold in the diced butter and season with salt and pepper. Mix the peas vigorously to mash them but leave them with some texture. Grease six individual pudding basins with butter (or alternatively, six teacups will do the job).

Fold the beaten egg thoroughly through the peas and spoon the mixture into the pudding basins. Place foil over the top of each pudding basin and place them into a deep tray ready for steaming.

Lift the ham knuckles out of the stock with a slotted spoon and place them to one side so they cool down enough to be handled. While the ham is cooling, strain the stock through a fine-mesh sieve and place to one side.

Heat a frying pan over a medium heat. Add 50g of the butter to the pan followed by the girolles. Season the mushrooms with salt and pepper and cook gently for 2-3 minutes, until soft. Place to one side.

In a separate saucepan melt the remaining butter over a medium heat and cook the onion for 4–5 minutes, until soft. Reduce the heat to very low and stir in the flour to form a roux. Cook for about 2 minutes, stirring constantly. Slowly pour in $1\frac{1}{2}$ litres of the reserved warm ham stock, a little at a time, stirring constantly to avoid lumps forming. Once the ingredients have amalgamated, cook the sauce over a low heat, stirring often, until the taste of flour has gone. This should take about 5 minutes.

Add the cream and stir in the mustard. Simmer the sauce gently, continuing to stir regularly, until it reaches the consistency of thick gravy. The sauce must be the right consistency. If it is too thin the pastry on the sides and bottom of the pie will not cook sufficiently, and if too thick, the pie will be dry and stodgy. Taste the sauce and adjust the seasoning accordingly.

Once the ham knuckles are cool enough to handle, discard any skin and fat from the outside and flake the meat from the bone into a large bowl carefully to ensure any gristle is removed. Pour the sauce over the flaked ham and fold in the parsley and girolles. Allow the pie filling to cool.

While the pie filling is cooling, cut the block of pastry into six even slabs. From each slab cut away one quarter of the pastry to be used for each pastry lid. Dust a work surface and your rolling pin liberally with flour and roll out the pastry lids first. They will need to be about $\frac{1}{2}$ cm thick and the perfect size to fit inside the rim of the pie dishes, so it's a good idea to use the rim of a pie dish itself as a stencil, trimming around it with a small sharp knife. Using a small round pastry cutter, cut a 2cm hole into the centre of each lid, so that as the pies cook, they can release a little steam. Dust the lids lightly with flour and place them to one side.

Lightly grease the pie dishes with butter. Line the base of each pie dish with greaseproof paper so that the pies can turned out easily. Roll out the pastry bases one at a time to about $\frac{1}{2}$ cm thick and large enough to line your pie dishes. Lay the rolled pastry sheets into each of the pie dishes, trimming the edges of the pastry so they only overlap the sides by 1cm.

Fill each pie dish to the top with the cooled filling. Place the pastry lid on top. Using a pastry brush, lightly brush a little egg yolk around the edge of each lid and fold over the overlapping pastry, pinching it all the way around to seal the pie. Brush the top of each pie with egg yolk. The pies can be prepared in advance and stored in the fridge overnight before cooking.

Preheat your oven to 150ºC/Gas Mark 2.

Boil a kettle of water and pour it carefully into the tray holding the pease puddings. The water level should come halfway up the side of the basins. Cover the tray with foil and carefully place in the oven for 35 minutes. Remove the puddings from the oven but leave them foiled in the tray of water so they stay warm while the pies are cooking.

Turn the oven up to 200ºC/Gas Mark 6 and bake the pies on the middle shelf for 30 minutes, until the pastry is golden brown. Rest the pies for 3–4 minutes before attempting to turn them out. While the pies are resting, place the puddings back into the oven to ensure they're hot.

Before turning the pies out, carefully run a small knife around the sides of the pie dish to make sure they aren't stuck. Do the same when turning out the puddings.

Slow-roasted pork belly with mashed potato and Bramley apple sauce serves 8

This is by far our most popular dish at Roast. We cook approximately 120 bellies per week, and due to the long cooking time our ovens are constantly full. During the busier festive season, we actually need to have a chef working through the night, roasting pork bellies, in an attempt to alleviate congestion in the ovens during the day!

4kg boneless pork belly
15 sage leaves, roughly chopped
3 garlic cloves, roughly chopped
vegetable oil, for rubbing the pork belly
1 carrot, peeled and roughly chopped
1 celery stick, roughly chopped
½ leek, roughly chopped
1 onion, peeled and roughly chopped
2 quantities Mashed Potato
   (see page 281), to serve
1 quantity Bramley Apple Sauce
   (see page 289), to serve
Gravy for Pork (see page 296), to serve
sea salt and freshly milled black pepper

Preheat your oven to 220°C/Gas Mark 7.

Score the pork belly skin crossways to a depth of about a ½ cm at 2 cm intervals using a sharp retractable Stanley knife. The idea is to score through the skin but not all the way through the layer of fat under it. Turn the belly over and season its underside with salt and pepper, then scatter over the chopped sage and garlic, covering the underside evenly.

Roll up the belly lengthways, with the skin to the outside, and tie it with cooking string. You'll need to make about 6–8 ties to hold it together securely.

Place the pork belly on a wire rack over the kitchen sink. Pour over a large kettle of boiling water. As the water is poured over the skin, the skin will tighten up and the pores will open, allowing the heat and salt to penetrate more easily, enhancing the quality of the crackling.

Pat the rolled belly dry and rub it with vegetable oil and a generous amount of salt. Place it on a wire rack inside a roasting tray and place the tray in the oven. The reason for the wire rack is to lift it off the bottom of the roasting tray so the hot air circulates all the way around the belly for even crackling. After about 45 minutes, the skin of the pork should be golden brown and crackled. Turn the oven down to 160°C/Gas Mark 3 and roast for 1 hour.

After 1 hour remove the roasting tray from the oven and lift out the rack with the pork on it. Scatter the chopped carrot, celery, leeks and onion into the roasting tray and mix them with the fat that has rendered out of the pork during cooking. Place the rack with the pork back into the roasting tray over the vegetables. Roast for a further 1 hour, until the pork is tender. While the pork is finishing roasting, prepare the mashed potato and Bramley apple sauce.

Remove the pork from the oven and allow it to rest for at least 10–15 minutes before carving. Meanwhile, make the gravy according to the recipe on page 296.

Carve with a large serrated knife so you're able to saw through the crackling.

Braised pork cheeks in cider with black pudding and butter beans
serves 6

Pork cheeks are the best braising cut from a pig. The cheek is a complex muscle that is broken up by several thin layers of sinew running through it. When slow-cooked, this sinew breaks down into the most divine jelly that just melts in your mouth. Cheeks are very popular in Spain, and when I first tried this dish it was made with morcilla, my favourite of all blood sausages.

Despite being one of the best braising cuts, pork cheeks are still under-utilised and if you're buying them in any quantity it may be an idea to give your butcher advanced warning. They have a good fat coverage that will require trimming to reveal the burgundy-coloured jewels of meat beneath.

If pork cheeks are to your liking, then you'll also enjoy ox cheeks. They would make an ideal substitute for the shin of beef in the Beef Shin and Ale Pie recipe on page 176.

100g dried butter beans, soaked
   overnight (see below)
18 pork cheeks, trimmed of outer fat
100g plain flour
3 tbsp vegetable oil
45g butter
1½ onions, roughly chopped
2 carrots, roughly chopped
1 leek, roughly chopped
3 celery sticks, roughly chopped
4 garlic cloves, roughly chopped
6 sprigs of thyme
2 bay leaves
1½ tbsp tomato purée
750ml good-quality dry cider
2 litres Chicken Stock (see page 298)
750ml Beef Stock (see page 297)
300g good-quality black pudding
   (at Roast we use Ramsay of Carluke)

3 tbsp chopped flat-leaf parsley
sea salt and freshly milled black pepper
crusty sourdough bread, to serve
buttered winter greens (such as sprout
   tops, curly kale and Savoy cabbage),
   to serve

The butter beans will need to be soaked in water overnight. Make sure you cover them with three times the amount of water as beans as they will swell substantially and need to stay submerged.

Preheat your oven to 150°C/Gas Mark 2. Season the pork cheeks with salt and pepper and place them into a large plastic bag (without holes). Add the flour to the bag and holding the bag closed at the top, give them a good shake, coating them with the flour. Remove the cheeks from the bag and save the flour for later.

Heat a large saucepan over a high heat. Add the vegetable oil and fry the floured pork cheeks until evenly browned. You may need to do this in two batches so as not to overcrowd your pan. Remove each batch, transferring the sealed cheeks to a braising dish or a casserole. Once the second batch has been removed from the pan, turn the heat down to medium and add the butter, onion, carrot, leek, celery, garlic, thyme and bay leaf. Allow to cook for about 4–5 minutes, stirring regularly to release any tasty morsels left behind by the pork cheeks. Cook until the vegetables are soft and slightly caramelised.

Stir in the reserved flour and tomato purée and cook for another minute, stirring continuously so they don't catch on the bottom of the pan. Stir in the cider, a little at a time so that lumps don't form. Once all of the cider has been added, pour in the stocks and bring to the boil.

Pour the liquid and all the vegetables over the pork cheeks, then cover the dish with a lid or foil. Place in the oven, and cook for 2 hours, until the cheeks are tender.

While the cheeks are braising, drain the butter beans in a colander and give them a rinse under cold water. Place the beans into a saucepan and cover with cold lightly salted water. Bring to the boil, then reduce the heat to a simmer. Cook the beans for 45 minutes or so until soft, topping up with water to cover the beans as required. Check the beans from time to time as the cooking time may vary from product to product. Once they're cooked, drain the beans through a colander and place them to one side.

Once the pork cheeks are tender, remove them from the oven and lift out of the braising dish with a slotted spoon. Strain the sauce through a fine-mesh sieve into a large saucepan or casserole. Bring the sauce up to the boil over a medium heat, before reducing to a simmer. Give the sauce a good skim with a ladle, removing any fat that may be collecting on the surface. If the sauce appears a little thin, reduce it slightly until it has reached the desired consistency, then season it with salt pepper and add the beans.

Break the black pudding into large nuggets and add them to the pan. Allow the black pudding to cook for 2–3 minutes only – this is enough time for it to impart flavour into the sauce but not so long that it disintegrates. Add the chopped parsley and serve with crusty sourdough and a mixture of buttered winter greens.

Breaded pork cutlet with a fried duck's egg, anchovies and capers

serves 4

This posh pork schnitzel and fried egg is a great one if you're short of time. Make sure you buy quality outdoor-reared pork, and ask your butcher to French-trim the rib bones, scraping them clean of meat, for a tidy finish. This recipe is also suitable for veal cutlets or even a flattened out skinless chicken breast. And best of all it should only take you a few minutes to prepare.

four 250g pork cutlets, French trimmed
100g plain flour
4 eggs, beaten
200g Japanese panko breadcrumbs
200ml extra virgin rapeseed oil
50g butter
4 duck eggs
12 salted anchovy fillets
80g capers
1 tbsp chopped flat-leaf parsley
sea salt and freshly milled black pepper

Remove the rind and fat from the edge of each cutlet. Lay a sheet of clingfilm down on a solid area of work surface and place a cutlet down upon it with the bone facing away from you. Place another sheet of clingfilm over the cutlet and using a meat tenderiser or the bottom of a small solid saucepan, give the cutlet a few solid taps, flattening it out to about half its original thickness. Don't bash it too hard. Many lighter taps are more effective than a few hard taps, or you risk tearing the meat. Repeat the process with the remaining cutlets.

Put the flour on to a large plate; the beaten eggs on a second and the breadcrumbs in a third. Press one of the cutlets into the flour on both sides, coating it well, then carefully shake off any excess. Dip the floured cutlet into the egg and then into the breadcrumbs. Cover the cutlet with a pile of crumbs and then press down on it with the palm of your hand so the crumbs stick to the egg. Once you're happy with the coating of crumbs on the first cutlet, repeat the process with the remaining three.

Preheat your oven to 180°C/Gas Mark 4.

Heat large frying pan over a medium-high heat and add the rapeseed oil. Rapeseed oil is great for this as it cooks at a high temperature without burning, and has a delicate nutty flavour. To test if the oil is hot enough, add a couple of breadcrumbs. If the breadcrumbs start to sizzle, season the crumbed cutlets with salt and pepper and place them carefully into the oil. If your frying pan is large enough you may be able to fry 2 cutlets at once. Shallow-fry the cutlets for about 3 minutes on each side, until they're golden and crispy. Drain on kitchen paper to soak up any excess oil. Then place them on to a tray and into the oven to keep warm while you fry the eggs.

Drain the rapeseed oil from the pan and add the butter. Place the pan on a low heat. Once the butter has melted crack all four duck eggs into the pan. Lay three anchovy fillets into the raw white of each egg, so that as the eggs cook, the anchovies set into the surface of the white. Season the eggs with pepper. They won't need any salt as the salty anchovies serve this purpose.

Once the eggs have cooked, remove the cutlets from the oven and place them on to four warmed plates. Place the eggs on top of the cutlets, then add the capers and parsley to the butter left in the frying pan to briefly warm through, before drizzling over the egg and cutlet.

Roast suckling pig serves 10

Thursday at Roast is suckling pig day – it's my favourite day of the week. The pigs we cook in the restaurant weigh about 10–12kg, which yield about 16–20 portions. These would not fit into your oven at home, though, so I've adjusted the recipe slightly to suit a smaller pig. At Roast we have an open kitchen, so once the little pigs are cooked, we line them up on the kitchen pass, facing out into the restaurant. The reaction from the guests as they are being led past them to their tables is brilliant, remarking and often even taking photos.

If you've not tried suckling pig before, then you're in for a treat. The thin crispy crackling is to die for, and the meat underneath so tender and juicy. Serve it with Bramley apple sauce (see page 289) and mashed potato or roasties (see pages 281 and 282).

one 6–7kg suckling pig
about 100ml vegetable oil
2 carrots, roughly chopped
2 celery sticks, roughly chopped
1 leek, roughly chopped
1 large onion, roughly chopped
sea salt

Preheat your oven to 220°C/Gas Mark 7.

Place the pig on a wire rack over the kitchen sink. Pour a large kettle of boiling water over it. As the water is poured over the skin, the skin will tighten up, opening the pores, which will allow the heat and salt to penetrate more easily, enhancing the quality of the crackling.

Pat the pig dry and rub it with vegetable oil and a generous amount of sea salt. Place the pig into a large roasting tray. Wrap the pig's ears and tail with foil so they don't burn and place the pig in the oven. After 35 minutes at this heat the skin should be starting to crackle. Remove the roasting tray from the oven and scatter the chopped vegetables around the pig. Turn the oven down to 160°C/Gas Mark 3 and cook for a further 1½ hours.

After about 45 minutes, remove the roasted vegetables and place them to one side for the gravy. When putting the pig back into the oven, turn the tray around so the pig is facing the opposite direction from before. This way the crackling will cook evenly.

To check that the pig is cooked, peel a small piece of crackling back from the shoulder and press into the flesh with a fork. It should feel soft and pull easily from the bone. Remove the foil from the ears and tail and prick a few holes in the crackling with a skewer to release some steam so that the crackling stays crisp. Carefully remove the pig from the roasting tray to rest for 20 minutes. While the pig is resting, prepare the gravy (see page 296). Place the pig back into the oven for 5 minutes before serving.

Honey-glazed leg of ham serves 18

For me, Christmas brings back memories of hot summer holidays and barbecues. Though the traditional roast Christmas dinner is still an institution in New Zealand for us it was usually followed by a bowl of fresh strawberries and cream rather than steamed Christmas pudding. In New Zealand it's also very popular to prepare a glazed ham for Christmas. The leftover ham would be picked to the bone and eaten cold over the few days following our celebration. The week after Christmas, as a family, we would often go camping. Taking the leftover ham with us was our plan 'B' in case we didn't catch any fish. Never has a plan 'B' been so well received!

If you're not a confident carver, ask your butcher to bone the ham and tie it up, leaving the small knuckle bone attached for presentation. At Roast, we often serve the ham with Bubble 'n' Squeak (see page 41), but it is also good with roasted pumpkin or squash and some steamed Savoy cabbage. Note that you need to soak the ham for two days before you can cook it.

one 4–5kg leg of raw smoked ham
2 large onions, halved
4 carrots, halved
1 leek, white part only
½ head of celery, leaves removed
2 bay leaves
10 peppercorns
30 whole cloves
350ml clear honey
150g wholegrain mustard
250ml double cream

Soak the ham in water for 2 days to desalinate, changing the water daily. Place the ham into a large stockpot and add the vegetables, bay leaves and peppercorns. Cover the ham with cold water and bring to the boil before turning the heat down to a simmer. Simmer the ham for approximately 3–4 hours, topping up the pot with water so the ham stays submerged.

If you have a temperature probe test the ham's core temperature. Ideally it should reach a temperature of 55ºC before being removed from the stock. If not, check the temperature with a thin bladed knife. When the knife is pulled out, the tip should feel warm to touch. If you boil the ham for too long it will fall apart when carving.

Preheat your oven to 200ºC/Gas Mark 6.

Once the ham has been removed from the stock, rest it and leave it to cool down slightly so it can be handled comfortably. While the ham is cooling strain the stock. Put 2 ½ litres of stock aside for the sauce and the rest can be chilled and frozen for a rainy day. It makes a great base for Ham and Garden Pea Soup (see page 165).

Once the ham is cool enough to handle, remove the string. With a sharp knife, shave the skin from the ham leaving a layer of approximately 1cm of fat still attached to the joint. Score the fat with a knife in a cross-hatched pattern and stud the intersection of each cross with the cloves. Place the ham in a large roasting tray and drizzle the honey all over it. It's a good idea to spoon the honey that collects in the bottom of the tray back over the ham a few times while cooking to achieve an even glaze. Place in the oven and bake for 15–20 minutes until the honey has caramelised well.

Meanwhile, place 2 litres of the ham stock in a saucepan over a high heat, add the mustard and bring to the boil. Once the ham has achieved an even caramelised glaze, pour the stock over the ham.

Place the ham back in the oven and bake for a further 1½ hours, basting the ham stock over the ham every 10 minutes or so. As the ham cooks, the ham stock, honey and mustard will reduce down to a dark, sticky glaze and coat the ham. Once you're happy with the glaze, remove the ham from the oven tray to rest while you make the sauce.

Pour a little more ham stock into the roasting tray to boil, and scraping the tin clean with a wooden spoon to loosen all the flavoursome, sticky glaze that is left in the bottom. Transfer to a saucepan and add the cream. Bring the sauce up to a gentle simmer and reduce it to a desired consistency and flavour. Add more honey and mustard if you feel it would enhance the sauce for your taste. Go easy on the honey though as you risk making the sauce too sweet. Don't add any salt as the ham has sufficient salt content.

Take the impressive honey glazed ham to the table to carve, and serve the sauce on the side in a sauce boat.

Crispy pork and wild herb salad with cobnuts and elderberries

serves 4 as a starter

You will need to think ahead for this one as the pork belly needs to be soaked in the brine for at least 48 hours to season it through. The brine works a treat, infusing the pork with the flavours of star anise and fennel. You can also brine larger joints. One of our butchers sent us in some tied pork rib eyes as a sample a few months back. We brined them in this solution for five days before boiling them gently with a few vegetables until the core temperature reached 45°C. We allowed them to cool in the liquor so they stayed moist, before cutting them into thick steaks and pan-frying them. They were delicious with some baby carrots and pea shoots.

This recipe may seem complex but the final result is a colourful autumnal salad of big flavours and varying textures. Pea shoots and bull's blood or ruby chard leaves are a good substitute if you can't get hold of the wild herbs.

600g boneless pork belly
1 pig's ear
800ml duck or goose fat
50g plain flour
1 egg, beaten
50g Japanese panko breadcrumbs
selection of wild herbs (such as bitter cress, chervil, sorrel, wood sorrel)
50g shelled fresh cobnuts
80ml Elderberry Dressing (see page 192)
vegetable oil, for frying
sea salt and freshly milled black pepper

For the brining solution
1 litre water
40g granulated or caster sugar
75g table salt
2 sprigs of thyme
1 bay leaf
5 black peppercorns

1 tsp fennel seeds
1/2 star anise

To prepare the brining solution, warm all the ingredients in a pan without boiling. Stir occasionally, until the sugar and salt have dissolved, then remove from the heat and leave to cool. The flavour of the spices and herbs will infuse into the brine. Once the brine has cooled completely, soak the pork belly for 48 hours.

Preheat your oven to 150°C/Gas Mark 2. Bring a small pan of lightly salted water to the boil. Add the pig's ear and simmer gently for 2 hours, until soft.

Remove the pork belly from the brine and dry it well. Place the pork into a small roasting dish. Melt the duck fat in a saucepan and pour it over the belly, submerging it completely. Cover the tray with foil and place it in the oven for 2½ hours. After this time the pork belly should be tender. Carefully remove it from the fat and lay it on to a large plate between two sheets of greaseproof paper. Place another plate on top of the belly and press it down with the weight of a few tins of baked beans or the equivalent. Once it's cooled, place it into the fridge, still under its weights, to set completely so it is slices easily without falling apart.

Meanwhile, slice the cooked pig's ear into thin strips and dust with flour. In a small bowl whisk the egg and add the strips. Shake off any excess egg and drop the strips into the breadcrumbs coating generously. Set aside for deep-frying.

Once the pork belly has set completely, slice off the rind and most of the fat, leaving a thin layer of only a few millimetres. Cut the belly into strips about 1cm thick.

Set your deep-fat fryer to 190°C. If you don't have a fryer, place the oil into a large, deep saucepan, leaving enough room at the top to allow for rapid boiling when the ear strips are added. Place the oil over a high heat but be very careful that it doesn't get too hot. If you have a cooking thermometer, use it so you can regulate the temperature. If not, test the heat by dropping a cube of bread into the oil; it should bubble on entry and start to brown after about 15 seconds.

Have to hand some kitchen paper and a slotted spoon to remove the crispy pig's ear strips from the hot oil. (Don't try to use spring-loaded tongs; this can be very dangerous for obvious reasons.)

Preheat your oven to 170°C/Gas Mark 3½ then very lightly roast the cobnuts for about 4–5 minutes to bring out their oils and enhance their mild flavour. Remove, transfer to a small plate and season them with a little salt.

Heat a large frying pan over a medium-high heat. Fry the strips of pork belly in 2–3 tablespoons of vegetable oil until crisp and golden on both sides. They won't need any seasoning as the brine will have done the job. Once cooked, keep them warm in the oven while you fry the pigs ears.

Deep-fry the crumbed pig's ears until golden. Drain on kitchen paper and season well with salt.

To serve, toss the wild herbs in the dressing and season. Arrange on serving plates with strips of pork belly among the leaves. Scatter the cobnuts, elderberries and crispy ear strips over the top.

Wicks Manor Farm, farmer of happy pigs

Pigs are very intelligent, inquisitive animals that need freedom and stimulation. At Fergus Howie's Wicks Manor Farm in Essex, it is plain to see just by looking at their expressive faces that his are very happy pigs. Fergus's pigs are born and bred on his farm and live in large open straw yards with plenty of space to express their natural behaviour. The yards, which have adjoining sheds, are mucked out twice a week and relayed with fresh straw produced right there on the farm. It's a great way to keep pigs as they can choose to be outside in the rain or sunshine or be tucked up in the comfort of the warm dry straw when they're cold. They even have toys to keep them stimulated. Hanging from a rope on the outside of the shed in each yard is an old Wellington boot for the pigs to gnaw on.

Unfortunately however, not all pigs are as well cared for. Intensive pig farming is going on in most parts of the world with appalling standards of animal welfare. In many cases, these intensive farms house the pregnant sows in stalls so small they can't even turn around. The animals live a horrible, undignified, stressed existence. I've seen footage of these intensive pig farms and it turns my stomach. It's so important to know what you're eating and to take responsibility for which products you choose to buy. Sow stalls have been illegal in Sweden and the UK for over a decade, and thankfully, due to consumer pressure, from 2013 they are now also illegal across the rest of the EU. However many EU countries, including France, Ireland and Spain, are not fully compliant and still farm pork using these methods. Whether or not these new EU standards will be properly policed remains to be seen.

At the end of the day, the consumer can make a difference. If you're buying intensively farmed pork you are directly supporting this horrific method of farming. Please avoid the 'bog-standard' cheap pork on the supermarket shelf. This is where you'll find intensively farmed pork being sold. If you're buying pork, bacon or sausages from the supermarket, buy UK outdoor reared. Look for information on the packaging explaining where and how the pork is produced. The packet will often even supply information about the farmer.

At Wicks Manor wheat and barley are grown and milled on the farm, which they process into feed for the pigs. They produce different feeds designed for different stages of a pig's development. Each yard holds pigs of a different age with a different nutritional requirement. The feed produced for the piglets straight from the sow, is produced with milk powder and biscuits to remain as similar in nutrients as that they would naturally receive from their mother's milk. They are then slowly weaned on to a higher protein diet of wheat and barley to develop muscle structure. Wicks Manor rear a Large White/Landrace crossbreed. The Large White is an English breed with good muscle structure and the Landrace, originally a Scandinavian breed, is a longer, leaner animal, which has a longer loin for a better yield of back bacon.

The pigs are sent to a local abattoir before being returned to the licensed cutting plant on the farm for butchery. A short trip to the abattoir is very important for meat quality. Pigs travel badly and are easily stressed by transport. They do not have sweat glands and are particularly susceptible to heat stress during their time on the truck. Once back at the farm, the carcass is processed and sold either as a fresh product or cured to produce Wicks Manor's award-winning bacon and ham.

Fergus and his team have actually developed a sausage recipe exclusively for Roast, made to our specifications, which we serve as part of our 'Full Borough' (our full English breakfast that I challenge anyone to finish!). They also supply us with dry-cured bacon, ham and the numerous pork bellies we sell.

I have a real soft spot for pigs. They are well natured animals with so much personality, so it's such a pleasure to spend time at Wicks Manor Farm and see first hand how well cared for are their animals. This care and attention is directly linked to the quality of the product, and it's with great pride that we can share it with our guests at Roast.

Ham and garden pea soup
serves 8–10

'London Particular' is a traditional ham and pea soup made with dried green split peas. It was named after the thick fog (resembling 'pea soup') that blanketed London. Such fogs were prevalent in UK cities, especially London, where the smoke from thousands of chimneys combined with the mists and fogs of the Thames valley. Legislation was passed in the 1950s banning the use of coal for domestic fires.

London Particular is a great winter warmer, but in the warmer months I prefer to make a lighter version with frozen garden peas. The sweet peas perfectly balance the salty ham stock.

You can either make this soup from scratch, making your stock from, and garnishing with, ham hocks. But it's also a good way of using up any ham stock you may have left over from a boiled ham. Any leftover soup can be frozen for up to 3 months.

1.2 litres ham stock
50g butter
½ leek, white part only, roughly
*   chopped*
½ onion, sliced
1kg frozen garden peas, defrosted
300g cooked ham, flaked
sea salt and freshly milled black pepper

Taste the ham stock before you start. If it's too salty, dilute it with a little water.

Heat a large soup pan over a medium heat, add the butter and gently cook the leeks and onions for 4–5 minutes, until soft. Add the ham stock and raise the heat, bringing it up to the boil.

When boiling, add the peas and season to taste with salt, if required, and pepper.

Once the peas have been in the stock for about 3 minutes, remove the soup from the heat and blend until smooth. It's important to blend the soup while it's still hot so it doesn't lose its vibrant green colour, but don't add too much hot soup to the blender at one time, or it will end up spraying all over yourself and your kitchen when you switch the blender on. Once the soup is smooth place it back into the saucepan and on to the heat, adding the flaked ham to warm it through before serving immediately.

beef

Roast fore rib of beef
Serves 10–15 depending on the size of your joint

A roast fore rib of beef is definitely the Rolls Royce of roast dinners. The 5-bone fore ribs we serve at Roast weigh in at about 7kg and will feed 15 people comfortably. For 10 people ask the butcher for a 3-bone joint. If you are serving fewer than 10, I suggest you go with something off the bone. Try strip loin, topside or even fillet. When cooking joints off the bone however, the timings are a little different to those on the bone. For every 500g, allow 20 minutes for rare, scaling up to 25 minutes for well done.

When buying your fore rib, don't go for the freshest looking bright red joint. This will not have been aged sufficiently and will shrink in the oven and lack flavour. Remember, good beef will have been dry-aging for 3–4 weeks where it will have lost 12–15 per cent of its weight (for more about this, see pages 184–185). Look for a joint with a good creamy-coloured fat coverage. A good fat coverage means the beef will self-baste and you won't have to go back and forth to the oven every 15 minutes. The outside should look dark and dehydrated. Don't be afraid of a little furry mould, this is normal and does no harm. The process of dry-aging promotes the growth of certain fungal (mould) species on the external surface of the meat. This does not cause spoilage. The mould works in conjunction with the beef's natural enzymes to help tenderise and increase flavour. Just wipe the mould off with a clean, damp cloth before preparing the beef for the oven.

The cooking time will of course depend on the weight of the fore rib. If you like your beef rare, calculate 14 minutes per 500g, and scale up to 20 minutes for well done. I personally prefer to use a temperature probe. These are fairly cheap and available from any good kitchenware supplier. At Roast we cook our joints of beef to medium–rare removing them from the oven once the core temperature reaches 35°C.

1 well-hung 3-bone fore rib of beef
2 carrots, peeled and roughly chopped
2 celery sticks, roughly chopped
1 leek, roughly chopped
1 large onion, peeled and roughly chopped
4 garlic cloves, unpeeled
sea salt and freshly milled black pepper

Gravy for Roast Beef (see page 294), to serve
Roast Potatoes (see page 282), to serve
Yorkshire Puddings (see page 287), to serve
Horseradish Cream (see page 291), to serve

Preheat your oven to 220°C/Gas Mark 7.

Score the covering fat of the beef in a criss-cross pattern to a depth of about 5mm. Season thoroughly with salt and pepper and rub the seasoning into the scored fat. Don't be shy with the salt. Crispy, salty beef fat is absolutely divine, and your guests will be asking for second helpings!

Place the fore rib in your largest roasting tray, resting it on the flat chine bone with the ribs pointing upwards. Place in the oven and roast at this high temperature for the first 25 minutes before turning the oven down to 160°C/Gas Mark 3. This initial blast on a high temperature will seal the outside of the beef so that it retains its juices as it roasts. When you turn down the oven, remove the beef.

You will notice that the fat has started to render out of the joint. Add the vegetables to the roasting tray, placing them around the joint, and mix them in the fat, coating them well. Place the beef back into the oven to roast for the weight-specified time (see above).

Check the vegetables after 15 minutes and give them a stir so they caramelise evenly. Remove the vegetables after about 30–35 minutes, once nicely browned, and place them to one side for the gravy (follow the recipe on page 294).

Once the beef is ready, remove it from the oven to rest in a warm part of the kitchen for a good 15–30 minutes. A 3-bone joint should rest for at least 15 minutes and 5-bone joints about 25–30 minutes. Before taking the joint to the table to carve, place it back into the oven for 5 minutes to bring it back to a suitable serving temperature.

Serve your beef with the gravy, roast potatoes, Yorkshire puddings and horseradish cream.

Salt beef croquettes with whipped peas and dandelion serves 8

These croquettes make a fantastic starter and are very economical and versatile. Don't limit yourself to salt beef; try smoked haddock, shredded ham hock or, for something more luxurious, crab or lobster. I use Tewkesbury mustard here, which is similar to Dijon but has the added kick of a little horseradish – a great pairing with the salt beef. You should be able to find it at a good supermarket but if not, Dijon mustard is a substitute.

For the salt beef
600g salt beef brisket, soaked in water
    for 12 hours (600g of uncooked
    brisket will yield 300g once cooked)
1 onion, peeled and roughly chopped
1 large carrot, peeled and roughly chopped
1 leek, roughly chopped
3 celery sticks, roughly chopped
a few sprigs of thyme
1 bay leaf
10 peppercorns

For the béchamel sauce
300ml milk
1/2 onion, sliced
1 bay leaf
50g plain flour
50g butter
1 tsp Tewkesbury mustard
300g boiled salted beef brisket, shredded
    into 3cm strands
2 tbsp chopped flat-leaf parsley
salt and freshly milled black pepper

For the croquettes
200g plain flour
3 eggs, beaten
200g Japanese panko breadcrumbs
2 litres vegetable oil, for deep-frying

To serve
100g pea shoots
100g dandelion leaves

*Lemon and Rapeseed Oil Dressing
    (see page 292)*
Whipped Peas (see page 286)

Start by preparing the salt beef. Place all the ingredients in a large saucepan and cover with cold water. Over a high heat, bring to the boil and then turn it down to a gentle simmer. Simmer for 2–3 hours until the brisket is soft and able to be pulled apart easily. Skim any scum off the surface as it rises, and top up with water as it evaporates ensuring the beef stays covered. Allow the brisket to cool in its cooking liquor so it doesn't dry out.

For the béchamel sauce, place the milk, onion and bay leaf in a small saucepan and bring to the boil. Once boiling, remove from the heat and set aside to infuse for 10 minutes before straining through a fine-mesh sieve.

In a separate saucepan over a low heat, melt the butter and stir in the flour (to form a roux). Cook the roux on a very low heat for about 2 minutes stirring constantly. Slowly pour in the warm milk infusion a little at a time to make a béchamel, stirring constantly to avoid lumps forming. Once the béchamel has come together to form a sauce, cook it over a low heat until the taste of flour has gone. This should take about 5 minutes and the resulting béchamel sauce should be quite thick. Whisk in the mustard but do not add any seasoning at this stage. Fold in the shredded beef and chopped parsley, season with salt and pepper and pour the mixture on to a tray to cool in the fridge until set. Cover with clingfilm to avoid a skin forming.

To make the croquettes, put the flour into a shallow bowl; the beaten eggs in a second and the breadcrumbs in a third.

Set your deep-fat fryer to 190°C. If you don't have a fryer, place the oil into a large, deep saucepan, leaving enough room at the top to allow for rapid boiling when the croquettes are added. Place the oil over a high heat but be very careful that it doesn't get too hot. If you have a cooking thermometer, use it so you can regulate the temperature. If not, test the heat by dropping a cube of bread into the oil; it should bubble on entry and start to brown after about 15 seconds.

Have to hand some kitchen paper and a slotted spoon to remove the croquettes from the hot oil. (Don't try to use spring-loaded tongs; this can be very dangerous for obvious reasons.)

Once set, roll the béchamel croquette mixture into 16 even-sized logs. You may find this easier with a little flour on your hands.

Coat the croquettes in flour and shake off any excess, then dip them into the beaten eggs, a few at a time, and finally roll them in the breadcrumbs. If you don't feel the croquettes are coated in enough breadcrumbs, dip them back into the egg, and again into the crumbs for a second coat. Deep-fry the croquettes for a couple of minutes until golden and crispy. You will need to do this in two batches so as not to overload the fryer. Once ready, drain the croquettes on kitchen paper to soak up any oil. The croquettes won't require any more salt as the béchamel has already been seasoned.

To serve, combine the pea shoots and dandelion to make a small salad and dress it with the lemon and rapeseed oil dressing, and serve with the hot croquettes and whipped peas.

Borough Burger serves 4

Iqbal Wahhab, our illustrious founder, is quite the connoisseur when it comes to burgers. We spent months eating at different places around London to see what take other chefs had on the humble burger, until finally he introduced me to my now good friend, Wyatt Shevloff. Wyatt was to be the head chef at one of Iqbal's new ventures and has a vast knowledge of Southern soul food and American barbecue. Who better to help me out in our quest to come up with our mighty Borough Burger?

In my opinion a burger is predominantly about the quality of the meat. After trial and error, playing around with fat percentages and even having a go at mixing raw bone marrow with the beef, the best result was a burger of minced rib trim with a fat content of 30 per cent. Wyatt came up with a fantastic spice mix to season the burger, which enhanced the smoky barbecue flavour from the grill. He also had a recipe for the mayonnaise-based burger sauce using the spice mix as a seasoning in the sauce itself. We also trialled a few different buns. I initially wanted a classic sesame seed bun but we ended up going with a half brioche style, which incorporates a little sugar and butter into the dough resulting in a slight but not overpowering sweetness, and a superb soft texture. It was well worth all the experimentation. We now have a very well executed classic that flies out the door on a busy market Saturday.

The seasoning is not only great for burgers. If you make up a batch and store it in a sealed jar in a cool dark cupboard it will keep for a year. You can pull it out when you're having a barbecue and use it for dusting chicken wings or seasoning steaks. The burger sauce can be kept in the fridge, covered, for 1 week.

four 200g beef burgers, 30 per fat content (ask your butcher about this)
4 half-brioche burger buns or classic sesame seed burger buns
½ iceberg lettuce, shredded
4 large thick slices of mild Cheddar cheese
2 large ripe tomatoes, sliced
2 large gherkins, sliced
½ small red onion, thinly sliced into rings
sea salt and freshly milled black pepper
Thrice-cooked chips (see page 283), to serve

For the burger seasoning
4 tbsp soft light brown sugar
1 tbsp caster sugar
3 tbsp smoked paprika
1 tbsp sweet paprika
2 tsp freshly milled black pepper
4 tbsp sea salt
1 tbsp table salt
1 tbsp garlic salt
1 tbsp onion salt
1 tbsp celery salt
2 tsp ground cumin
2 tsp ground cinnamon
½ tsp cayenne pepper

For the burger sauce
100g Mayonnaise (see page 290)
1 large gherkin, finely diced and squeezed dry
1 large tomato, deseeded and finely diced
½ red pepper, roasted, peeled and finely diced (to roast the peppers yourself, follow the instructions in the Wild Sea Bass with Dublin Bay Prawns recipe on page 82, or there are some good quality preserved roasted peppers available off the shelf)
1 red chilli, deseeded and finely diced
5 drops of Tabasco sauce
1 tbsp American-style mustard
1 tbsp tomato ketchup
1 tsp Burger Seasoning (above)

First, make the burger seasoning by mixing all the ingredients together, then transferring to a sealed jar.

Mix all the mayonnaise ingredients in a bowl, then cover with clingfilm and place in the fridge until ready to use.

Preheat your oven grill to high.

Heat a large griddle over a high heat. Season the burgers liberally with the burger seasoning and place them carefully in the hot dry pan. You won't need to use any oil as the fat in the burgers will gradually release. Seal the burgers until well caramelised on both sides, then turn the heat down to low. If you like your burgers medium-rare, as I do, allow the burgers to cook for 2 more minutes, turning them a couple of times so they cook evenly. For well done add another 3 minutes to the cooking time. Remove the griddle from the heat and allow the burgers to rest in the pan.

While the burgers are resting, slice the burger buns in half horizontally. Toast the buns lightly under the grill. Mix four tablespoons of the burger sauce with the shredded lettuce and distribute the dressed lettuce evenly between the bases of the buns.

Place the cheese on the burgers and put them under the grill until the cheese melts, then place the burgers on top of the lettuce. Place the sliced tomatoes on next, followed buy the sliced gherkins and red onion rings. Pour over a little ketchup and place the bun lid on top. Enjoy your burger with the thrice-cooked chips.

Chargrilled 1kg T-bone steak with scrumpy-battered onion rings serves 4–6

At Roast we offer this 'Flintstones'-sized steak for two people to share. On occasion someone will order the whole thing for themselves. Realistically there is more than enough beef here to feed three comfortably but some still manage on their own!

T-bone steaks are made up of two types of steak. On one side of the T-shaped bone is the larger sirloin steak and on the other is the smaller fillet steak. The fillet muscle, because of its situation on the carcass, does less work than the sirloin, which means it is more tender and tends to cook slightly quicker than the sirloin. So the main thing to watch out for when cooking a T-bone steak is not to overcook the tender fillet.

If you're having a barbecue, these are a must-have! Your friends and family will be blown away by the gargantuan slabs of beef hissing away over the hot coals. Because they are so big though, it's a good idea if you want them cooked further than medium-rare to finish them in the oven for a few minutes rather than char them too much on the barbecue.

2 T-bone steaks, about 1kg each
sea salt and freshly milled black pepper
1–1½ quantities Scrumpy-battered
  Onion Rings (see page 175), to serve
Béarnaise Sauce (follow the recipe for
  Hollandaise Sauce on page 32 and
  add 3 tablespoons of chopped fresh
  tarragon), to serve

Preheat your oven to 200°C/Gas Mark 6.

Season the beef generously with salt and pepper and let it rest for 20 minutes, so that the seasoning penetrates the meat and it has time to come to room temperature. Large steaks such as this are much better cooked from room temperature. Meanwhile, prepare the barbecue. Allow the flames on the barbecue to die down so you're left with hot glowing coals. Push the hot coals to one side of the barbecue, in order to create a hot side and a cooler side.

Place the steaks on to the barbecue over the hot coals to sear and seal the meat. The strip of fat on the edge of the larger sirloin may flame a little as the fat drips on to the coals, so keep moving the steaks around so the flames don't burn the meat. Seal both sides of the steaks until you are happy with the caramelisation you have achieved. If you wish to cook the steaks to medium well or well done, place them on a tray in the oven for 15 minutes or so. If you wish to cook the steaks less, pull them to the cooler side of the barbecue and finish the cooking here, turning them regularly so they cook evenly but don't burn. Given the different cooking times of the sirloin and fillet sides of the steak (see above), it's a good idea at this stage to hang the fillet off the edge of the barbecue from time to time so it doesn't overcook. It's impossible to give an accurate cooking time for the steaks because it depends on the heat of the barbecue. A good indicator for medium–rare is that when the steak has reached this stage it will start to bleed slightly, and should be removed from the heat source to rest for at least 8 minutes.

Once rested, carve the sirloin and fillet carefully off the bone using the bone to guide your knife. Carve the steak into slices about 1cm thick and place them back against the bone in their correct position for your guests to help themselves. Serve with the onion rings and Béarnaise sauce.

Beef shin and ale pie with a suet crust and baked bone marrow serves 4

In this pie I've replaced the traditional 'pie bird' with a tasty stuffed marrow bone to lift the pastry off the pie mixture and keep it crispy. Not only does the baked marrow bone complement the pie, but it's visually impressive too. It works most effectively with individual pies, but you could try placing all four marrow bones into one larger dish to share – it may just end up resembling Battersea Power Station! Try adding a little horseradish cream to your mashed potato for a bit of kick.

1.4kg beef shin, cut into 4cm dice
100g plain flour
80ml vegetable oil
40g butter
2 onions, peeled and chopped
2 garlic cloves, finely chopped
4 sprigs of thyme, leaves only, chopped
1 bay leaf
1 tbsp tomato purée
150ml good-quality red wine
250ml good-quality dark ale
1 ½ litres hot Beef or Veal Stock
   (see page 297)
1 tsp cornflour (optional)
four 7cm lengths of marrow bone,
   at room temperature
2 tbsp chopped flat-leaf parsley
4 slices of white bread, crusts removed
   and blended to coarse crumbs
1 quantity of Suet Pastry (see page 288)
4 egg yolks, beaten
sea salt and freshly milled black pepper
Mashed Potato (see page 281), to serve

You will also need: 4 x 15cm individual pie dishes

Preheat your oven to 150°C/Gas Mark 2.

Season the diced beef shin with salt and pepper and place the meat into a large plastic bag (without holes). Add the flour to the bag and holding the bag closed at the top, give it a good shake, coating the beef pieces with the flour. Remove the beef from the bag and save the flour for later.

Preheat a large saucepan over a high heat. Add the vegetable oil and fry the floured beef shin in three batches, until evenly browned. Remove each batch, transferring the sealed beef to an ovenproof casserole before adding the next. Once the last batch has been removed from the pan, lower the heat to medium and add the butter, onion, garlic, thyme and bay leaf. Allow to cook for about 4–5 minutes, until the onions are soft and slightly caramelised, stirring regularly with a wooden spoon to release any tasty morsels left behind by the beef. Stir in the flour and tomato purée and cook for another minute, stirring continuously so they don't catch on the bottom of the pan. Stir in the wine and ale a little at a time so lumps don't form.

Once all of the alcohol has been added, pour in the hot stock and bring it to the boil. Pour the gravy over the beef shin, and cover your casserole with a lid or foil. Place in the oven and braise for 2 hours, until the meat is tender. It's difficult to put an exact time on braising or stewing meats, sometimes an extra half an hour may be needed depending on the cut. The best way to check is by tasting the meat.

While the beef is braising, make the suet pastry (see page 288), leave it to rest as per the recipe, then roll it into four sheets on a floured surface, each just over ½ cm thick and a suitable size to cover your pie dishes. If you have any pastry left over it will keep in the freezer, well wrapped, for 2–3 months. Rest the sheets of pastry in the fridge for a few minutes, with a layer of greaseproof paper between each one. Resting the pastry in the fridge after rolling will reduce shrinkage during cooking.

Once you've rolled out the pastry, push the marrow out of the centre of each bone using your thumb. You will find this easier if the marrow bones are at room temperature. Chop the marrow into large chunks and place in a mixing bowl. Add the parsley and breadcrumbs and mix well. Season well with salt and pepper. Bone marrow has a very high fat content and the breadcrumbs are essential to absorb the fat as it melts during cooking, so it doesn't seep out and flood the pie. Stuff the seasoned marrow back into the bones.

Once the beef shin is cooked, carefully remove the meat from the gravy with a slotted spoon. If your gravy seems too thin then pour it into a saucepan, and over a medium heat, bring it up to a simmer. Stir in a teaspoon of cornflour dissolved in a little cold water and continue to simmer, skimming off any fat that may rise to the surface. Once the gravy has reached the correct consistency, taste it to check the seasoning and pour it back over the beef shin. Allow the mixture to cool completely before building the pies.

To assemble the pies, stand a stuffed marrow bone in the centre of each pie dish. Surround the marrow bones with enough braised beef shin and gravy to fill the dishes. Cut a hole in the middle of each pastry sheet and place it over each

pie so the marrow bone pokes through the hole. Cut off the extra pastry and with wet fingers, press the edges of the pastry to the outside of each pie dish so it is sealed.

Finish one pie at a time, leaving the other pastry sheets in the fridge so that they stay cold and workable. Once all the pies are covered with pastry, brush a generous layer of the beaten egg yolks over the pastry of each pie. Rest the pies in the fridge for at least 1 hour before baking. If you're entertaining, the pies can be prepared well in advance.

Preheat your oven to 200°C/Gas Mark 6. Before placing the pies in the oven, cover the exposed tops of each bone marrow with a small piece of foil so they don't burn. Bake the pies for 20 minutes before removing the foil and continue to bake for a further 10–15 minutes, until the pastry is crispy and golden. Serve with mashed potato and don't forget a teaspoon to scoop out the marrow!

Steak and kidney pudding
serves 6

This traditional hearty pudding is great on a cold winter's day. Adding a little stout or red wine to the braise will result in a richer, deeper flavour if you wish. You also have the option of serving one large pudding or 6 individual puddings turned out into bowls. Serve with Mashed Potato (see page 281) with the added kick of a little creamed horseradish.

1 veal or ox kidney (surrounding suet removed)
2½ kg braising beef (chuck or shin work well), cut into 5cm dice
200g plain flour
5 tbsp vegetable oil, for frying
100g butter, plus extra for greasing
3 medium onions, peeled and finely chopped
4 garlic cloves, peeled and finely chopped
1 tbsp chopped fresh thyme
2 bay leaves
3 litres hot Beef or Veal Stock (see page 297)
2 tsp cornflour (optional)
1 quantity of Suet Pastry (see page 288)
4 egg yolks, beaten
sea salt and freshly milled black pepper

You will also need:
a 2-litre pudding basin

Preheat your oven to 150°C/Gas Mark 2.

To clean the kidney, cut it in half lengthways and from each half, carefully peel off the thin membrane covering the outside of the kidney. Using a small knife, remove any fat from the inside of each half and cut all of the cleaned kidney into 5cm dice.

Season the diced beef with salt and pepper and place it in a large plastic bag (without holes). Add the flour to the bag and holding the bag closed at the top, give it a good shake, coating the beef with the flour. Remove the beef from the bag, shaking off any excess flour into the bag. Repeat the process with the diced kidney and save the flour for later.

Preheat a large saucepan over a high heat. Add the vegetable oil and fry the floured beef in three batches, until evenly browned. Remove each batch, transferring the sealed beef to an ovenproof casserole before adding the next. Once the last batch has been removed from the pan, lower the heat to medium and add the butter, onion, garlic, thyme and bay leaves. Allow to cook for about 4–5 minutes, until the onions are soft and slightly caramelised, stirring regularly with a wooden spoon to release any tasty morsels left behind by the beef. Stir in the reserved flour and cook for another minute or so, stirring continuously so it doesn't catch on the bottom of the pan. Stir in the hot beef stock a little at a time so lumps don't form, and bring to the boil. Pour the gravy over the diced beef, and cover your casserole with a lid or foil. Place in the oven and braise for 2 hours, until the meat is tender. It's difficult to put an exact time on braising or stewing meats, sometimes an extra half an hour may be needed depending on the cut. The best way to check is by tasting the meat.

While the beef is braising, make the suet pastry and leave it to rest as per the recipe. Remove the pastry from the fridge, cut off a quarter to use for the lid and return this to the fridge. Dust a work surface and your rolling pin liberally with flour and roll the pastry out into a circle large enough to line a 2-litre pudding basin. The pastry should be just under 1cm thick. Butter the pudding basin well and drop the pastry in leaving the edges of the pastry overlapping the sides.

Once the beef is cooked, carefully remove the meat from the gravy with a slotted spoon. If your gravy seems too thin then pour it into a saucepan, and over a medium heat, bring it up to a simmer. Stir in 2 teaspoons of cornflour dissolved in a little cold water and continue to simmer, skimming off any fat that may rise to the surface. Once the gravy has reached the correct consistency, taste it to check the seasoning and pour it back over the beef. Add the kidney and allow the mixture to cool completely before building the pie.

Roll out the reserved quarter of pastry to the correct size for the lid. Spoon the cooled filling into the pudding basin and lay the pastry lid on top. Fold in the overlaping edges and with wet fingers press the edges together so that the filling is sealed in. Cut a circle of greaseproof paper just large enough to sit on top of the pudding but inside the rim of the basin. Cut a piece of foil big enough to fit over the top of the basin and come halfway down the sides. Fold a pleat down the middle of the foil to allow for expansion, then place it over the basin. Tie it in place with some string, making a string handle so it can be lifted out of the steamer easily once cooked.

Bring a large pan half-filled with water to the boil and lower the pudding into it. The water must come at least halfway up the side of the basin. Cover the pan with a lid or more foil and leave to simmer for 2 hours. If the water level gets low, top it up with more boiling water.

You can either serve the pudding by spooning portions straight out of the bowl, or slide a palette knife carefully round the edge and turn the whole pudding out on to a serving dish.

Batch 01181212
Rib beef five rib
Delivery Date: 18/12/2012

Batch 01181212
Rib beef five rib
Delivery Date: 18/12/2012

Batch 01181212
Rib beef five rib
Delivery Date: 18/12/2012

Batch 05030113
Rib beef four rib
Delivery Date: 03/01/2013
Stock Number:

Batch 05030113
Rib beef four rib
Delivery Date: 03/01/2013
Stock Number:

Batch 05030113
Rib beef four rib
Delivery Date: 03/01/2013
Stock Number:

Braised short ribs in porter with battered rock oysters serves 6

This dish is a tribute to the numerous Oyster and porterhouses that emerged in London in the 1700s. Oysters were consumed by the poverty-stricken masses, often as an accompaniment to porter, a dark beer popular with the street and river porters of London, made with roasted malts.

Short ribs, also known as a Jacob's Ladder, are a fantastic braising cut. They are the rib bones that would extend further from the classic roasting joint the 'fore rib', and they have a very generous portion of meat attached. The flavour can be compared to that of oxtail but they're a lot less work to eat. Ask your butcher to cut them to 7½ cm lengths so they're easier to manage. The battered oysters are a great accompaniment to this dish, adding the occasional crunch!

*3kg bone-in short ribs, cut to 7½ cm
    lengths (ask your butcher to do this)*
100g plain flour
3 tbsp vegetable oil
*2 large onions, peeled and cut into
    quarters*
4 garlic cloves, unpeeled
1 tbsp tomato purée
200ml good-quality red wine
500ml good-quality porter
*2 litres hot Beef or Veal Stock
    (see page 297)*
4 sprigs of thyme
1 bay leaf
1 tsp cornflour (optional)
*1½ quantities of Mashed Potato
    (see page 281), to serve*
sea salt and freshly milled black pepper

For the battered oysters
*1 quantity of Scrumpy-battered Rock
    Oysters (see page 96, but substitute
    the scrumpy in the batter for porter
    and there's no need to make the
    dipping sauce)*

Preheat your oven to 200°C/Gas Mark 6.

Using a heavy knife, cut down between each rib bone, separating them into individual ribs. Season with salt and pepper and place them into a large plastic bag (without holes). Add the flour to the bag and holding the bag closed at the top, give them a good shake, coating them with the flour. Remove the ribs from the bag and save the flour in the bag for later.

Place the ribs into a large roasting tin and rub them with the vegetable oil. Add the onions and garlic to the tray and place on the middle shelf of the oven to roast for 30–40 minutes, until the meat is golden brown and retracting from the bone. Turn the ribs and onions over halfway through roasting so they colour evenly.

Remove from the oven and lift the ribs, onions and garlic cloves into an ovenproof casserole. Drain off half of the fat left in the roasting tin, and place the tin over a medium heat to make the gravy. Stir in the flour and tomato purée using a wooden spoon and cook for 1 minute, stirring constantly so they don't catch on the bottom of the tin. Stir in the red wine and the porter a little at a time so lumps don't form. Once all the alcohol has been added, pour in the hot stock and bring it to the boil, using your spoon to release any tasty morsels left on the bottom of the tin by the ribs.

Pour the gravy over the ribs, onions and garlic and add the thyme and bay leaf. Cover your casserole with a lid or foil and place it back in the oven, turning the temperature down to 150°C/Gas Mark 2. Braise for 2–2½ hours, until the meat is tender.

While the ribs are braising, prepare the batter for the oysters following the recipe for Scrumpy-battered Onion Rings on page 175 but substitute the scrumpy in the batter for porter and leave to rest.

Remove the meat carefully from the gravy with a slotted spoon and strain the sauce through a fine-mesh sieve. If your gravy seems too thin then pour it into a saucepan, and over a medium heat, bring it up to a simmer. Stir in a teaspoon of cornflour dissolved in a little cold water and continue to simmer, skimming off any fat that may rise to the surface. Once the gravy has reached the correct consistency, taste it to check the seasoning and pour it back over the ribs.

Keep the ribs hot in a low oven while you deep-fry your oysters (see page 96) and when the oysters are ready, serve the beef with the mashed potato and the oysters on the side.

Oxtail and root vegetable soup
serves 12

As I sit here and write this recipe, outside there's about 10cm of snow on Clapham Common. It's making me hungry just thinking about this soup. I think I'll have to strap some tennis racquets to my feet and pop down to M. Moen & Sons, my superb local butcher and pick up some oxtail.

This is definitely a hearty winter warmer. It takes some time to prepare but it's well worth the wait. Oxtail has such a unique flavour and its gelatinous meat flaked from the bone warms you from the inside on a cold winter's day.

2kg oxtail, cut into $7^1/_2$ cm pieces and
    trimmed of fat
200g plain flour
3 tbsp vegetable oil
1 onion, peeled and roughly chopped
2 carrots, peeled and roughly chopped
2 celery sticks, roughly chopped
1 leek, roughly chopped
3 litres Beef Stock (see page 297)
1 tbsp tomato purée
a few sprigs of thyme
1 bay leaf
sea salt and freshly milled black pepper
crusty bread, to serve

For the garnish
50g butter
2 large carrots, peeled and cut
    into $1/_2$ cm dice
$1/_2$ small swede, peeled and cut
    into $1/_2$ cm dice
$1/_2$ small celeriac, peeled and cut
    into $1/_2$ cm dice

Preheat your oven to 200°C/Gas Mark 6.

Season the pieces of oxtail with salt and pepper and place them in a large plastic bag (without holes). Add the flour to the bag and holding the bag closed at the top, give them a good shake, coating them with the flour. Remove the oxtail from the bag and save the remaining flour for later.

Rub the floured oxtail with vegetable oil then place it in a roasting tray. Add the onion, carrot, celery and leek and roast in the oven for 20–30 minutes, until the meat and vegetables are well caramelised. Place the roasted oxtail and vegetables into a deep casserole and cover with the beef stock. Stir in the tomato purée and add the thyme and bay leaf. Cover with foil and place in the oven, turning the temperature down to 150°C/Gas Mark 2.

After 2 hours the oxtail should be cooked and falling off the bone. Lift out the meat with a slotted spoon and set to one side to cool. Skim off any fat that has settled on the top with a ladle and discard. Strain the stock through a fine-mesh sieve into a saucepan and reserve the stock for the soup. Keep the stock warm over a low heat.

Heat a large saucepan over a medium heat. Melt the butter in the saucepan and add the garnish ingredients and season. As the root vegetables are cooking, flake the meat from the oxtail bones leaving it in chunks large enough to fit on a soup spoon. Once the root vegetables are starting to soften, add 4 tablespoons of the reserved flour and continue to cook for a minute or so. Add the warm reserved stock a little at a time, stirring

constantly to avoid lumps forming. Bring the soup to the boil then turn it down to a simmer. Simmer until the vegetables are tender then add the flaked oxtail. Bring the soup back to the boil and season to taste with salt and pepper. Serve with crusty bread and butter. This soup will keep in the fridge for 4–5 days.

Aubrey Allen, the chef's butcher

The scale of the quality of beef available on the UK market is very broad. Much of this is down to the fact that cattle are bred for two reasons: milk production and beef. The simple fact is that dairy breeds produce poor-quality beef as they are genetically bred for a completely different purpose. However, some of the beef sold for consumption in the UK is a by-product from the dairy industry.

Only a small fraction of our male dairy cows are used to produce UK rose veal. Many of the remaining dairy bull calves are fed a high protein diet to build muscle mass and are then killed at 12–14 months to be sold as beef. The size maybe right but the meat has no marbling (inter-muscular fat), its light in colour, and lacks flavour. Even beef from older dairy cows finds its way into the market. These cows can be up to 12 years old and have been working hard every day of their lives to produce milk. The meat from these animals, as you can imagine, is inferior and tough. The best beef comes from the breeds bred specifically for that purpose. This is known as suckler beef.

The fact that there are such differing standards of quality product on the market makes it important that at Roast we find the right supplier to provide us with a meat we are proud to serve to our customers. Aubrey Allen is just that supplier. They are 'the chef's butcher'. Their passion to find the best-quality product parallels the passion a chef has to turn that product into a memorable meal. Our relationship is integral.

Aubrey Allen don't have their own farms as they would then be committed to selling everything they produced. They strive for consistent quality and this means cherry-picking their stock from the best UK farmers have to offer. Their quality specifications are precise and strict: only 10 per cent of UK beef meets the Aubrey Allen grade. Much of the beef in the UK is killed too young. Some animals are as young as 12 months. Aubrey Allen prefer animals over 24 months. 'Slow-grown' beef that has reached its kill weight over time has a fuller, deeper flavour, and has had the time to develop marbling and texture.

Aubrey Allen realise that the environment is a huge factor in producing great beef. Areas in the country where there are a lot of vehicles have a higher pollution level. The pollution floats up into the atmosphere and is rained down on to the grass the herds graze from and into the water they're drinking.

This in turn affects the flavour of the meat. With this in mind there is all the more reason for Aubrey Allen to be very specific when it comes to where they source their beef. They prefer to source it from rural areas, favouring the heart of Scotland or the coastal regions of the South West, where the air is cleaner and the environment more comfortable for the livestock. Pollution isn't the only problem though. The noisy road networks also affect the stress levels of the animals which in turn affects the end product.

The next important factor critical to quality is the treatment of the animal from the time it leaves the farm to the time it is slaughtered. A farmer's care and hard work can all be for nothing if the animal is stressed when slaughtered at the abattoir. Aubrey Allen will only buy beef that has travelled for less than two hours from farm to abattoir. They will also not take anything that has travelled with animals from other farms. Cattle are very hierarchical and will become stressed during the journey if they have to socialise with unfamiliar animals. Many abattoirs slaughter the animals within an hour of their arrival. Aubrey Allen's beef is from animals that have been rested at the abattoir, providing enough time to alleviate any stress they may have experienced during their journey.

The aging process is the next step in ensuring the flavour of the beef has reached its full potential. At Aubrey Allen, all of their beef has been dry-aged (hung in a cold room) for 21–28 days. This allows the beef to mature. After 21–28 days the joint has lost between 12 and 15 per cent of its weight in water content, which intensifies the flavour. This weight loss is also reflected in the cost of the beef as we buy at a price per kilo. You could choose to buy cheaper wet-aged beef but this has spent much of its maturation time in a vacuum pack where the water is retained and accounts for the supplier's ability to charge a lower price for it. The value-for-money issue between beef aged in a vacuum and beef that is properly dry-aged is balanced out however, when the meat is cooked. If you were to cook two steaks of the same weight side by side, one dry-aged and the other wet-aged, you will find that the cheaper wet-aged steak will shrink to a fraction of the size of the dry-aged beef. The flavour and texture of the dry-aged beef will also be far superior.

Not only are Aubrey Allen's standards reflected in the quality of meat they supply, but also in the quality of their butchery.

(1) Fillet on the bone; **(2)** short ribs or Jacob's ladder; **(3)** shin of beef and marrow bone; **(4)** 1kg T-bone.

Aubrey Allen started the business in 1933 shortly after becoming the youngest man in Coventry (aged 18) to obtain a slaughter licence. Aubrey went on to grow the business, and when he finally handed it over to his son, Peter in the late 1970s, they had six butcheries in and around Coventry. Peter had done much of his training in different butcher's shops around the UK, but also ventured into Europe to gain more education in the butchery schools of Holland, Germany and France. On his return to the UK he started to meet with and listen to chefs who, like Peter, had been educated abroad. Peter's knowledge of international cutting techniques, creating more tender cuts from a single carcass, is inspirational. I for one am always looking for new ideas and different, interesting cuts to put on the menu at Roast.

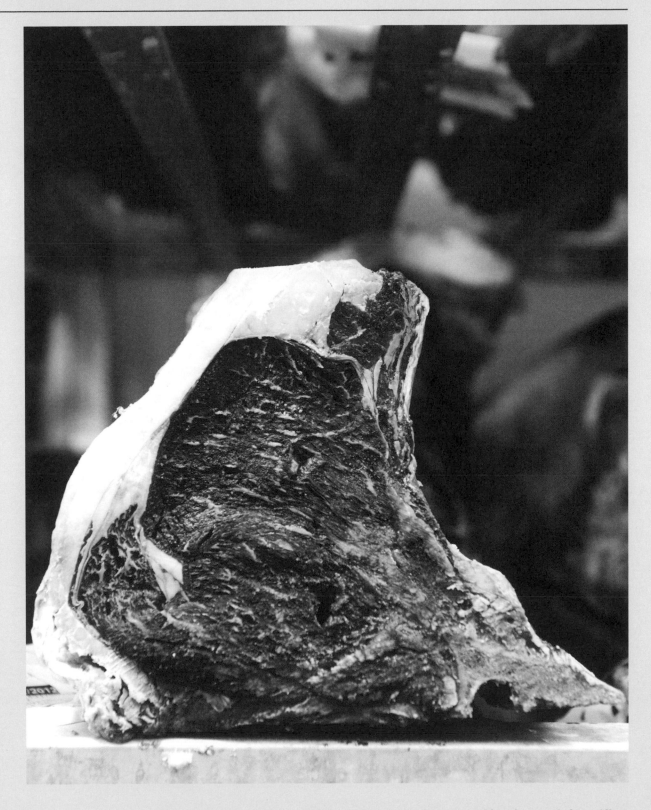

This page and opposite: examples of the wonderful meat and butchery at Aubrey Allen.

Jellied ox tongue with pickled beets and horseradish serves 12

I was unsure how this old classic would sell when I put it on the menu. I thought it would be a slow mover, but I wanted to put it on anyway for interest's sake. Our customers proved me wrong and it we ended up selling out on the first night!

You may need to put in an advanced order with your butcher for the salted tongue as they will need to soak it in brine for about 8–10 days to cure it properly. One tongue will make about 12 individual jellies but if you have a few slices left over save them for sandwiches with a little piccalilli.

If you like, you could make the jelly in a terrine and cut it into slices. If so, increase the gelatine by 50 per cent so the terrine can be sliced.

one 1½ kg salted ox tongue, soaked in
*   water overnight to desalinate*
1 large carrot, peeled and cut into 4
1 onion, peeled and halved
1 leek, white part only
2 celery sticks, cut in half
1 bay leaf
8 sprigs of thyme
1 litre Beef Stock (see page 297)
1 bunch of baby beetroot, with tops
about 100ml extra virgin rapeseed oil
150ml good-quality cider vinegar
75g caster sugar
8 gelatine leaves (16g)
sea salt and freshly milled black pepper
100g Horseradish Cream (see page 291),
*   to serve*
toasted bread, to serve

Place the soaked tongue into a casserole with the carrot, onion, leek, celery, bay leaf and 4 sprigs of the thyme. Add the beef stock. The stock gives the jelly some added flavour and a golden colouring. Top up with cold water to cover the tongue, and place over a high heat.

Bring to the boil before turning the temperature down to a simmer. Simmer gently for 2–3 hours depending on the size of the tongue, topping up with water as required to keep the tongue covered. The simmer must be very gentle or you'll end up with a cloudy stock that won't be suitable for the jelly. Test that the tongue is cooked with a sharp pointed knife. The blade should slide in with little resistance.

Preheat your oven to 180°C/Gas Mark 4.

While the tongue is cooking, cut the tops from the beets, saving them if they are in good enough condition to use as a garnish. Wrap the beetroot and remaining thyme in foil, seasoning well with salt and pepper and with a generous drizzle of rapeseed oil. Add a little water to the parcel so the beetroot also steams as it bakes. Place the parcel in the oven for 40 minutes. Test the beetroot is cooked with the blade of a small pointed knife; it should be soft. Allow the beetroot to cool slightly so you can handle it, then under cold running water, rub the skins off the beets. They should peel easily if the beetroot is properly cooked.

Bring the cider vinegar and sugar to the boil in a small saucepan then remove from the heat to cool. Slice the cooked beetroot into thin discs. For uniformity, use a Japanese mandoline, if you have one. Once the pickling vinegar has cooled add the sliced beetroot. Kept covered in the fridge, the pickled beets will keep for a month or so. Serve them at room temperature.

Once the tongue is cooked, remove it from the stock to cool enough to be handled. Strain the stock through a fine-mesh sieve. If the stock is clear it can be used for the jelly. If it is cloudy, you may want to clarify it using the same technique as for the clear game broth on page 205.

Soak the gelatine leaves in cold water for about 5 minutes until they're soft. Bring the clear stock to the boil and check the seasoning. Don't be too heavy-handed with the salt as the tongue is already salty. Remove the stock from the heat and add the soft gelatine, stirring to dissolve it. Pass the stock through a fine-mesh sieve again then place it to one side.

Peel the leathery skin off the ox tongue while it is still warm; it is much more difficult when cold. Now, if you have a good relationship with your local butcher, ask them to slice the tongue into thin full length slices on their meat slicer. If not, do your best with a sharp carving knife, slicing as thinly as possible.

You can either set the jellies individually using tea cups for moulds, or you can make one large jelly in a terrine or container to be sliced.

Pour 1cm of jellied stock into your chosen mould or moulds and allow them to set in the fridge for about 1 hour. Once the jelly has set, fill the mould with loosely folded slices of tongue and then fill all the way to the top with the remaining stock. Set the jellies in the fridge. They will need a good 3–4 hours before they will be set firm enough to turn out.

To turn out your jellies for serving, dip the mould/s briefly in a bowl of boiling water to release them.

Serve with a small pile of pickled beets, the reserved leaves drizzled with rapeseed oil, the horseradish cream and crispy toasts.

Wild rabbit and dandelion salad with elderberries and pea shoots serves 4

Being from New Zealand, where our farms are plagued by rabbits that fill the lush paddocks full of holes, I feel that by eating wild rabbit we are also doing our noble farmers a favour. Besides, rabbits are very tasty and also economical. At Roast, one of my favourite dishes is the wild rabbit, cider and snail pie. For the pie we use only the legs so we often offer this salad as a special to use the fillets, belly and offal.

2 wild rabbits, with offal
  (heart, liver and kidneys)
100g plain flour
1 egg
100g Japanese panko breadcrumbs
vegetable oil, for deep-frying
30g butter

1 head of dandelion, cut the long leaves
  in half
50g pea shoots
sea salt and freshly milled black pepper

For the elderberry dressing
4 tbsp extra virgin rapeseed oil
1 tbsp good-quality cider vinegar
1 tsp Dijon mustard
1 tsp caster sugar
60g fresh elderberries

Start by making the dressing to allow it time to infuse. Whisk the oil, vinegar, mustard and sugar together with half the berries, crushing them slightly to release the juices. Leave to infuse for an hour before adding the remaining berries to serve.

Next, you will need to butcher the rabbits. (You can follow these steps in the photos on pages 208–209, to which the numbers in brackets, below, correspond.) Lay the rabbit down on its back and with a sharp filleting knife remove the belly flaps and reserve (1). Remove the livers, kidneys (2) and heart (3) from inside the rabbit and set them to one side. Turn the rabbit over and lay it down with the legs at the top of your chopping board. To remove the legs, run your knife down one side of the tail between the leg and base of the spine using the spine to guide your knife (4). Follow the defined leg muscles all the way round to remove it from the rest of the carcass (5). Do the same with the second leg.

To remove the fillets, turn the rabbit around so the head is now at the top of the chopping board. Run your knife down one side of the spine, again using the spinal column to guide you **(6, 7)**. For the tapered end of the fillet, closest to the shoulder, you will need to follow the rib cage with your blade to remove it completely **(8)**. Repeat these steps with the second fillet. Finally, carefully remove the sinew from each fillet **(9)** so they don't curl up when frying. Your rabbit is now quartered **(10)**.

Boil the belly in well-salted water for 30 minutes to soften. Remove from the water and leave to cool, then slice the cooked belly into thin strips and dust with flour. In a small bowl whisk the egg. Place the breadcrumbs in a separate shallow bowl. Dip the rabbit strips in the egg then shake off any excess before dropping them into the breadcrumbs, coating them generously. Set aside for deep-frying. Start to heat the vegetable oil in the deep-fat fryer or in a deep saucepan to 180°C.

Season the rabbit fillets, melt half of the butter in a heavy-based frying pan and cook the fillets over a medium-high heat. For medium-rare they should only take about a minute on each side. Remove from the pan and set aside to rest. Season the kidneys, hearts and livers, add the remaining the butter to the pan and fry them for about 30–40 seconds on each side, keeping them nice and pink.

While the offal is cooking, deep-fry the breadcrumbed belly slices until golden and crisp. Drain on kitchen paper and season well with salt.

To serve, cut the fillets and livers into bite-sized slices. Toss the dandelion and pea shoots in the dressing and season. Arrange on serving plates with the fillet and offal in amongst the leaves. Scatter the remaining elderberries and crispy belly strips over the top.

Gamekeeper's terrine
Makes 16 slices if served as a starter

Building a terrine is a tricky business, which requires time and patience. Don't be put off by the seemingly complex task ahead. The rewards greatly outweigh the labour involved. There is nothing like the feeling of anticipation, when you cut the first slice and reveal your mosaic masterpiece! There are step-by-step photographs to assist you over the page.

4 skinless partridge breasts, fillets removed
2 skinless pheasant breasts, fillets removed and split in half lengthways
2 skinless mallard breasts
2 rabbit fillets, plus the offal (heart, liver and kidneys) from 1 rabbit
1 venison under-fillet or tenderloin (the same length as the terrine)
2 tbsp vegetable oil
30g butter
3 shallots, finely diced
1 small garlic clove, finely chopped
5 sprigs of thyme, leaves only, chopped
4 juniper berries, finely chopped
150ml Madeira
100ml port
200g fatty pork mince
300g marrow bones (to yield about 80g bone marrow)
300g unsmoked streaky bacon, thinly sliced
8 roasted chestnuts, peeled and each cut into 3
sea salt and freshly milled black pepper
chargrilled slices of toast, to serve
Rowan Berry Jelly (see page 293), to serve
green salad, to serve

You will also need: a 30 x 10 x 7cm terrine mould

(You can follow the step-by-step photos for this recipe on pages 196–197.)

Preheat your oven to 150°C/Gas Mark 2.

Season the partridge breasts, pheasant breasts, mallard breasts, rabbit fillets and venison with salt and pepper. Heat a large pan over a high heat and when very hot add the vegetable oil, then the seasoned meat, leaving it just long enough to seal and caramelise the outside. Remove immediately, place in a bowl and cool quickly in the fridge so the meat doesn't overcook.

Heat the butter in a frying pan, add the shallots, garlic, thyme and juniper and cook over a medium heat for about 10 minutes, until soft. Add the Madeira and port, increase the heat and bubble to reduce to a jam consistency. Set aside and place in the fridge to chill.

To make the farce, which will bind the terrine, dice the rabbit offal into rough chunks and place in a mixing bowl with the pork mince.

To extract the marrow from the bones, bring them to room temperature. This will make it easier to push out the marrow with your thumb. Roughly chop the bone marrow and the reserved fillets from the pheasant and partridge breasts with a sharp knife and add to the pork mince along with the chilled Madeira and port reduction. Mix thoroughly and season generously. Make a small burger with the farce and pan-fry it in vegetable oil to check if the seasoning is to your liking.

Line the terrine mould with the bacon rashers leaving lengths draped over the side of the mould to fold across the top once filled. Trim the bacon ends to be the same length.

To fill the terrine, wet your fingers so the farce is easier to handle. Start with a very thin layer of farce, then add the partridge, pheasant, mallard and rabbit pieces, and in the very centre, the venison fillet. Between each piece of meat add a thin layer of farce to hold everything in place. Make sure that as you add to the terrine you press it with your fingers as you go, so that it remains tight and free from air pockets. Distribute the chestnuts evenly throughout the terrine as you go. As you build up the layers, think about how it will appear once sliced. You want to aim for an even distribution with the venison fillet running directly through the centre, so it stays pink once cooked. Once the terrine is full, fold over the overhanging bacon encasing the terrine tightly all the way round and trim with scissors if necessary.

Cover the terrine with its lid and place in a deep roasting tin. Fill the tin with boiling water until it reaches 2½ cm below the level of the terrine. This is best achieved with the tin already in the oven so you don't have to transfer it once filled.

Bake for 30–40 minutes or until a probe inserted into the centre reads 50°C. If you don't have a probe, check the temperature with a small knife. The blade should feel lukewarm when touched on the back of your hand.

Carefully remove the terrine from the water bath and allow it to rest for 30 minutes at room temperature. It will then need to be pressed as it chills in the fridge (while still in the mould) under a moderate weight. If the weight is too heavy, the juices will be forced out leaving the terrine dry. Place a piece of

clingfilm over the terrine, then cut out a piece of heavy card the same size as the terrine filling. Cover with your weights (a couple of tins of baked beans or pulses will do nicely) and leave in the fridge for 24 hours. Pressing the terrine ensures it retains density and will force out any air holes.

Slice and serve with the chargrilled toast, rowan berry jelly and a small green salad.

Making Gamekeeper's Terrine

See pages 194–195 for recipe.

(1–3) Lining the terrine mould with the bacon rashers; (4) the first layer should be a thin layer of farce; (5–7) adding ingredients to layer the terrine; (8) adding a thin layer of farce between each meat layer and pressing as you go so the terrine remains tight; (9) laying the venison fillet in the centre of the terrine; (10) distributing the chestnuts evenly throughout; (11) adding a layer of partridge breasts; (12) pressing down the final layer of farce; (13–15) folding in the overhanging strips of bacon to encase the terrine; (16) trimming off the excess bacon; (17) ready for cooking.

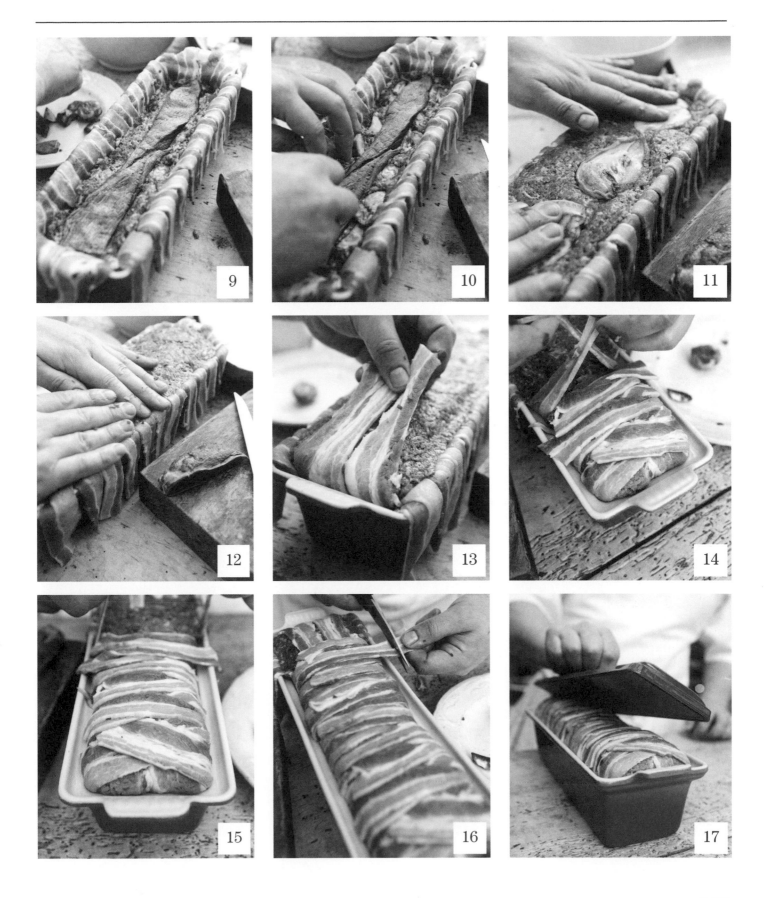

Traditional roast grouse with parsnip crisps and rowan berry jelly serves 4

A wise woman once said, when roasting grouse: 'we would strongly recommend the toast to be laid in [the dripping pan] under the birds, as it will afford a superior relish, even to the birds themselves' *Eliza Acton, 1853*

4 oven-ready grouse, plus the heart, liver and kidneys from the grouse (offal are optional)
4 sprigs of thyme
150g butter
4 slices of crusty white bread (cut into 2½ cm-thick slices)
1 large banana shallot, finely chopped
1 small garlic clove, finely chopped
150g chicken livers, cleaned and patted dry
150ml port
1 tbsp double cream
300ml hot Game Gravy (see page 295)
sea salt and freshly milled black pepper
Rowan Berry Jelly (see page 293), to serve
Bread sauce (see page 289), to serve

For the parsnip crisps

2 large parsnips
2 litres vegetable oil, for deep-frying, plus extra to fry the grouse

Start by making the parsnip crisps. Set your deep-fat fryer to 190°C. If you don't have a fryer, place the oil into a large, deep saucepan, leaving enough room at the top to allow for rapid boiling when the parsnip shavings are added. Place the oil over a high heat but be very careful that it doesn't get too hot. If you have a cooking thermometer, use it so you can regulate the temperature. If not, test the heat by dropping a cube of bread into the oil; it should bubble on entry and start to brown after about 15 seconds.

Have to hand some kitchen paper and a slotted spoon to remove the crisps from the hot oil. (Don't try to use spring-loaded tongs; this can be very dangerous for obvious reasons.)

Using a peeler, shave the parsnips into full-length strips until you are left with only the core. Test the oil with one shaving. It should boil on entry and gradually turn golden. If it goes dark too quickly, your oil is too hot and you'll need to turn the heat off and allow it to cool to the correct temperature.

Once you've tested the oil and are happy with the temperature, drop in half the parsnip shavings and move them around gently with the slotted spoon so that they cook evenly. Once they have reached an even golden colour and are no longer producing much steam (this will take about 90 seconds), remove them carefully with the slotted spoon and drain on kitchen paper. Repeat this process with the rest of the parsnip shavings and then season them with salt.

Preheat your oven to 200°C/Gas Mark 6.

With a small knife, remove the wishbone from each bird for ease of carving once cooked, and place a sprig of thyme inside the cavity of each one. Season the grouse liberally with salt and pepper. In a large frying pan over a medium-high heat, fry the birds in a little vegetable oil to seal them, first on each side and then directly on the breast. Once the skin of each grouse is nicely caramelised add 100g of the butter to the pan. Place the bread slices into a roasting tin and place a bird, lying on its back, on top of each slice. Pour the melted butter from the frying pan over the birds so it drips over each one and soaks into the sliced bread underneath. Place the grouse into the oven and roast for approximately 8–10 minutes if you like them nice and pink. As the birds are roasting, spoon the melted butter over them a few times to keep them and the bread moist. Halfway through the cooking, turn each slice of bread over to ensure both sides become crispy and place the birds back on top. As the grouse roast, the juices soak straight into the underlying bread or 'trencher' as it is called, packing it full of flavour.

Remove the grouse from the oven and set them to one side to rest for at least 6 minutes. It's best to turn the birds over on to their breast while resting so they retain their juices.

You need to work quickly for the next stage so that the chicken livers and grouse offal (if using) don't overcook and your grouse don't cool down too much.

While the grouse are resting, heat the remaining butter in a small frying pan over a medium heat and cook the shallot and garlic until they are soft. Remove from the pan and set to one side. Return the pan to the heat and increase the heat to high. Season the grouse offal and chicken livers with salt and pepper and coat them in a couple of tablespoons of vegetable oil. Place all the offal into the hot pan and fry it quickly until it's sealed on both sides. Add the port carefully as it may spit, and boil to reduce it until there is virtually no liquid left. Add the cream, cooked shallot and garlic and about 100ml of the hot game gravy. There should be just enough gravy to coat the offal but not so it's swimming in sauce. By this stage the offal will be cooked. Tip the cooked offal out on to a chopping board and chop it roughly with a large knife before returning it to the pan. Check the seasoning and adjust if necessary.

To serve, spread the offal liberally onto each trencher, and serve alongside the grouse, hot bread sauce, parsnip crisps and rowan berry jelly.

***more* roast**
Scan the QR code to see
Marcus dressing a grouse.
http://roastcookbook.com/how-to-dress-a-grouse/

Roast partridge with creamed spelt, rainbow chard and winter chanterelles

serves 4

If you're not accustomed to strong gamey-flavoured meat then partridge is a good place to start. Its meat is much paler and has a more delicate flavour than the likes of grouse or wild duck.

The spelt in this dish is cooked in the same way as you would cook a risotto and should be the same consistency. Make sure you use 'pearled' spelt. It has had the hard outer shell removed allowing the grains to absorb the stock more effectively.

600ml Chicken Stock (see page 298)
80g butter, plus an extra knob for the
*   chanterelles*
½ onion, finely diced
200g pearled spelt (no need to soak)
4 tbsp double cream
4 partridge
4 sprigs of thyme
about 4 tbsp vegetable oil
4 large rainbow chard leaves, with stalks
200g winter chanterelles, brushed clean
sea salt and freshly milled black pepper
100ml Game or Chicken gravy
*   (see page 295), optional*

Preheat your oven to 200°C/Gas Mark 6.

Firstly, bring the chicken stock to the boil and keep hot over a low heat. Melt half the butter in a small saucepan over a medium heat, add the onion and cook for about 5 minutes until it's translucent and soft. Add the spelt and season with salt. Continue to cook for 1–2 minutes, stirring constantly. It is important to season at this stage so that when you add the hot chicken stock and it starts to be absorbed by the spelt it takes the salt with it, seasoning the inside of each grain instead of just the outside. As a result you'll find you use less salt.

Slowly add the hot chicken stock a ladle at a time, stirring constantly. Once each ladle of stock is absorbed, add a little more until the spelt is soft but still retains some bite. Add the double cream and season with salt and pepper. Remove from the heat and place to one side; keep any remaining stock warm as you'll need it to reheat the spelt.

Using a small sharp knife, remove the wishbone from each bird for ease of carving once cooked, and place a sprig of thyme inside the cavity of each one. Season the partridge liberally with salt and pepper. In a large frying pan over a medium-high heat, fry the birds in 3 tablespoons of the vegetable oil to seal them, first on each side and then directly on the breast. Once the skin of each partridge is nicely caramelised, add the remaining butter to the pan. Transfer the birds to a roasting dish, pour over the melted butter and place them into the oven. Roast for 6–8 minutes if you like them nice and pink. As the birds are roasting, spoon the melted butter over them a few times to keep them moist.

While the partridge are roasting, bring a pan of lightly salted water to the boil. Remove the stalks from the chard and cut them into 4–5cm batons. Blanch the colourful chard stalk batons in the boiling water for about 1 minute, remove with a slotted spoon and set to one side. Cut the leaves into manageable pieces and blanch these for 30 seconds only. Refresh the leaves in cold water so they retain their vibrant green colour and drain well.

Remove the partridge from the oven and allow them to rest for at least 4 minutes. It's best to turn the birds over on to their breast while resting so they retain their juices.

Once the partridge has rested remove the legs and breasts from each bird and place them in four sets on to an oven tray.

Heat about a tablespoon of vegetable oil in a frying pan over a high heat and cook the chanterelles for about 30 seconds, until just wilted, before adding a knob of butter and the blanched chard batons. Cook for a further few seconds to warm the chard batons through.

Put the creamed spelt back on to the heat, adding a little stock to regain the correct consistency. Add the blanched chard leaves and fold them through the hot creamy spelt. Check the seasoning and set to one side.

Place the tray of partridge back into the oven and while it is warming through, divide the creamed spelt between four bowls. Sit the breasts and legs of each bird on top of the spelt and then spoon the chanterelles and colourful chard batons over them. In the restaurant we finish this dish with a drizzle of gravy for gloss and flavour but it is not a necessity.

Fillet of red deer Wellington with haggis, girolles and bashed neeps

serves 8

Initially I was going to include a recipe for the more traditional beef Wellington. However, having researched the origins of the dish there were many differences of opinion. I had always assumed it was named after the Duke of Wellington, which seems to be the general consensus. Clarissa Dickson Wright, however, claims the dish was invented for a civic reception in Wellington, New Zealand's capital city. Now being a Kiwi, I automatically wanted to back Clarissa, out of pure pride, but in an effort to delve deeper and be sure, I only encountered dead ends. I resorted to sending my mum a message to ask her opinion. She was unsure of the dish's origin but went on to explain that when we were kids she used to cook 'beef Verberne' using a minced beef farce for the Wellington as we couldn't afford the luxury of beef fillet. I finally decided that rather than take the conventional route, I'd come up with a Scottish version of the dish. Being a huge fan of haggis, I personally prefer this one to the original.

When you purchase the red deer from your butcher, ask for a piece of striploin cut from the centre so it doesn't taper at one end. This will ensure the cooking is even over the length of the Wellington.

The recipe for the Savoury Pancakes does in fact make eight and you only need four for this recipe, but you will need to make the full quantity of batter as it's not good if made in smaller amounts. Simply store it in the fridge overnight and you've got pancakes for breakfast the next day.

1.6kg red deer striploin
100ml rapeseed oil
10 juniper berries, chopped
6 sprigs of thyme, leaves only, chopped
500g spinach, stalks removed
1kg good-quality haggis
  (We use Macsween's)
about 100g plain flour, for rolling out
  the pastry
1.2kg good-quality ready-made puff
  pastry
4 large thin Savoury Pancakes
  (see page 285)
8 egg yolks, beaten
30g butter
500g girolles, brushed clean
1 tbsp chopped flat-leaf parsley
sea salt and freshly milled black pepper
Bashed Neeps (see page 280), to serve
500ml Game Gravy (see page 295),
  to serve

You will also need: a rolling lattice cutter (optional)

With a thin-bladed filleting knife, trim any sinew from the striploin. If the sinew is left on, it will contract causing the loin to curl up when it is seared. Once the meat has been trimmed, in a small bowl, mix the rapeseed oil, juniper berries and thyme together and rub all over the meat. Place the meat on a plate and cover it with clingfilm. Allow it to marinate in the fridge overnight.

The next day, leave the haggis out of the fridge and allow it to come to room temperature – you will find it less crumbly and easier to work with.

Preheat a large frying pan on a high heat. Carefully sear the marinated striploin until it is sealed well on all sides. This will help it to retain its juices while cooking so it won't bleed and cause the pastry to go soggy. When the meat is seared, place it straight in the fridge to cool down quickly – it is easier to work with if cold.

Bring a large pan of lightly salted water to the boil and blanch the spinach for a few seconds before plunging it into iced water so it retains its vibrant green colour. Drain the leaves in a colander and then lay them out in an even layer on a clean tea towel to dry.

You now need to roll out the haggis to a sheet about 1cm thick and large enough to wrap around the striploin. The easiest way to achieve this is between 2 sheets of clingfilm. Lay the first sheet of clingfilm on your worktop and cut the haggis into slices about 2cm thick. Remove the casing from the haggis slices and lay them out on the clingfilm. Place another sheet of clingfilm over the top and with a rolling pin, roll out the haggis into an even layer about 1cm in thickness. Transfer the haggis carefully on to a large tray and set aside (not in the fridge).

Dust your worktop with flour and with your rolling pin, roll out two thirds of the pastry into a rectangle of a suitable size to wrap your Wellington (roll it large enough to allow for any trimming as well). Save the remaining pastry for the decorative lattice. When rolling the pastry, rub the rolling pin with a little

continued on page 204

continued from page 203

flour so it doesn't stick, and turn the pastry over a couple of times, dusting with more flour, to keep it from sticking to the work top.

To build the Wellington, cut the rounded edges off each pancake to make squares and lay them on the pastry like tiles. Lift the tea towel containing the spinach and carefully turn the spinach out in a neat layer over the pancakes. Remove the top layer of clingfilm from the haggis and carefully lay it out over the spinach, pulling off the rest of the clingfilm once it is in place. Patch up any holes as you go. Place the striploin in the very centre of the layers so you are looking across it, not down its length. Calculate how much pastry you will need to wrap the meat and trim off any excess before you start, making sure the pastry at the top of the work top, furthest from you, slightly extends the layers of pancake, spinach and haggis. Using a pastry brush, brush this strip of pastry with the egg yolk so when you wrap the Wellington it acts as a glue to stick the two layers of pastry together. Lift the pastry and all the layers on the side closest to you, carefully over the meat. Repeat the process with the side furthest from you lifting it towards you, stretching it over and sticking it down as tightly as possible. With a pair of kitchen scissors, trim the pastry at each end round as far as the work top, but leaving a rectangular flap of pastry at the bottom. Brush these flaps with the egg yolk and stretch them over each end of the Wellington, sealing it neatly.

The side of the Wellington facing you with all the seams of joining pastry is the underside. Your next step is to carefully roll the Wellington over on to a baking tray covered with a layer of non-stick baking parchment.

Once the Wellington is sitting the right way up on your tray, look down the length of it, and using both hands, tuck any loose pastry underneath in an attempt to tighten it. Brush the Wellington all over with egg yolk and set it to one side.

Dust the work top with flour and roll out the rest of the pastry into a length slightly longer than the Wellington and slightly wider than the width of your lattice roller. Dust the lattice roller with a little flour so it doesn't stick then roll it firmly along the length of the pastry. If you don't have a lattice roller you could get creative with your pastry decoration using a small knife to cut leaves or what ever else takes your fancy.

Stretch the pastry lattice over the Wellington to cover it completely, and trim the edges with kitchen scissors. Ensure the lattice is stuck fast to the Wellington and then brush with a final layer of egg yolk. Place your beautiful creation in the fridge to allow the pastry to relax for at least 30 minutes, before you bake it.

Preheat your oven to 180°C/Gas Mark 4. Bake the Wellington for 50 minutes, until the pastry is golden brown. Cover loosely with foil if the pastry is browning too much. If you have a temperature probe the core temperature should reach 35°C for the deer to be medium-rare. If you don't have a probe, pierce the meat with a metal skewer or a small pointed knife and touch it on the inside of your forearm; it should feel warm but not hot. When the Wellington is ready, remove it from the oven and rest it in a warm place for 8–10 minutes before carving.

While the Wellington is resting, heat a large frying pan over a medium heat, add the butter and cook the girolles gently. Season with salt and pepper and finish with the chopped parsley just before serving. Serve the Wellington with the girolles, bashed neeps and game gravy alongside.

Clear game broth with pearl barley and Laphroaig single malt serves 8

At Roast, during the game season, Nick, our butcher stockpiles any game bones in the freezer. Whether they be carcasses from wild fowl, deer or on occasion even hare, they can all be used to make this flavoursome, healthy broth. If you often cook game at home, you should do the same and try your hand at the classic technique of clarifying your stock with egg whites to achieve this crystal clear broth. The whisky is of course optional but well worth a try. The reason I use Laphroaig is for its smoky character but any quality single malt will do. The whisky really does add another dimension to the broth.

For the game stock
4kg game bones
3 tbsp vegetable oil
1 onion, roughly chopped
1 leek, trimmed and roughly chopped
2 carrots, roughly chopped
2 celery sticks, roughly chopped
2 garlic cloves, peeled
5 juniper berries, crushed
10 peppercorns
a few sprigs of thyme
1 bay leaf
2 tbsp concentrated tomato purée
1 tbsp redcurrant jelly
sea salt

For the clarification
1 carrot, roughly chopped
1/2 leek, roughly chopped
1 celery stick, roughly chopped
300g minced game meat (at Roast we
    tend to use venison trimmings)
8 egg whites

For the garnish
8 pheasant thighs, on the bone
1/4 small swede, peeled and cut into
    1cm dice
1 large carrot, peeled and cut into
    1cm dice
1/4 small celeriac, peeled and cut into
    1cm dice
100g pearl barley (soaked in water
    for at least 2 hours)
50ml Laphroaig single malt whisky
    (optional)
sea salt and freshly milled black pepper

Preheat your oven to 220°C/Gas Mark 7. Roast the game bones for 20–30 minutes, until they have lightly browned. Remove from the oven and set aside to rest.

While the bones are roasting, place a large heavy-based stockpot on a medium-high heat, add the vegetable oil and cook the onion, leek, carrots, celery and garlic for 7–10 minutes, stirring occasionally, until they are soft and nicely caramelised. Add the juniper berries, peppercorns, thyme, bay leaf and tomato purée and cook for a further 2 minutes, stirring often so the rawness of the tomato purée cooks out sufficiently. Add the roasted game bones and cover with cold water just to the level of the bones. Turn the heat up to bring the liquid to the boil before turning down to a gentle simmer. Stir in the redcurrant jelly and simmer for 2½ hours, skimming off any impurities or fat that collects on the surface.

Once the stock is ready, strain it through a sieve into a clean saucepan and place over a high heat to reduce it, tasting it on occasion until you are happy with the intensity of the flavour. At this stage season the stock to your liking with salt. Set the stock to one side and allow it to cool.

While the stock is cooling, prepare the clarification. Place the carrot, leek and celery in a food processor and pulse to very small pieces. Transfer to a large mixing bowl and mix thoroughly with the minced game and egg whites.

When the stock has cooled it is ready for clarifying. Pour the stock into a tall saucepan, and stir in the clarification mixture thoroughly. Gently bring it up to a simmer over a medium heat, stirring gently and often so the egg whites don't catch on the bottom. As the stock heats, the egg whites will solidify, binding with the minced game meat and rising to the surface creating a raft. As the raft rises it takes all the impurities with it, leaving a crystal clear broth. Break a small hole in the raft to allow steam to escape and simmer gently for 3–4 minutes to ensure the stock is completely clear.

Lift the raft off very gently using a slotted spoon and discard it. Strain the clear broth through a fine-mesh sieve or, if you have it, through muslin cloth as an even better option. Taste the broth to check the seasoning. You'll find the flavour has developed with the help of the clarification. Remove from the heat and set aside while you prepare the garnish.

continued on page 206

continued from page 205

Turn your oven back on at 220°C/
Gas Mark 7. Place the pheasant thighs on
to an oven tray and season with salt and
pepper. Roast the thighs for 20–25 minutes,
then remove from the oven and allow
them to cool. Once they are cool enough
to handle remove the skin and flake the
meat into pieces that would sit
comfortably on a soup spoon.

Bring a saucepan of lightly salted water
to a rapid boil and add the swede.
After 2 minutes add the carrot and
celeriac and boil the root vegetables
until they are cooked but still have a
little bite. Remove them from the water
using a slotted spoon and add the pearl
barley. The barley should only take
about 15 minutes to cook on a rapid boil
if it has been soaked properly. Strain the
barley and in a mixing bowl mix it
together with the root vegetables and
flaked pheasant thighs.

To serve, reheat the broth in a saucepan
over a high heat with all the garnish
ingredients. Being a thin broth it needs
substantial garnish. Just before serving,
check the seasoning again and add a few
drops of Laphroaig per portion, if using.
Don't add too much as the strength of its
flavour will overpower the broth.
It would be best to add a little at a time
until you're happy with the flavour.

Braised red deer shanks with dried sour cherries   serves 8

There are six different species of deer in the UK, red deer being the largest. One shank from a red deer is more than enough for a hearty portion for one person, but if you are cooking shanks from a smaller deer such as a roe or fallow deer, you will probably have to serve two per person and slightly reduce the cooking time by about 30–45 minutes.

The morello cherries in this recipe work a treat with the deer. If you marinate the deer shanks overnight in red wine in addition to the cherries, the flavour really permeates through the meat. The cherries can be difficult to get hold of. Your best bet would be to try a health food shop selling different dried fruits, but if all else fails, you could resort to what we had to do and buy them from amazon.co.uk.

140g dried morello cherries
1 bottle of good-quality red wine
8 red deer shanks
130g plain flour
1 large onion, peeled and cut into
  quarters
1 large carrot, peeled and cut into large
  pieces
3 celery sticks, roughly chopped
4 garlic cloves, unpeeled
2 tbsp tomato purée
2½ litres hot Beef or Veal Stock
  (see page 297)
4 sprigs of thyme
1 bay leaf
1 tsp cornflour (optional)
vegetable oil
sea salt and freshly milled black pepper
Bashed Neeps (see page 280), to serve

Place the dried cherries into a large mixing bowl. In a saucepan, bring the red wine to the boil and pour it over the cherries. Allow the wine and cherries to cool, then place the shanks in the liquid. Cover the shanks and let them marinate in the fridge in the cherry-infused wine for 24 hours. During the marinating process, turn the shanks a couple of times as the wine will not totally cover them.

The next day, remove the shanks and pat then dry with kitchen paper. Strain the wine, reserving both it and the cherries separately.

Season the shanks with salt and pepper and place them into a large plastic bag (without holes). Add the flour to the bag and holding the bag closed at the top, give them a good shake, coating them with the flour. Remove the shanks from the bag and save the flour for later.

Preheat your oven to 200°C/Gas Mark 6. Place the shanks into a large roasting tin and rub them with a little vegetable oil. Add the onions, carrot, celery and garlic to the tin and place it on the middle shelf of the oven to roast for 30-40 minutes, until the meat is golden brown and retracting from the bone. Turn the shanks over halfway through roasting so they colour evenly. While you're turning the shanks, give the vegetables a good stir as well. When ready, remove from the oven and carefully lift the shanks and vegetables into an ovenproof casserole.

Place the roasting tin over a medium heat to make the gravy. Stir in the reserved flour and tomato purée and cook for 1 minute, stirring constantly with a wooden spoon so they don't catch on the bottom of the tray. Stir in the reserved red wine a little at a time so lumps don't form. Once all of the alcohol has been added, pour in the hot stock and bring it to the boil, using your wooden spoon to release any tasty morsels left on the bottom of the tin by the shanks.

Pour the gravy over the shanks and vegetables and add the thyme and bay leaf. Cover your casserole with a lid or foil and place it back in the oven, turning the oven setting down to 150°C/Gas Mark 2. Braise for 2½–3 hours, until the shanks are tender and just falling from the bone. Remove the shanks carefully from the gravy with a slotted spoon and strain the sauce through a fine-mesh sieve. If your gravy seems too thin pour it into a saucepan and, over a medium heat, bring it up to a simmer. Stir in a teaspoon of cornflour dissolved in a little cold water and add the reserved cherries. Continue to simmer, skimming off any fat that may rise to the surface. Once the gravy has reached the correct consistency, taste it to check the seasoning and pour it back over the shanks. Serve with the bashed neeps.

Preparing rabbit

See pages 192–193 for step-by-step instructions.

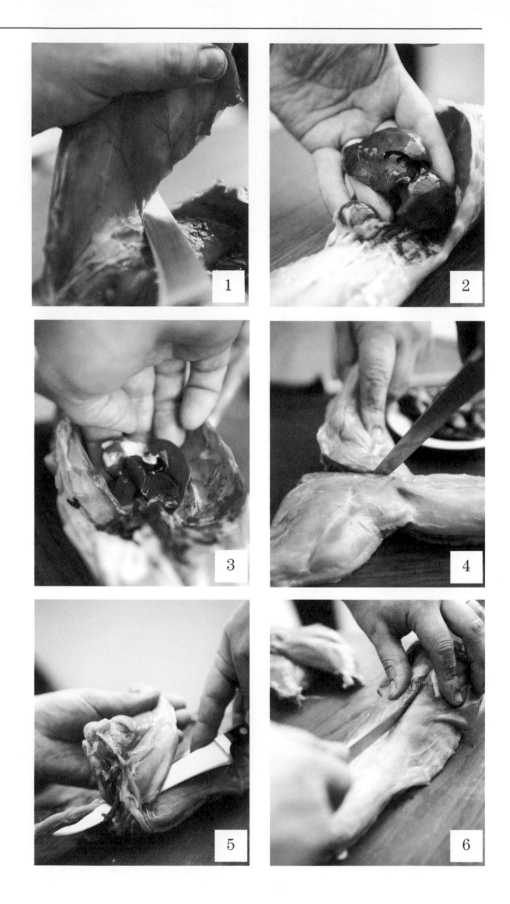

roast a very british cookbook

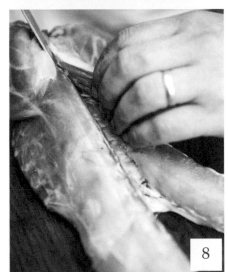

***more* roast**
Scan the QR code to see
Marcus butcher a rabbit.
http://roastcookbook.com/how-to-butcher-a-rabbit/

Wild rabbit and cider pie with snails and ramsons serves 6

We receive our snails weekly from Tony Vaughan who runs Credenhill Snail Farm in Herefordshire. The snails are washed, and then blanched for five minutes in boiling water with lots of salt and vinegar (the salt raises the temperature of the water and with the aid of the acidic vinegar helps dislodge the mucus).

If you haven't had snails before, don't be squeamish. They have an earthy flavour and a texture similar to cooked mushrooms.

Try to source wild rabbit for this recipe rather than farmed. The flavour is stronger and more gamey – far superior – to that of farmed rabbit, which to me is really just like chicken.

Rather than constructing individual pies, you may like to make one pie for the family to share in a larger pie dish.

12 wild rabbit legs (or 10 farmed)
150g plain flour
3 tbsp vegetable oil
200g butter
2 large onions, peeled and sliced
5 sprigs of thyme
1 bay leaf
300ml good-quality dry cider
2 litres hot Chicken Stock (see page 298)
150ml double cream
1 tbsp Dijon mustard
50g ramsons (wild garlic), roughly chopped
30 snails (you can find quality prepared snails in tins from a good delicatessen)
2 large garlic cloves, finely chopped
two 500g blocks good-quality ready-made puff pastry
6 egg yolks, beaten
sea salt and freshly milled black pepper
6 clean snail shells, to garnish (optional)
1½ quantities of Mashed Potato (see page 281), to serve
green salad leaves, to serve

You will also need: 6 individual pie dishes

Preheat your oven to 150°C/Gas Mark 2.

Season the rabbit legs with salt and pepper and place them into a large plastic bag (without holes). Add the flour to the bag, and holding the bag closed at the top, give them a good shake, coating with the flour. Remove the legs from the bag and save the flour for later.

Preheat a large saucepan over a high heat. Add the vegetable oil and fry the floured rabbit legs six at a time, turning them over halfway, until evenly browned. Remove the first six legs, transferring them to an ovenproof casserole before adding the next six.

Once the last six legs have been removed from the pan, turn the heat down to medium and add 100g of the butter and the onion, thyme and bay leaf. Allow to cook for about 4–5 minutes, stirring regularly with a wooden spoon to release any tasty morsels left by the rabbit. Cook until the onions are soft and slightly caramelised. Add the flour and cook for another minute stirring continuously so it doesn't catch on the bottom of the pan. Stir in the cider a little at a time so lumps don't form. Once all of the alcohol has been added, pour in the hot stock and bring to the boil. Taste the sauce, and season with salt and pepper accordingly. Pour the sauce over the rabbit legs, and cover your casserole with a lid or foil. Place in the oven, and braise for 1½–2 hours, until the meat is falling from the bone. Once the rabbit legs are cooked, lift them out of the braising sauce with tongs and place them to one side so they can cool down enough to be handled.

While the legs are cooling, strain the sauce through a fine-mesh sieve into a saucepan. Bring to the boil over a medium heat, stirring regularly so the sauce doesn't catch on the bottom. Add the cream and stir in the Dijon mustard. Simmer the sauce gently, continuing to stir regularly, until it reaches the consistency of thick gravy.

continued on page 212

continued from page 210

The sauce must be the right consistency. If it is too thin the pastry on the sides and bottom of the pie will not cook sufficiently, and if too thick, the pie will be dry and stodgy.

Once the rabbit legs are cool enough to handle, flake the meat from the bone, making sure any gristle is also removed from the meat. Pour the sauce over the flaked rabbit meat and stir in the chopped ramsons. Allow the pie filling to cool completely.

While the pie filling is cooling, melt the remaining butter in a small saucepan over a low heat, with the chopped garlic. Add 24 of the snails. Cook the snails in the garlic butter for 1–2 minutes, making sure the garlic doesn't brown. Remove the saucepan from the heat and place to one side.

Cut each block of pastry into three even slabs. From each slab cut away one quarter of the pastry to be used for each pastry lid. Dust a work surface and your rolling pin liberally with flour and roll out the pastry lids first. They will need to be about ½ cm thick and the perfect size to fit inside the rim of the pie dishes, so it's a good idea to use the rim of a pie dish itself as a stencil, trimming around it with a small sharp knife. Using a small round pastry cutter, cut a 2cm hole into the centre of each lid, so that as the pies cook, they can release a little steam. Dust the lids lightly with flour and place them to one side.

Lightly grease the pie dishes with butter. Line the base of each pie dish with greaseproof paper so that the pies can be turned out easily. Roll out the pastry bases one at a time to about ½ cm thick and large enough to line your pie dishes. Lay the rolled pastry sheets into each of the pie dishes, trimming the edges of the pastry so they only overlap the sides by 1cm.

Fill each pie dish with the cooled rabbit filling almost to the top. Place four snails and a teaspoon of garlic butter into each pie before laying the lid on top. Reserve the remaining garlic butter for the snail garnish.

Using a pastry brush, lightly brush a little egg yolk around the edge of each lid and fold over the overlapping pastry, pinching it all the way around to seal the pie. Brush the top of each pie with egg yolk and rest in the fridge until ready to bake. The pies can be prepared a few hours in advance.

To cook the pies, preheat your oven to 200°C/Gas Mark 6. Bake on the middle shelf of the oven for 30 minutes, until the pastry is golden brown. Rest the pies for a couple of minutes before attempting to turn them out. Before turning the pies out, carefully run a small knife around the sides of the pie dish to make sure they aren't stuck.

To serve, warm the six remaining snails in the reserved garlic butter and place one snail into each garnishing shell along with a spoonful of garlic butter. Place a shell resting in the hole of each pie. Serve with the mashed potato and a green salad.

Gamekeeper's pie serves 6

This is a play on a shepherd's pie, using minced game and parsnip instead of minced lamb and potato. The combination is wonderful. We actually use this recipe in the restaurant more often as a miniature accompaniment for game, rather than a main course in its own right, as demonstrated in the recipe for Roast Mallard with Elderberry Sauce on page 222.

3 tbsp vegetable oil
1kg minced game meat
50g butter
1 large onion, peeled and finely diced
2 garlic cloves, peeled and very finely chopped
4 juniper berries, finely chopped
2 tsp chopped thyme leaves
3 tbsp plain flour
1 tbsp tomato purée
100ml red wine
500ml Beef Stock (see page 297)
sea salt and freshly milled black pepper
buttered winter greens, such as sprout tops or kale, to serve

For the mashed parsnip topping
3 large parsnips, peeled and roughly chopped
2 floury potatoes (such as Maris Piper), peeled and halved
50g butter
2 egg yolks

Heat the vegetable oil in a large saucepan over a high heat until very hot. Season the minced game meat and fry it in two batches until lightly browned. Remove the mince from the pan and place it in a sieve to drain any excess fat.

Heat the butter in the same pan but over a medium heat and cook the onion, garlic, juniper and thyme for about 5 minutes, until soft. Add the flour and stir well, then stir in the tomato purée. Gradually add the red wine, stirring constantly to avoid lumps. Add the beef stock, and the cooked game. Bring the game sauce to the boil and then turn it down to a simmer. Season with salt and pepper and simmer gently for 30 minutes or so giving it the occasional stir. It may need topping up with a little water towards the end of cooking if too much liquid has evaporated. The final consistency should be that of a rich Bolognese sauce.

Fill a baking dish with the game sauce, leaving enough room at the top of the dish for the layer of mashed parsnip. Allow the game sauce to cool completely in the fridge so it sets before you attempt to apply the mashed parsnip.

For the mashed parsnip, place the parsnip and potatoes into a saucepan of lightly salted cold water and bring to the boil. The parsnips will cook slightly faster than the potatoes, so once these are cooked through remove them with a slotted spoon into a colander to drain. Rest the parsnips for a couple of minutes in the colander to dry out before blending them to a smooth purée in a food processor. If there are lumps in your purée, rub the purée through a sieve with the back of a large spoon.

By this stage the potatoes will be cooked. Drain them in the colander and allow them to sit for a couple of minutes to release their steam and dry out. Mash the potatoes using a potato ricer or with a hand-held potato masher. Add the parsnip purée and the butter to the potato and mix well. Taste the mash for seasoning and add salt if required. Finally, fold in the egg yolks thoroughly. The egg yolks will help the top of the pie glaze in the oven.

While the topping is still hot spread it onto the pie evenly in a layer about 1–2cm thick. Score the top with the back of a fork so the ridges crisp up in the oven as it bakes. If you have a piping bag, I suggest you pipe the mash to top the pie as it's easier to gain even coverage.

When you're ready to cook, preheat your oven to 180°C/Gas Mark 4. Bake the pie for 30–40 minutes, until the topping is crispy and the meat sauce hot in the middle. If the parsnip top colours too quickly, cover the dish with foil. Serve with some buttered winter greens such as sprout tops or curly kale.

Grouse shooting: A day on the moors with Ben Weatherall

The 'Glorious Twelfth' of August marks the beginning of an exciting time in the British culinary calendar. It's the first day of the grouse-shooting season, which kicks off the game season for another year. One of the most poignant moments in the kitchen for me is the distinctive smell of the first grouse being pulled from the oven. It means that summer is coming to an end and autumn, with its bounty of interesting ingredients, is just around the corner.

There are few experiences more satisfying for me than cooking with ingredients I have caught, foraged or hunted myself, and having cooked game supplied by Ben Weatherall every year for over 12 years, I was thrilled at the opportunity to travel north to visit his heather-clad hill farm in southwest Scotland in an attempt to bag a grouse or two.

We rose early on a crisp misty morning to a hearty breakfast of local kippers before heading out with guns and a dog. As we drove through the hills to our destination the mist gradually lifted revealing a beautiful clear windless day.

I am by no stretch of the imagination an experienced gunman, so on our arrival, in an attempt to preserve his and Audrey, his black labrador's lives, Ben ran me through the importance of safe gun handling.

There are two methods of grouse shooting. 'Driven grouse-shooting' refers to the way in which the grouse are pushed or driven over the waiting guns by beaters. There are usually 8–10 guns stood in a line in butts (a hide for shooting screened by a turf or stone wall usually dug into the ground) and the birds are flushed out of the heather towards them by beaters. As there were only two of us shooting we opted for the 'walk-up' approach, wandering up the hill waiting in anticipation for the grouse to fly out of the heather, often in pairs.

As we walked up through the heather, Ben explained to me the processes involved in maintaining the perfect environment for a healthy grouse population. Gamekeepers burn patches of heather on the moorland to create a variety of heather heights. The longer heather provides the grouse with cover and shelter from the elements and predators, such as aerial raptors, foxes and stoats. A burnt patch allows fresh heather shoots to come through, which are ideal nutrition for the grouse.

The birds begin to pair up during the spring and stay together as a pair with their young. Their nest is a shallow scrape (where soil has been scraped away), up to 20cm across, lined with vegetation. About six to ten eggs are laid, mainly during April and May. The eggs are incubated for three weeks before hatching and after two to three weeks the young birds are already on the wing to escape predators.

There was a constant 'chut, chut, chut' on the moor, the distinctive call of the grouse, coming from distant patches of heather. These were broken every few minutes by a frantic whirring of wings as the birds were disturbed from their resting places. Grouse fly at over 125km per hour so are notoriously difficult to shoot. After about an hour or so, despite having fired off plenty of rounds, our bags were still empty. Audrey, Ben's astute gun dog, managed to flush out a blue mountain hare right at Ben's feet, which he swiftly pounced on, snapping its neck in an instant. Although unconventional, we now had at least something to take back to the house and prepare for dinner, but it was Audrey: one, Ben and Marcus: nil. This would not do.

After a few more minutes making our way slowly up the steep hill, I disturbed a bird about 15–20 metres ahead of me. I raised my shotgun quickly to my shoulder, flicking off the safety catch, and followed the bird carefully with the barrels as it flew off at great speed to my left. Once in my sight, I let off a shot and to my ecstatic disbelief, the grouse dropped from the sky like a stone. I can't describe the feeling of exhilaration. It was a 'bucket list' moment. Ben quickly sent Audrey off down the hill to retrieve my prize. On examining the bird, Ben expertly deduced by the length of its wing feathers that it wasn't a young bird suitable for roasting, but suggested that it would make fine pâté. Grinning from ear to ear, I popped it into my bag and we continued up the hill.

Ben managed to shoot two more birds that morning, and we fired off many shots at the numerous mountain hares as they darted out of the safety of the heather, but to no avail. Once we reached the top of the hill we stopped for a cool refreshing drink from a cascading brooklet before making our way back down to Ben's car.

Once back at the house Ben produced four grouse he had been hanging for a few days allowing the flavour to mature and the meat to tenderise. The length of hanging time is entirely down to personal preference. The meat on a young bird is already very tender so, for my personal taste, only needs hanging with

the viscera left inside for 3–4 days to develop the flavour. Older birds however are a little tougher so require hanging for longer. We ate very well that evening. Cooking on the Aga back at the house was an absolute pleasure. With the hare (which would have benefited from being hung for a few days) I prepared a salad using the offal and fillet with some poached quince and wild herbs (see page 219). For our main course I roasted the grouse traditionally and served it with Bread Sauce, Rowan Berry Jelly (see page 198) and a rustic pâté made from the offal. And to accompany the grouse we had Sprout Top Hearts with Roasted Chestnuts and Wild Boar Pancetta (see page 238). It was a day I will never forget.

Taking aim (*left*) and ejecting the spent cartridges (*this page*).

Hare and poached quince salad with foraged herbs and crispy bacon

serves 4

I prepared this lovely starter at Ben Weatherall's farmhouse in Dumfries after he'd taken me grouse shooting (see pages 214–217). The hare was unfortunately not shot by either of us – it was caught by Ben's gun dog Audrey! A bit embarrassing, but at least it wasn't riddled with shot.

Game is often accompanied by red fruit such as elderberries, currants, cherries or even plums. I think the fragrant poached quince in this recipe works equally well cutting through the strong gamey hare and contrasting well with the salty bacon.

As an alternative to using wild herbs you could use ruby chard, pea shoots and watercress as your salad leaf selection.

1 large quince
200g caster sugar
juice of 1/2 lemon
2 hare fillets, plus the offal (heart, kidneys and liver) from 1 hare
4 thin rashers of smoked streaky bacon
30g butter
sea salt and freshly milled black pepper
100g selection of picked and washed wild herbs (such as bitter cress, chervil, sorrel and wood sorrel)
4 tbsp Lemon and Rapeseed Oil Dressing (see page 292)

To prepare the poached quince, peel the quince and place it in a small saucepan. Only just cover the quince with cold water and add the sugar and the lemon juice. Place a disc of baking parchment directly over the quince and bring it up to a gentle simmer on a medium heat. Don't boil the quince or it will overcook on the outside and still be hard in the centre. The cooking time will depend on the size and ripeness of the fruit. The harder the quince, the longer it will take to cook. For a large ripe quince 20 minutes should be sufficient. Check it's ready with a small knife, then allow the quince to cool in its poaching liquor. Once the quince is cool, slice the flesh from the core and cut it into slices about 1cm thick.

Preheat your oven grill to its highest setting.

If you have a whole hare and need instructions to butcher it follow those for the rabbit on pages 192–193 (and pictures on pages 208–209), or scan the QR code below to watch the video. Once the hare has been prepared, cut each bacon rasher into three strips and grill them on a tray for about 3 or 4 minutes, until crispy. Switch off the grill and close the oven door to keep the bacon warm.

Season the hare fillets with salt and pepper. Melt half the butter in a heavy-based frying pan and cook the fillets in the butter on a medium-high heat, turning them regularly. They should take about 4 minutes to seal and warm through but still be nice and rare in the middle. Remove the fillets from the pan and place to one side to rest.

Season the kidneys, heart and liver, add the rest of the butter to the pan, and fry the offal for about 1 minute on each side, keeping it nice and pink.

To serve, slice the hare fillet into strips. Slice the kidneys and heart in half and the larger liver into a few pieces. Scatter the hare, quince, bacon strips and wild herbs onto a serving platter and drizzle with the lemon and rapeseed oil dressing. Serve immediately.

more **roast**
Scan the QR code to see Marcus filleting a hare.
http://roastcookbook.com/filleting-a-hare/

Roast pheasant breast with creamed Brussels sprouts, smoked bacon and roasted chestnuts serves 4

Pheasant is one of the trickier game birds to cook. I wouldn't recommend roasting a whole pheasant, as by the time the legs are cooked, the breast meat will be overcooked and dry; and there is nothing worse than overcooked pheasant. When cooking the breast off the bone, cook it slowly in plenty of butter, basting it regularly to keep the breast moist. Save the thighs for a gamey curry or a slow-cooked casserole – they are ideal for this as they don't dry out as the breasts would if you cooked them for too long. The skinny sinuous legs, however, are only worth keeping to enhance a game stock or gravy.

I used to detest sprouts as a child, sneaking them on to my dad's plate while mum was in the kitchen. My mum is awesome in the kitchen but her sprouts were so overcooked, they used to collapse under their own weight on the plate. (Sorry Mum, love you loads, but I couldn't resist!)

Pheasant season in the UK runs from 1st October to 1st February.

300g Brussels sprouts, trimmed
8 large fresh chestnuts
50g butter
6 rashers of rindless smoked streaky
   bacon, cut crossways into thin strips
200ml double cream
4 large pheasant breasts (cock breasts
   are larger than hens')
2 tbsp vegetable oil
150ml Gravy for Game (see page 295)
sea salt and freshly milled black pepper

Preheat your oven to 200°C/Gas Mark 6.

Bring a large saucepan of well-salted water to the boil. Blanch the Brussels sprouts for 3–4 minutes until cooked but still a vibrant green with a slight bite. Once the sprouts are cooked, drain them in a colander over the sink and plunge them into iced water. This will stop the cooking and they will retain their vibrant green colour. Once the sprouts are cold, remove them from the water and slice each one into three. Place the sliced sprouts back into the colander and set them to one side.

To peel the chestnuts, use a small sharp knife to score a cross into the pointed end of each chestnut. Roast the chestnuts in the oven for 15 minutes until the crossed end starts to splay open revealing the golden nut inside. Allow the chestnuts to cool slightly so they can be handled, but do not let them cool completely or you will have a torrid time trying to peel them. Remove the hard casing and also the membrane between the casing and the nut. Once peeled, break each chestnut in half and place to one side.

Heat a saucepan over a medium heat. Add a teaspoon of the butter and the bacon and cook, stirring regularly, until the bacon is crispy. Add the cream and bring it to the boil before reducing the heat to a gentle simmer. Reduce the cream for 2 minutes or so until it thickens slightly.

As the cream is reducing, heat a large frying pan over a medium-high heat. Season the pheasant breasts on both sides with sea salt and freshly ground pepper. Add the vegetable oil to the hot pan and place the breasts, skin-side down, inside. Once the skin is crispy reduce the heat to low-medium and turn the breasts over. Add the remaining butter and the chestnuts. Cook the pheasant breasts in the butter for about 5–7 minutes turning them and basting them regularly so they cook evenly. Once the chestnuts have browned slightly remove them from the pan. Remove the frying pan from the heat leaving the breasts in the butter to rest for a few minutes.

Add the sliced Brussels sprouts to the reduced cream and bacon and heat through thoroughly. Season with salt and pepper.

In a small saucepan bring the game gravy to the boil, add the roasted chestnuts and remove from the heat. Divide the creamed sprouts and bacon between four serving plates and place a pheasant breast on top of each. Spoon the chestnuts and a little gravy over each one and serve.

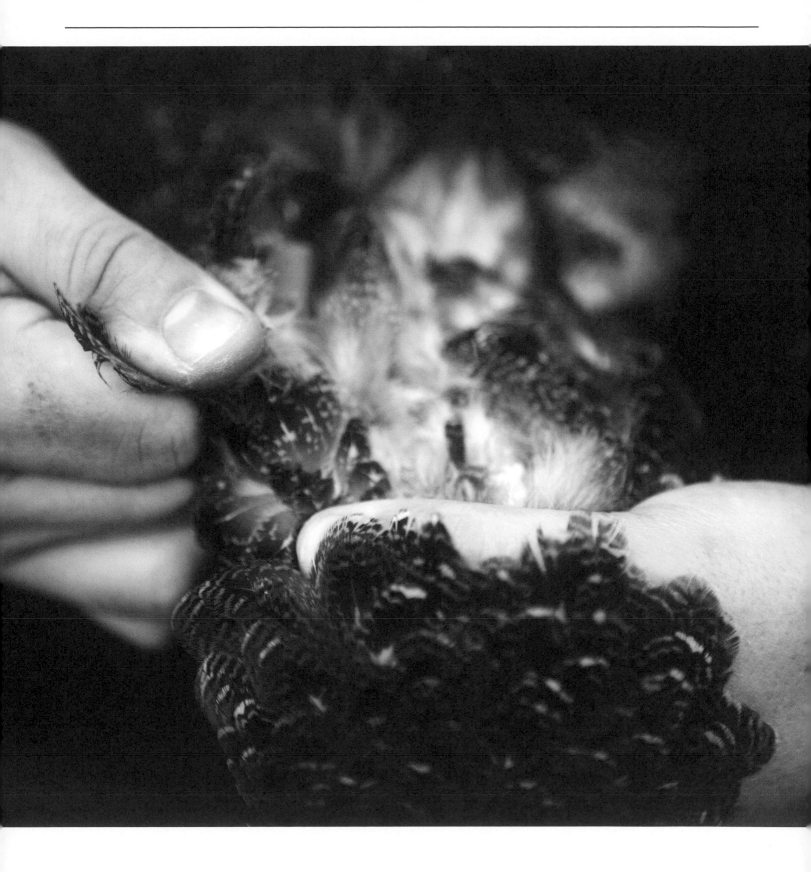

Roast mallard with a gamekeeper's pie and elderberry sauce serves 4

Even a large mallard breast is fairly small and not really enough protein to use as a main course on its own. At Roast we pride ourselves on our generous portions so in this dish we offer the mallard breast alongside a tasty miniature gamekeeper's pie. The pie can also be served as a dish in its own right (following the recipe on page 213).

In the restaurant, we bake the miniature pies in a stainless steel ring lined with a collar of greaseproof paper so that they can be removed easily during service. If you haven't got rings, the pies can be assembled and served on the plate in a small ceramic ramekin. Even if you only want to make a few miniature pies, I suggest you still make the full recipe on page 213 and freeze whatever you don't use for a later date (the recipe is more successful made in larger quantities).

Domestic duck has a thick fat coverage and should be cooked slowly on the skin side to render out this fat. Mallards, however, are wild and spend much of their time on the wing burning fat like athletes, so they simply need to be sealed quickly. If you attempt to cook a mallard breast off the bone you will find that the already small breast will shrink even further during cooking so at the restaurant we cook the breasts on the bone and remove the bone before they go on the plate.

For this recipe I've suggested cooking two crowns. The term crown is used for all fowl and refers to the two breasts on the bone, minus the legs, wings and tail. Remember to remove the wishbone from the crowns before roasting (see page 20 for how to do this) or you'll leave much of the breast still on the bone when carving.

The elderberries cut through the duck wonderfully. When they're in season I always fill small containers and freeze them to be used throughout the year.

*1 quantity Gamekeeper's Pie
    (see page 213), placed in four 7cm
    ramekins or stainless steel rings*
3 tbsp vegetable oil
2 mallard crowns
100g curly kale
30g butter
2 tbsp elderberries
sea salt and freshly milled black pepper

Preheat your oven to 180°C/Gas Mark 4.

Place the miniature pies in the oven. The smaller pies will only take about 25 minutes to heat through.

About 15 minutes before the end of the pies' cooking time, heat a large ovenproof frying pan over a medium-high heat and add the vegetable oil. Bring a saucepan of lightly salted water to the boil for the kale.

Season the duck crowns with salt and pepper and seal the breasts in the oil until the skin is crispy all over. Turn the crowns on to their backs and place them in the oven. For medium-rare, roast the crowns for 8 minutes and then pull them out of the oven to rest for about 6 minutes before carving the breasts off the bone.

While the mallards are resting, blanch the kale in the boiling water for 1–2 minutes. Drain the kale well and toss it back into the pan with the butter, seasoning it well. Heat the game gravy in a small saucepan and add the elderberries. To carve the crowns, run a small sharp knife down either side of the breast bone. Follow the rib cage with the blade of the knife, down and around to remove each breast. Take your time to ensure minimal meat is left on the bones. Reserve the bones for stock.

To serve, place a mallard breast and a portion of kale on to warmed serving plates. Remove the pies from the oven and serve immediately.

vegetables

Heritage tomatoes on toast with celery hearts and shaved Berkswell serves 4

Heritage tomatoes have become increasingly popular and more readily available in recent years. Old tomato varieties are grown from a historical seed bank in a more traditional manner with open pollination and no hybridisation. The range is endless and diverse, and when the different varieties are combined the result is an interesting mix of colours, textures, acidity and sweetness.

Celery salt is a lovely seasoning for tomatoes, and making it at home is not only very easy, but the outcome is far superior to that of any bought product. Just save all the dark green leaves from a head of celery and dry them out for a few days in the airing cupboard or another warm dry place. Once they are completely dry and crumble when touched, blend or grind to a dust with a heaped tablespoon of good sea salt.

Berkswell is a hard sheep's milk cheese, named after the village in the West Midlands in which it is made. Ask your cheesemonger for one that is well aged, as its texture and saltiness will resemble that of a good aged pecorino, making it perfect for this play on the classic Italian 'bruschetta pomodoro'. If you can't find it, just use pecorino or Parmesan.

500g heritage tomatoes of different varieties, cut into chunks
4 thick slices of crusty sourdough bread
1 garlic clove, halved
a good handful of celery leaves (picked from the heart)
Lemon and Rapeseed Oil Dressing (see page 292)
80g Berkswell cheese
olive oil, to drizzle
celery salt and freshly milled black pepper

Place the tomatoes, seeds and all, into a bowl, and season them with the celery salt and pepper. If you have time, allow the tomatoes to stand for an hour, so the salt has a chance to draw some of the juice from the tomatoes, breaking them down slightly.

Heat a griddle pan until very hot. Drizzle the bread with olive oil and grill in the pan, pressing on it lightly to achieve the flavoursome burnt bar marks from the hot griddle. (Use a barbecue for an even better flavour.) Once the toast is grilled on both sides, rub it lightly with the garlic clove half.

Toss the celery leaves with the tomatoes and dress with the lemon and rapeseed oil dressing. Scatter the tomatoes, celery leaves and all the juices over the toast, then using a vegetable peeler, shave the Berkswell over the top.

Chilled golden tomato soup with buffalo mozzarella and basil serves 8

During the warmer summer months we always have a refreshing chilled soup on the menu. This recipe is of a gazpacho style, using fresh, raw tomatoes. It's so easy to prepare but does benefit greatly from spending 24 hours in the fridge to macerate before blending so the salt can draw out the juice and start breaking down the tomatoes. Of course, if you can't find good ripe golden tomatoes use the best red tomatoes available. The most important thing is the quality of the tomato. There's no point in even trying this soup unless it's during the warmest months of summer or the tomatoes just won't be up to scratch. I remember a tomato supplier we used when I worked in Melbourne. You could literally smell him coming!

1/2 garlic clove, peeled
2kg ripe golden tomatoes, roughly chopped
1 green chilli, deseeded and roughly chopped
40ml white balsamic vinegar
2 slices of fresh white sandwich bread, roughly torn
one 200g ball buffalo mozzarella, roughly torn
4 ripe red tomatoes, deseeded and diced
sea salt and freshly milled black pepper

For the basil oil
1 bunch of basil, leaves picked (reserve the stalks)
200ml extra virgin olive oil

Blanch the garlic in boiling water for 5 minutes to reduce its raw intensity. Place the golden tomatoes in a deep bowl with the garlic, chilli, balsamic vinegar and torn bread. Season well with salt and pepper and mix thoroughly. Cover with clingfilm and refrigerate for 24 hours.

Once the soup has been allowed to macerate, blend until very smooth. Use a blender, as a food processor won't do the required job. Check the seasoning. Depending on the tomatoes you may need to add a touch more vinegar as well. Once you're happy with the flavour, pass the soup through a fine-mesh sieve and chill until ready to serve.

To make the basil oil, bring a saucepan of water to a rapid boil. Fill a small bowl with water and add a few ice cubes. Blanch the basil leaves in the boiling water for 10 seconds, then plunge them straight into the iced water so they retain their vibrant green. Strain the basil leaves and squeeze out all the excess water.

Blend the blanched basil leaves with the olive oil and a good pinch of salt until smooth. Be careful not to blend for too long or the friction from the blender will heat the oil and the basil will lose its colour.

To serve, mix the soup well before pouring into bowls as it will separate in the fridge. Garnish with the chunks of mozzarella. Sprinkle with the basil stalks and diced red tomatoes and finally, drizzle with the basil oil.

Steamed asparagus with St George's mushrooms and wild garlic serves 4

St George's mushrooms usually start to appear near the end of April, but like any mushroom, they pop up when they feel like it. These mushrooms have a relatively short season that tails off at the beginning of June. They grow on permanent grassland, whether it be old pastures or even a grassy verge in an urban setting. If you're picking your own mushrooms, ensure you are certain of what you are collecting and don't take any chances. There are many good guidebooks available.

For a special St George's Day menu we took a bit of a gamble in promoting this dish in advance as the starter. The week prior, I was on the phone every day to Tony Booth, our wild mushroom supplier, asking if he'd had any news from his foragers, and every day I got the same answer: 'Nothing yet I'm afraid.' Finally, the 23rd rolled around and Tony phoned me first thing to say he'd received only 2kg and was sending me the lot. We were probably one of the only restaurants in London lucky enough to have them on the menu that day.

The fact that St George's mushrooms grow in fields means they are usually fairly clean and may just need a gentle rub with a damp cloth to free them of any dirt or grit. Don't wash them in water. Mushrooms are like sponges and are ruined if they get too waterlogged. Being a spring mushroom means they are almost always free from maggots, which can be one of the hazards with autumnal mushrooms such as ceps.

400g English asparagus, woody ends removed
250g St George's mushrooms, cleaned (see above; girolles or ceps are a good alternative if St George's are unavailable)
8 wild garlic leaves, roughly chopped, (or 1 garlic clove if unavailable)
100g butter
sea salt and freshly milled black pepper

Cut your cleaned mushrooms into large pieces, trying to show off their natural form. Some may only require cutting in half or even not at all.

Bring a large pan of well-salted water to the boil and heat a frying pan over a medium heat.

Plunge the asparagus into the boiling water. Place the butter into the frying pan, add the mushrooms and cultivated garlic, if using, and cook gently. Season the mushrooms with sea salt and pepper at the beginning – the salt will draw water out of them, which will emulsify with the butter and create a lovely mushroom sauce. After a couple of minutes the asparagus and the mushrooms should both be cooked. Lift the asparagus from the water and drain on kitchen paper. Add the chopped wild garlic, if using, to the mushrooms just before serving.

Chilled, minted pea soup with preserved lemon and goat's curd
serves 4–6

The key to success with this soup is speed. Any soup made with green vegetables, unless being served hot and straight away, needs to be chilled as quickly as possible in order for it to retain its colour.

The preserved lemons are definitely something you should try. They are great with grilled fish, lamb or chicken. However, if you don't have a couple of months to wait, they are available from good supermarkets and delicatessens.

½ onion, peeled and roughly chopped
50ml rapeseed oil
550ml vegetable stock
500g frozen peas, defrosted
10 mint leaves
1 preserved lemon (shop-bought or see page 288 for how to make your own), flesh and pith removed, rind finely diced
100g goat's curd
extra virgin olive oil
sea salt and freshly milled black pepper

If you're making your own preserved lemons, you will need to allow 2–3 months and follow the recipe on page 288.

In a large saucepan, gently cook the onion in the rapeseed oil over a low-medium heat until it's soft and translucent. Add the vegetable stock, season with salt and pepper and bring to the boil. If using a stock cube, a quarter will be enough.

Have ready your blender and fill a zip lock plastic bag with ice cubes and seal it tightly. Place the bag of ice into a large bowl and have a fine-mesh sieve to hand.

Add the peas and mint to the boiling stock and after 1 minute, remove from the heat and blend in batches. Be careful not to overload the blender or you may end up cleaning soup off your ceiling! Allow the soup to blend until very smooth before straining it through the sieve into the bowl containing the bag of ice. Keep stirring the soup in the bowl as you blend the next batch, so the ice cools it quickly and it retains its vibrant green colour. Correct the seasoning with salt and pepper if required.

Serve the soup straight from the fridge and sprinkle with the diced lemon rind. Add a few dollops of goat's curd and a drizzle of olive oil to each bowl.

Crisp summer vegetable salad with shaved Caerphilly serves 4

I live on this refreshing salad in the hotter weeks of summer, when the overwhelming desire to be healthy comes over me. It's perfect for a barbecue with grilled meats or fish. Use raw vegetables that haven't lost any of their goodness in boiling. You'll feel like you're doing your body a huge favour with every crunchy mouthful.

Caerphilly is a hard cow's milk cheese, named after the village in which it originated, in South Wales. Its salty flavour and crumbly texture are increased with age. If you have trouble locating it, use Parmesan instead.

400g broad beans, in their pods (will yield about 100g of podded broad beans)
1 fennel bulb, halved lengthways and cored
6 radishes, finely sliced into discs
300g peas, in their pods (will yield about 100g of podded peas)
100g mangetout, very finely sliced into long strips
8 asparagus spears, woody ends removed, very finely sliced on the diagonal
60g capers
1/2 red onion, finely sliced
8 mint leaves, shredded
12 basil leaves, torn
a few sprigs of dill or fennel tops, roughly picked
a generous handful of pea shoots
Vinaigrette (see page 292)
80g aged Caerphilly cheese
sea salt and freshly milled black pepper

Blanch the broad beans for 1 minute in boiling water and then refresh in iced water. Once the beans are cold, pop them out of their bitter skins.

Slice across the fennel, shaving it very finely with a sharp knife, or if you have a Japanese mandoline, this will do the best job. Plunge the shaved fennel into a bowl of iced water. The cold water shocks the fennel and it will emerge very crispy. It only needs about 30 seconds though, or it will lose flavour. Drain in a colander.

Toss all the ingredients except the cheese in a large bowl, dressing liberally with the vinaigrette and seasoning to your liking.

To serve, lay the salad out in a large shallow dish so you can see all the different components and vibrant colours. Using a vegetable peeler, shave the Caerphilly over the top.

Chicory and apple coleslaw with kohlrabi and golden raisins serves 8

We came up with this coleslaw while trying to find a light garnish to serve with duck during the warmer months. The sweet, crisp slaw is the perfect match to cut through the fat of the duck; it also works very well with barbecued pork chops.

There is a wonderful balance between the sweetness of raisins and apple and the bitter crunch of chicory and kohlrabi. Don't prepare this slaw in advance – the chicory isn't quite as robust as the shredded white cabbage usually associated with coleslaw and will wilt.

100g golden raisins
2 white chicory heads, halved
  lengthways and cored
3 red chicory heads, halved lengthways
  and cored
1 kohlrabi, peeled
2 Granny Smith apples, cored
2 tbsp sweet apple vinegar or 1 tbsp
  cider vinegar
2 tbsp flat-leaf parsley, chopped
100g Mayonnaise (see page 290)
sea salt and freshly milled black pepper

Soak the raisins in water overnight to rehydrate and swell.

The next day, slice across the chicory at 1cm intervals and place in a large mixing bowl. Slice the kohlrabi into long thin strips – about 3mm wide – and add to the bowl. Slice the apple, leaving the skin on, into strips the same size as the kohlrabi. If you have a Japanese mandoline, use it to slice the kohlrabi and apple for a more uniform finish. Toss the apple in the apple vinegar and mix with the kohlrabi and chicory. The vinegar stops the apple from turning brown.

Finally, drain the plump raisins and add to the coleslaw, along with the parsley and mayonnaise. Fold all the ingredients together gently and season to your liking with salt and pepper.

Shaved asparagus, fennel and blood orange salad serves 4 as a starter

This simple, easy-to-prepare salad is suitable as a refreshing starter in its own right but at Roast we also serve it as an accompaniment for fish. It works particularly well with oilier fish such as sea bass, sea bream, salmon or mackerel. The blood orange dressing (see page 293) makes the dish. Don't worry if you can't find blood oranges as the season is fairly short; just substitute with standard oranges.

16 asparagus spears
2 fennel bulbs
3 blood oranges
1 small bunch of fennel tops (dill is a
 good alternative)
Blood Orange, Honey and Mustard
 Dressing (see page 293)
sea salt and freshly milled black pepper

Remove the woody ends from the asparagus and slice each spear very finely on the diagonal.

Cut the bulb of fennel in half lengthways and remove the core. Slice across the fennel as finely as possible with a sharp knife (it should be shavings), or if you have a mandoline, this is even better. Plunge the shaved fennel into a bowl of iced water. The cold water shocks the fennel and it will emerge very crispy. It only needs about 30 seconds though, or it will lose flavour. Drain in a colander.

To segment the oranges, cut both ends off each orange using a small sharp knife. One at a time sit each orange on its flat end, and in a curved motion, cut off the skin all the way down to the flesh, removing all of the bitter white pith. Holding the now peeled orange in the palm of your hand carefully cut out each segment, removing them one at a time and removing any pips.

Toss all the ingredients together in a large bowl. Dress liberally with the blood orange dressing and season to your liking. Serve immediately.

Mixed beetroot and blood orange salad with foraged herbs and Ragstone goat's cheese serves 4

New-season beetroot is best in late spring and into summer, but crops sown as late as June reach full maturity in October and are stored as a winter crop along with other root vegetables, such as parsnips and carrots. The fact that it stores well makes it available throughout the year.

Beetroot's sweet but earthy flavour makes it a perfect partner for cheese. Goat's cheese, with its sharp, tangy characteristics, works particularly well, and Ragstone, when ripe, is in my opinion, the best the UK has to offer. Be aware though, that it is made with animal rennet and unsuitable for vegetarians. Good vegetarian alternatives for this salad are Childwickbury or fresh goat's curd.

As an alternative to using wild herbs you could use ruby chard, pea shoots and watercress.

400g baby beetroot (red, golden and candy)
80ml extra virgin rapeseed oil
5 sprigs of thyme
selection of picked and washed wild herbs (such as chervil, sorrel, wood sorrel)
2 blood oranges
Blood Orange, Honey and Mustard Dressing (see page 293)
150g Ragstone goat's cheese, at room temperature
sea salt and freshly milled black pepper

Preheat your oven to 180°C/Gas Mark 4.

Remove the stems and leaves from the beetroot saving any delicate new leaves for the salad. Wash the beetroot and place it in the middle of a large sheet of foil. Drizzle over the rapeseed oil and add the thyme. Season liberally with salt and pepper. Lift the sides of the foil into the middle creating a trough and pour in about 80ml of cold water. Seal the foil at the top to create a small parcel. Place the parcel into the middle of your oven and bake for 40 minutes, until the beetroot are cooked through. Test one with a sharp knife. Allow the beetroot to cool a little so they can be handled. Once cool, the skins will rub off easily in your hands. Make sure you peel the red beetroot last or the dye on your hands will leave its distinctive mark on the other varieties. Cut the beetroot into bite-sized wedges and place to one side.

To segment the oranges, cut both ends off each orange using a small sharp knife. One at a time sit each orange on its flat end, and in a curved motion, cut off the skin all the way down to the flesh, removing all of the bitter white pith. Holding the now peeled orange in the palm of your hand carefully cut out each segment, removing them one at a time and removing any pips.

Serve the salad on a flat platter so all the vibrant colours can be seen. In a small bowl, dress the beetroot lightly with some of the blood orange dressing and season. Lay out the beetroot first and add the goat's cheese, breaking it into bite-sized nuggets as you go. Scatter over the wild herbs and then the orange segments. Finally, drizzle a little more dressing over the salad and serve.

Sprout top hearts with roasted chestnuts and wild boar pancetta

serves 4

I actually prefer the sweet sprout top hearts to the Brussels sprouts themselves. The sprouts grow clutching to the thick stem of the plant and the heart sits at the very top of this stem. Cut in half down the centre and opened up, the sweet sprouts act as a vessel for this dish, catching the chestnuts, pancetta and butter between their many layers. This recipe is great as an accompaniment for game birds such as pheasant and partridge but in the past, during the Christmas period I have even served it as a starter.

At Roast, we use Peter Gott's wild boar pancetta for this dish. His award-winning market stall, Sillfield Farm, is conveniently located directly underneath our site at Borough market, where he sells all his wild boar products and many others, all produced on his farm in Cumbria. His wild boar pancetta is phenomenal, rivalling anything produced on the Continent. However, if you can't get hold of wild boar pancetta, a good-quality standard pancetta would be fine as a substitute.

10 fresh chestnuts
8 sprout top hearts
1 tbsp vegetable oil
12 rashers of wild boar pancetta, cut into 5cm lengths
50g butter
sea salt and freshly milled black pepper

Preheat your oven to 200°C/Gas Mark 6.

To peel the chestnuts, use a small sharp knife to score a cross into the pointed end of each chestnut. Roast the chestnuts in the oven for 15 minutes until the crossed end starts to splay open revealing the golden nut inside. Allow the chestnuts to cool slightly so they can be handled, but do not let them cool completely or you will have a torrid time trying to peel them. Remove the hard casing and also the membrane between the casing and the nut. Once peeled, break each chestnut in half and place to one side.

Bring a large saucepan of lightly salted water to the boil. Cut each sprout top heart in half, splitting the stalk end down the middle. Rinse the tops under cold water to remove any undesirables lurking between the leafy layers.

Heat a large heavy-based frying pan over a medium-high heat, add the vegetable oil and fry the pancetta. When the pancetta is just starting to curl up and its flavoursome fat is rendering into the pan, add the chestnuts. When the pancetta is crispy add the butter. Continue to cook until the chestnuts caramelise in the foaming butter.

Meanwhile, add the washed sprout top hearts to the boiling water and cook for 2 minutes until tender. Drain the sprout top hearts in a large colander with their hearts pointing downwards, which will allow the water to drain off. Arrange the drained sprout top hearts on a flat serving dish with their open hearts facing upwards.

Generously spoon the chestnuts, pancetta and foaming butter into and over the sprout top hearts. Season them with salt and pepper. Don't be shy with the pepper – sprout top hearts love pepper! Serve immediately.

Celeriac and apple soup with toasted walnuts serves 8–10

This autumnal soup uses the same flavour combination as the classic American dish, Waldorf salad. Celeriac, an under-utilised and very versatile vegetable, makes the loveliest creamy soup. Sliced thinly it's also a welcome addition to a coleslaw.

Celeriac also has its health benefits. It's very low in calories and has high levels of vitamin K, which is important in children's development. It helps the blood to clot for all those scraped knees and elbows and also helps to keep their bones healthy and strong. Whenever you cook with celeriac, season it with celery salt to give it a boost in flavour.

50g butter
$\frac{1}{2}$ onion, thinly sliced
$\frac{1}{2}$ leek, white part only, roughly chopped
1 large celeriac, peeled and roughly chopped
2 Bramley apples, peeled, cored and roughly chopped
2 tsp celery salt
1.3 litres water
300ml milk
30g walnuts, lightly toasted and chopped
sea salt and freshly ground pepper

Melt the butter in a large saucepan on a moderate heat and gently cook the onion and leek for 4–5 minutes, until they're soft. Add the celeriac and apple and season with the celery salt. Continue to cook, stirring regularly, until the apple disintegrates and the celeriac starts to soften. Add the water and turn up the heat bringing the soup to the boil. Once it boils, reduce the heat and simmer for 30 minutes, until the celeriac is very soft. Season with salt and pepper. Once the celeriac is cooked through, remove the pan from the heat and stir in the milk. The milk helps to keep the soup white.

Allow the soup to cool slightly before processing it in a blender until smooth. If you try to process the soup while it's too hot, you'll end up with hot soup all over yourself and probably the ceiling. If the soup seems a little thick add some water to adjust the consistency and season again.

When reheating the soup do not boil it or you risk curdling the milk. Serve sprinkled with the chopped walnuts. Go easy on the walnuts – they have a very strong flavour and you don't want them to overpower the soup.

Sweetcorn and smoked haddock chowder serves 8–10 as a starter

This chunky rustic chowder is an adaptation of a recipe I used to cook while working in an Italian restaurant in Melbourne. The original recipe was a combination of sweetcorn and baccalà. Baccalà is a heavily salted cod used regularly in Italian, Portuguese and Spanish cuisine. The salty fish and sweetcorn marry very well in a harmonious balance. The same applies with smoked haddock, which is much easier to find in the United Kingdom.

5 ears of sweetcorn, husks removed
50g butter
1 large onion, finely diced
1 red chilli, deseeded and finely diced
1 tsp chopped thyme leaves
1 small red pepper, deseeded and finely diced
1 large Maris Piper potato, peeled and cut into 1cm dice
400g undyed smoked haddock fillet, skinned and chopped into 2½cm pieces
500ml Fish Stock (see page 299)
500ml Chicken Stock (see page 298)
100ml double cream
2 tbsp flat-leaf parsley, chopped
sea salt and freshly milled black pepper

Stand each corn ear on one end, holding it at the other and run a sharp knife down the cob, slicing off the kernels. Work your way around each ear removing all the kernels. Scrape out all the juices and any pulp left in the cobs carefully using the sharp edge of the knife.

Melt the butter in a large heavy-based saucepan over a medium heat and add the onion, chilli and thyme. Cook for 4–5 minutes, stirring regularly, until the onions are soft, then add the sweetcorn, red pepper, potato and half the smoked haddock.

Cook for a further 5 minutes stirring regularly before adding the fish and chicken stocks. Season with salt and pepper and bring it to the boil. Once boiling, reduce the heat to a simmer and cook for about 15 minutes, until the diced potato is soft.

Remove a third of the soup from the pan and blend it in a blender until smooth. Be careful not to overload the blender or you may end up cleaning soup off your ceiling!

Place the blended soup back in the pan along with the remaining smoked haddock. Simmer the soup for a further 5 minutes or so until the haddock is cooked and flaking. Add the cream and chopped parsley and bring the chowder back to the boil. Adjust the seasoning if necessary and serve.

Heritage squash and goat's curd tart with pickled walnuts
serves 10 as a starter or 6 as a main

This rustic tart looks awesome on the table but can be a little difficult to eat. The skin on some of the squash varieties is thin and tender enough to be eaten, but on others it's too tough. You could opt to peel the squash before you roast it but it will lose its visual impact, and with the smaller varieties you may find you don't have much squash left once they've been peeled and had the seeds removed. If you do decide to peel the squash, it might be a better option to make individual tarts and serve them on plates. Whatever method you decide on, you won't be disappointed – the squash are divine with the sweet pickled walnuts and the sharp goat's curd. Try sprinkling a few toasted pumpkin seeds over the top for added texture.

1 large butternut squash (for the
*   purée), halved lengthways, seeds*
*   scooped out*
1 quantity of Sage-roasted Heritage
*   Squash (but omit the bacon) page 281*
1kg good-quality puff pastry
2 eggs, beaten
200g pickled walnuts, sliced into discs
300g goat's curd
butter, for greasing
extra virgin rapeseed oil
sea salt and freshly milled black pepper

Preheat your oven to 180°C/Gas Mark 4.

For the squash purée, place the butternut squash in a roasting tin skin-side up. Rub the flesh with a little rapeseed oil and season it well with salt and pepper. Cover with foil and bake it in the oven for about 1 hour, until the flesh is soft and cooked through.

At the same time, roast the heritage squash, following the instructions for the Sage-roasted Heritage Squash on page 281, but omitting the bacon.

While the squash is roasting, roll out the pastry for your pastry case. On a floured work top, roll out the pastry with a rolling pin to a thickness of about 3–4mm. It's best to use a flat baking tray without raised sides for this, so the tart can be easily cut for serving. Cut out a large rectangle (about 35 x 25cm) to fit your tray. Grease the baking tray with a little butter and lay the sheet of pastry on to it. With the pastry you've trimmed from the edges, cut four strips about 2½ cm wide to form the sides of the tart. Using a pastry brush, brush the edges of the tart base with the beaten egg, then stick the four strips of pastry to the edges of the pastry base to form a frame. Prick holes all over the pastry base with a fork. Docking the base in this manner stops the pastry from rising so freely, enabling the undocked edges to rise up and frame the tart.

Brush the pastry case with the beaten egg, giving it a generous coat. Place the pastry base into the oven with the squash and bake it for 15–20 minutes, until the pastry is golden and crispy. Remove the tart case from the oven and if the centre of the base has risen, gently press it back down with a spatula.

Remove the butternut squash from the oven and scoop out the flesh with a spoon. Place the flesh in a food processor and blend to a smooth purée. Season the purée with salt and pepper and spread it on to the base of the pastry case. Place the roasted heritage squash, garlic and sage randomly inside the case. Make sure the squash is still hot as the tart, once assembled, will only be flashed through the oven briefly to warm the goat's curd and pickled walnuts.

Scatter the pickled walnuts over the tart, then spoon the curd among the roasted squash in random dollops and place the tart back in the oven for 5 minutes to warm through, and drizzle a little rapeseed oil over the top before serving.

Forager: leaders in the British wild food renaissance

The satisfaction and sense of achievement I feel when cooking with ingredients I've gathered myself is indescribable. In the grand scheme of things, until only a few thousand years ago we were a hunter-gatherer society.

I believe that this way of life is somehow naturally embedded in our genetic make up and only requires a little encouragement and know-how to be tapped into.

The nutritional benefits of eating wild food are vast. Wild plants are generally high in antioxidants, minerals and essential vitamins, particularly vitamin C. Through years of cultivation, in an attempt to grow large perfectly formed vegetables, in some cases we may have inadvertently bred out much of the nutritional value they once had.

At Roast we work with a company based in Kent called Forager. They supply us with a wide variety of leaves, stems, roots, flowers, seeds and fruits of wild plants.

I was first introduced to the owner, Miles Irving, and his foraged produce about 10 years ago when I was working as a sous chef at Le Caprice, and have been using them ever since. During that time I also moved out of London, living in Colchester for four years, where I spent much of my spare time scouring the woodlands, hedgerows and the seashore of Mersea Island for various herbs, fungi, vegetables and fruits. After four years I had gained a real knowledge of my local area and foraging had become something of an obsession, to the point where I once drove into a ditch having spotted a patch of parasol mushrooms growing on the side of the road. When I finally left Colchester, the hardest thing about moving back into London was leaving behind my wild garlic grove, the high yielding seashore of West Mersea and my secret mushroom spots.

Once a year we hire a van and I drive some of Roast's staff back out to Essex to visit my old foraging spots so they can see first-hand where and how abundantly some of these plants, which were once a very important part of our ancestors' everyday diet, actually grow.

Miles Irving and his foragers have been a driving force behind the foraging movement, enlightening many chefs over the past few years with their interesting, often forgotten bounty. These wild ingredients can be found on menus all over the country. I have been lucky enough to spend a morning on the East Kentish seashore foraging with Miles. His knowledge of British wild flora is astounding and he shares this wealth in his *The Forager Handbook* (Ebury Press, 2009), a must-have for any aspiring forager. We spent about two hours scouring the beach front and found 15 or so varieties of edible plants and seeds that would probably be looked upon as weeds by the unenlightened. The species I found most intriguing was the wild carrot we stumbled across. It's the parent plant of the carrot humans have been cultivating for centuries. Miles handed me the tender leaves – the tops – from the plant itself to taste. They had a light herbal flavour with a hint of carrot and would be an interesting addition to a salad.

But it was the small root that was the obvious champion. Miles scraped back the skin with a small knife to reveal the clean, creamy-coloured root which had the most intense carrot flavour. Other species we found were sea purslane and sea beet, which we often use at Roast as a garnish for fish. We also found some alexanders, which was a widely used herb and vegetable until the sixteenth century. Dried alexanders seeds were also used as a spice before pepper became available with the onset of the spice trade. Alexanders grows in abundance throughout England, there's even a healthy crop growing behind Clapham Common tube station in London, near where I live, which the council cut back every year or so but to no avail as it just keeps coming back.

Like many chefs, working with Miles and Forager has really opened my eyes to what is available right there at our feet if we only know what we're looking for. With the newfound knowledge I have eagerly developed, a walk or drive in the countryside holds so much more pleasure and meaning than before. Please note: if you are an amateur forager, I advise you to use a good handbook and that you know exactly what it is you have found before eating it!

vegetables

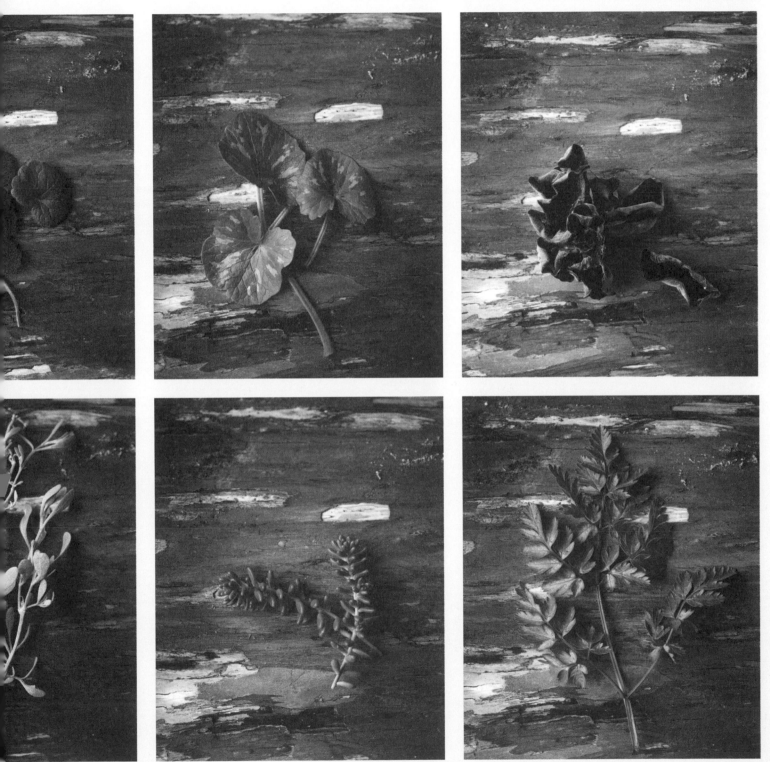

A selection of our finds from the day foraging:
top, left to right: alexanders, fennel, ground ivy, lesser salandine, Judas ear fungus
bottom, left to right: pepper wort, sea beet, sea purslane, stone crop, wild chervil

vegetables

Miles Irving and I scouring the Essex beach front.

puddings

Sticky date pudding with poached autumn fruits and clotted cream
serves 12

This comforting pudding is the most popular choice on the Roast pudding menu during the cooler months. It's rich, but still wonderfully light in texture.

600ml water
340g pitted dates
2 tsp bicarbonate of soda
120g butter, plus extra to grease
340g caster sugar
4 eggs
340g flour
2 tsp baking powder
1 tsp vanilla extract
clotted cream, to serve

For the poached autumn fruits

2 large quince (poached and sliced)
300ml water
300g caster sugar
1 vanilla pod, seeds scraped
a 2½cm piece of cinnamon stick
juice of 1 lemon
2 large Cox's apples, peeled, quartered
    and cored
2 large Comice pears, peeled, quartered
    and cored

For the toffee sauce

150g caster sugar
50ml water
80ml double cream
20g butter

For the hazelnut praline

50g toasted blanched hazelnuts
100g caster sugar
1 tbsp cold water

You will also need: a 30 x 20 x 5cm cake tin

Start with the hazelnut praline. Lay the toasted hazelnuts on to a small tray covered with greaseproof paper and place to one side. Place the sugar and water in a small clean saucepan and over a high heat, bring it to the boil. Boil rapidly until the sugar has turned into a dark caramel. Pour the caramel over the hazelnuts and allow to cool at room temperature for 2 hours, until set hard. Break up the praline into pieces and pulse in a food processor into course crumbs. Set aside until ready to serve.

While the praline is cooling, prepare the poached fruits. The quinces take much more cooking than the apples and pears, so it's a good idea to poach them separately beforehand and just add them to the cooked compote at the end.

To poach the quinces, peel them, leaving them whole, place in a saucepan and cover with the water and sugar. Add the vanilla seeds, cinnamon, and the lemon juice (this prevents the quinces discolouring). Cover the surface of the liquid with a disc of baking parchment and bring the mixture to the boil. Turn down to a gentle simmer and poach until soft. The poaching time will vary depending on the size and ripeness of the fruit but it may take up to 20 minutes. Once cooked, leave the quinces in the poaching syrup to cool.

Slice each apple and pear quarter into about 3 wedges. Place into a saucepan and add enough of the quince poaching syrup just to cover the apples and pears. Bring to the boil and turn down to a gentle simmer. Poach until the fruit is

soft – about 5–7 minutes – then remove from the heat. Remove the quinces from their poaching syrup, cut into wedges and add to the apples and pears. Set aside until ready to serve then gently reheat the fruit in the poaching syrup.

For the pudding, preheat your oven to 160°C/Gas Mark 3. Grease the inside of a the cake tin with butter, then dust with flour. Give the tin a couple of taps over the sink to release any excess flour.

Bring the water to the boil in a saucepan. Add the dates and simmer for a couple of minutes, until they have softened. Mix in the bicarbonate of soda and allow the dates to stand for about 10 minutes. The bicarbonate of soda will break the dates down further so they are easily distributed through the pudding.

Beat the butter and sugar until light and fluffy. Add the eggs, one at a time, mixing well after each addition, before adding the next. Sift the flour and baking powder together then stir them into the egg mixture. Add the date mixture and the vanilla extract and mix well until all the ingredients are well combined. I remember being worried that the mixture seemed a little wet the first time I made this pudding but rest assured, all was fine when it emerged from the oven.

Pour the mixture into the prepared tin, allowing plenty of room for the pudding to rise. Place the tin on the middle shelf of the oven and bake for 30 minutes. To test if it's ready push the blade of a small knife or a skewer into the centre. If it comes out clean, the pudding is ready.

continued on page 254

continued from page 252

Allow to cool in the tin for 30 minutes before turning out carefully on to a wire cooling rack. Once cool, trim the edges from the cake and slice into 12 evenly-sized squares. Wrap each portion in clingfilm and store in the fridge until serving.

When ready to serve, make the toffee sauce. Place the sugar into a heavy-based saucepan and mix in the water so all the sugar is wet. Heat the pan over a medium-high heat to melt the sugar and bring it to the boil. Have a pastry brush and a glass of water to hand to brush down the sides of the pan should any sugar crystals start to form. Once the sugar has reached a dark caramel, switch off the heat source and gently stir in the cream, followed by the butter. Be very careful as it will boil violently when the cream hits the hot caramel. Keep stirring until you have a smooth sauce, then keep warm over a low heat.

To serve, heat the number of pudding portions you need in the microwave, or if you don't have a microwave, cover with foil and reheat in a low oven. Remove the clingfilm carefully and cut a corner out of each steaming hot portion with a round biscuit cutter. Place in serving bowls with the corner slightly separated from the rest of the pudding. Spoon the warm poached fruits down between the two pieces of pudding and pour the toffee sauce liberally over the top. Finish with a generous spoonful of clotted cream and a light sprinkling of hazelnut praline. Any pudding you don't need with keep for 5 days in a sealed container in the fridge.

Warm tapioca pudding with rhubarb and stem ginger compote serves 8

British school children have aptly nicknamed this dessert 'frogspawn' due to its appearance. It has been served as school dinners for years at colleges and schools the length and breadth of the country. Being from New Zealand, I was never exposed to the school-dinner culture, but my mother used to make this on occasion at home. She would use sago instead of tapioca. Pearl sago is a very similar starch product and can be used as a substitute for tapioca.

I'm not a huge fan of candied stem ginger, but combined with rhubarb, it's wonderful. You could fold some of this compote through whipped cream and serve it in glasses, as a simple fool with shortbread fingers.

165g small pearl tapioca (not instant)
1½ litres whole milk
5 egg yolks
2 vanilla pods, split in half and seeds scraped
160g caster sugar
a pinch of table salt
100ml double cream

For the rhubarb and stem ginger compote
300g forced rhubarb
150g caster sugar
30g stem ginger, cut into fine strips
2 tsp stem ginger syrup

Soak the tapioca in 500ml of the milk for 1 hour.

Meanwhile, make the compote. Place the rhubarb, sugar, stem ginger and stem ginger syrup into a heavy-based saucepan and cook over a medium heat, stirring occasionally for roughly 4–5 minutes, until the rhubarb is soft but still holding its shape. Strain the rhubarb through a colander set over a bowl, to catch the liquid. Pour the liquid back into the saucepan and boil to reduce by about half, until a thick pink syrup is achieved. Place the strained rhubarb into a bowl and pour the reduced syrup over the top, stirring gently. Cool the compote to room temperature before serving.

In a medium heavy-based saucepan, whisk together the remaining litre of milk, egg yolks, vanilla pod and seeds, sugar and salt. Add the soaked tapioca and milk and bring the mixture slowly to the boil over a low-medium heat, stirring slowly but constantly with a wooden spoon. Once boiling point is reached, lower the temperature to a gentle simmer, stirring continuously. The pudding will gradually start to thicken. It will take about 20 minutes until the tapioca is completely translucent and cooked.

Remove the pudding from the heat and cover with a disc of baking parchment so it doesn't form a skin as it cools. Leave the pudding to stand until it's lukewarm.

Divide the pudding between serving bowls and top with a generous spoonful of the rhubarb and stem ginger compote.

Cox's apple and bramble crumble with custard serves 6–8

When I lived in Colchester, there was a huge belt of brambles growing just across the road from my local supermarket, which I used to raid every autumn. I remember one year a man walking past me with his groceries. He had a punnet of blackberries sitting on top. I asked him why he paid for them when they were growing here for free. He pointed to my purple stained hands and to all the scratches up my arms and said, 'That's why,' and kept walking. For me, it's a small price to pay for the personal satisfaction of cooking something you've foraged.

It's a good idea to use two varieties of apples for crumble. One that breaks down into a sauce and one that holds its shape well. The Bramley apple is a fantastic cooking apple with a big flavour. However, they disintegrate very quickly when cooked. But the addition of some Cox's or Granny Smith apple will give your compote those desirable chunks and more texture.

300g brambles
150g butter
2 Bramley apples, peeled, cored and cut into 2cm dice
1 vanilla pod, split in half and seeds scraped
200g caster sugar
4 Cox's or Granny Smith apples, peeled, cored and cut into 2cm dice
juice of 1/2 lemon

For the crumble topping
125g plain flour
125g caster sugar
75g ground almonds
75g cold butter, cubed

For the custard (a British staple)
300ml double cream
300ml milk
1 vanilla pod, split in half and seeds scraped
7 egg yolks
100g caster sugar
2 tbsp cornflour

To wash the brambles, fill the kitchen sink with cold water and drop them in. Move them around gently in the water. The berries will drop to the bottom and any twigs, leaves or other undesirables will float to the top where they can be scooped off. Drain the brambles on kitchen paper.

Melt the butter in a large saucepan over a medium-high heat. When the butter is hot and foaming, add the Bramley apples, vanilla pod and seeds and sugar. Cook until the apples are soft and broken down, stirring regularly to avoid them catching on the bottom of the pan.

Reduce the heat slightly and add half the Cox's apples to the purée. Add the lemon juice (this will help prevent the compote from discolouring). Cook the first batch of Cox's apples until they are starting to soften, then add the rest. Cook the compote, stirring regularly, until the diced apple is almost cooked and still holding its shape. Finally, fold in the brambles and pour into your chosen baking dish and allow to cool.

Preheat your oven to 180°C/Gas Mark 4.

Make your crumble topping. Place all the ingredients into a food processor and blend until the mixture looks like breadcrumbs. If you don't have a food processor, rub the butter into the dry ingredients with your fingers, until you reach the breadcrumb consistency. Sprinkle the crumble topping over the fruit. Use a bit more than you think you'll need, as it cooks down substantially. Bake the crumble for 25–30 minutes, until a golden crust has formed and the fruit is boiling over the sides of the dish.

Make your custard. Put the cream, milk and vanilla pod and seeds into a small saucepan and bring to the boil. Remove from the heat and leave to infuse for about 10 minutes.

In a bowl, mix the egg yolks, sugar and cornflour together with a whisk. Remove the vanilla pod from the cream and pour over the egg mixture, gradually whisking as you pour. Return the custard to the pan and cook gently over a low heat, stirring constantly with a wooden spoon until the custard thickens. Be patient with this and don't turn up the heat. If the custard gets too hot too quickly it will scramble. Remove from the heat and give a final mix with a whisk. Strain through a fine-mesh sieve into a clean bowl and serve hot on the side with the crumble. Any leftover custard can be stored in the fridge for up to 3 days, covered with a disc of baking parchment so a skin doesn't form.

Eton mess with strawberries and elderflower serves 4

This is without a doubt my favourite English pudding, and probably the simplest to prepare. It is traditionally served at Eton College's annual cricket match against the students of rival Winchester College and dates back to the early 19th century.

Traditionally served with strawberries, it also works well with other fresh summer fruits.

I love the addition of elderflower in this recipe. It adds a beautiful fragrance to the dish. The Scots have a similar dessert called cranachan, using whipped cream, raspberries, honey, whisky and toasted oats. This combination is equally successful.

500g strawberries, hulled
50g caster sugar
1/2 vanilla pod, seeds scraped
400ml whipping cream
50ml concentrated elderflower cordial
50g icing sugar
4 small meringue nests

Grade the strawberries into two even piles. Save the best presentation strawberries for the mess, and place the remaining half of the strawberries into a saucepan with the caster sugar. Add a couple of tablespoons of water and cook over a medium heat. As the strawberries cook they will release all their juices and boil down into a sauce. Push the sauce through a sieve using the back of a spoon, leaving only the seeds behind. Allow the strawberry sauce to cool in the fridge.

Put the vanilla seeds into a large bowl with the whipping cream, elderflower cordial, and icing sugar. Using a whisk, whip the cream until it reaches the soft peak stage. To check it's at the correct stage, when lifting out the whisk, the cream should stand to a peak with the tip just curling over.

Cut the remaining strawberries in half and if there are any large ones, into quarters.

To serve, crush the meringue nests into pieces and add to the whipped cream. Add a good drizzle of strawberry sauce, and most of the halved strawberries (saving a few for decorating the top). Fold the mess together to create a rippled effect and spoon into your serving dishes. Top with the reserved strawberries and a little more strawberry sauce.

Cinnamon ring doughnut with a Perry-poached pear and hot chocolate sauce
makes approximately 12 doughnuts

The inspiration for this dessert came when I was enjoying 'churros' at Thomasina Miers's restaurant, Wahaca, in Soho. Churros are South America's answer to doughnuts. The batter is squeezed straight from a piping bag into hot oil, where it's fried until crispy then tossed in sugar and served with a rich chocolate sauce.

Poached pears and chocolate are a beautiful partnership, and served alongside a hot crispy doughnut and a generous dollop of whipped cream, they complete this irresistible dessert. William pears are probably the best to use for the poaching due to the fact they are a bit smaller than Comice or Conference pears, and present well. However, if you can only find large pears, use half for each plate. Remember, the doughnut is the star of the show and the pear its 'Debbie McGee', not the other way round.

Try to find a good Perry for this recipe, rather than settling for a commercial pear cider. The Perry won't be quite so sweet and will have a more natural pear flavour.

100g caster sugar, plus about 200g
  to coat the doughnuts
1 tsp ground cinnamon
2 eggs
100g soured cream
1 tsp vanilla extract
350g plain flour
2½ tsp baking powder
1 tsp bicarbonate of soda
½ tsp salt
whipped cream to serve

For the Perry-poached pears
500ml Perry
100ml water
6 ripe Williams pears
300g caster sugar

For the chocolate sauce
150g dark cooking chocolate, chopped
  into small pieces
150ml double cream

To poach the pears, pour the Perry and water into a saucepan, just large enough to hold the 6 pears standing on their ends. Add the sugar, but don't heat yet. Poached pears should always be started in cold syrup.

Peel the pears leaving the stalk attached. Remove the core with a corer or melon baller, leaving the pears whole, and place them in the saucepan. If they are not submerged, add some more water and a little more sugar to just cover. Place a disc of baking parchment directly over the pears and bring them up to a gentle simmer over a medium heat. Don't boil the pears or they will overcook and become mushy. The cooking time will depend on the size and ripeness of the fruit. The harder the pear, the longer it will take to cook – 15–25 minutes should be enough time. Check for readiness with a small knife and allow to cool naturally in the poaching liquor. Reheat gently in the liquor when ready to serve.

Preheat your deep-fat fryer to 170°C.

Mix about 200g of caster sugar in a dry bowl with the ground cinnamon.

For the doughnut dough, beat the sugar and eggs together in a clean bowl with a whisk, until light and fluffy. Gently fold in the soured cream and vanilla extract. Sift the dry ingredients into the mixture and fold together to form a ball of soft dough. Knead the dough on a lightly floured work surface for about 6–8 minutes. As you knead you will feel the dough becoming more elastic. This is what you are trying to achieve. If the dough isn't worked sufficiently, when the doughnuts hit the hot oil they will develop cracks as they swell.

With a rolling pin, roll out the dough on a lightly floured work surface, to about 1cm thick. Using a 7cm round biscuit cutter, cut out 12 circles. To create the hole in your ring doughnuts use a 2cm cutter. Test the mixture by putting one of the small circles cut from the middle of the rings in the fryer to see if it cracks. If the test doughnut cracks, knead the dough for a couple more minutes.

For the best results fry the doughnuts straight after they've been cut so they don't develop a dry crust. Allowing them to dry out could also cause them to crack as they cook.

Deep-fry the rings for approximately 1½–2 minutes on each side. Using a slotted spoon, carefully remove the doughnuts from the fryer and drain them briefly on kitchen paper. Toss the doughnuts in the cinnamon sugar to coat them. Serve hot.

Meanwhile, make the chocolate sauce. Place the chocolate in a heavy-based saucepan with the cream. On a low heat, warm the cream until the chocolate starts to melt into it. Stir constantly until a smooth rich sauce is achieved. Serve while still hot.

Mrs Wade's plum and almond tart with bay leaf ice cream serves 4

I first cooked this tart when working in the small village of Nayland in Suffolk. Nayland lay in a shallow, very sheltered valley and seemed to have its own microclimate. Fruit ripened on the trees a good two weeks earlier than in other areas only a short distance away. Walking through the village one day, I noticed three huge Mirabelle trees growing in a yard that backed on to a paddock. I went up to the house to see if there was anyone home and the door was answered by Mrs Wade, a woman who had been living in the village for many years. She was more than happy for me to collect the fruit as there was too much for her to eat herself. I filled the freezer with individual tarts and had them on the menu for over a month. You can use any variety of plums for this recipe. In the past I've also used greengages, Victoria plums, and Marjorie's Seedling.

The recipe for the almond cream makes about 500g, which is more than required for this pudding . However it will keep in the fridge for about a week and can be used to enhance any fruit tarts. It works very well with apricots in particular.

400g ripe plums, halved and stoned
150g caster sugar
600g ready-made puff pastry, chilled
80g Almond Cream (see below),
    at room temperature
50g flaked almonds
3 egg whites beaten with 50g icing
    sugar
icing sugar, to dust
Bay Leaf Ice Cream (see page 273),
    to serve

For the almond cream
125g butter
125g caster sugar
2 eggs
½ tsp lemon juice
2 tsp Amaretto (optional)
125g ground almonds
1 tbsp plain flour

Start by making the almond cream. In a clean mixing bowl, whisk the butter and sugar until light and fluffy. Add the eggs, one at a time, mixing gently after each addition. Don't be too vigorous with your mixing at this stage as the mixture may curdle.

Carefully fold in the lemon juice, Amaretto, ground almonds and flour. Mix well and store covered in the fridge until required. Allow the mixture to come back to room temperature before using so it's softer and easier to work with.

Pre-heat your oven to 200°C/Gas Mark 6.

Lay the plums on a baking tray, flesh-side up, and sprinkle liberally with the caster sugar. Roast in the oven for 10–15 minutes. The cooking time will depend on the size of the plums – smaller plums will take less time to cook. Remove the plums from the oven once soft and leave to cool on the tray. Lower the oven setting to 200°C/Gas Mark 6.

Cut the chilled pastry into two even pieces and on a lightly floured surface, roll each out to a thickness of 3-4mm. Out of one, cut four 12cm discs for the tart bases and out of the other, use a rolling lattice cutter to cut one sheet of lattice approximately 35cm long, large enough to stretch across the four tart bases at once. If you don't have a lattice cutter you can create your own lattice by criss-crossing thin strips of pastry. Transfer the four bases to a sheet of baking parchment, and place the lattice on a separate sheet, then transfer the bases and the lattice to the fridge to rest for about 20 minutes (puff pastry has a high butter content and is much easier to work with when chilled).

Place the four bases (still on their baking parchment) on to a large baking tray. Using a fork, prick holes into the centre of each disc leaving a 1½ cm border around the edge free of holes. Docking the centre of each disc in this manner, stops the pastry from rising so freely, enabling the undocked edges to rise up and encase the tart.

Spread the almond cream evenly on to the centre of each pastry base, still leaving the edges clear. Lay the roasted plums, skin-side down, on to the thin layer of almond cream and sprinkle them with the flaked almonds.

Using a pastry brush, brush the exposed edge of each tart base lightly with the egg white mixture so the lattice tops have something to stick to. Stretch the piece of lattice pastry across the four tarts and press down gently around the edge of each tart so the lattice sticks into place. Using the same 12cm cutter used for the bases, cut around the tarts again and remove the wasted lattice. Brush the lattice tops with the egg white and rest again in the fridge until you're ready to bake.

Bake the tarts for 25–30 minutes, until the pastry is golden and crispy. Dust with icing sugar and serve hot, straight from the oven, with a ball of bay leaf ice cream.

Almond cake with poached apricots and yoghurt cream

makes 2 small loaf cakes

This recipe comes from the very first kitchen I worked in, The Beacon, in Wellington, New Zealand. I started in as a dishwasher, and knew literally on my first night that this environment would be my life. My head chef, Dean Clure, was a huge inspiration to me in the early days. He had a particular flare for desserts and this was one of my favourites. Please note you will need to make the yoghurt cream the day before you wish to serve the cake. Any almond cake surplus to requirements can be stored for 3 days in an airtight cake tin.

450g softened butter, plus extra to
     grease
450g caster sugar
6 eggs, separated
225g fine polenta flour, sifted
450g ground almonds
1½ teaspoons of baking powder
¼ tsp table salt
grated zest of 4 lemons, plus the juice
     of 1 lemon
2 tsp vanilla extract

For the poached apricots
500ml water
500g sugar
1 vanilla pod, split in half, seeds
     scraped
12 ripe apricots, halved and stoned

For the yoghurt cream
200ml double cream, whipped to soft
     peaks
200ml Greek-style yoghurt
100g soft light brown sugar

Start by making the yoghurt cream. In a small plastic storage container, spread the whipped cream and yoghurt in 1cm layers sprinkling brown sugar between each layer. Allow to rest in the fridge overnight so the sugar dissolves.

Make the poached apricots. In a saucepan, bring the water, sugar and vanilla seeds to the boil and turn down to a simmer. Add the apricots and simmer gently until they are soft. The cooking time depends on how ripe they are, but they shouldn't take longer than about 5–7 minutes.

Remove from the heat and allow the apricots to cool. Store them in their poaching syrup in the fridge until required. The apricots are best poached on the day of serving as they tend to discolour if left overnight.

Preheat your oven to 160°C/Gas Mark 3.

Beat the butter and sugar until light and fluffy. Add the egg yolks, one at a time, mixing well after each addition, before adding the next. Add the polenta flour, ground almonds, baking powder and salt, and continue to mix. Add the lemon zest and juice and vanilla extract and mix until all the ingredients are well incorporated.

In a very clean, dry bowl, whisk the egg whites until they reach the soft peak stage. To check they are at the correct stage, lift out the whisk – the egg whites should stand to a peak with the tip just curling over.

Fold half the whisked egg whites into the cake mixture until just incorporated, then fold in the second half. Try not to overwork the mixture or you risk knocking the air out of the egg whites. This air keeps the cake light and helps it to rise.

Grease the inside of two 450g loaf tins with butter and then dust with flour. Give the tins a couple of taps over the sink to release any excess flour. Divide the mixture between the two tins. They should only be half filled, leaving plenty of room for the cakes to rise.

Place the cakes on the middle shelf of the oven and bake for 45 minutes. To test they are ready push the blade of a small knife or a skewer into the middle of each loaf – if it comes out clean, the cakes are ready.

Leave to cool in the tins for 30 minutes before carefully turning out on to a wire cooling rack to cool completely.

To serve, place a slice of cake down on each plate. Spoon a little of the apricot poaching syrup over the slice to moisten it. Lay two apricot halves against the cake and finish with a generous dollop of yoghurt cream.

Soft-centred chocolate pudding with sea-salted caramel ice cream serves 8

This is one of our best-selling puddings at Roast. As you dig your spoon in, the molten centre oozes out on to the plate. It's a real crowd-pleaser at dinner parties and if you're planning on preparing it regularly, I strongly suggest you invest in a set of stainless steel rings about 7cm in diameter by 4cm in height. If you haven't got rings, but wish to prepare the puddings anyway, try baking and serving them in ramekins – they just won't have quite the same effect visually when you cut into them.

A great adaptation to this dessert, and one we've played with in the restaurant, is to make jelly (blood orange or raspberry work well with the chocolate) and freeze it into small ice cubes. Stuff the centre of each pudding with a frozen jelly cube so that as the pudding bakes, the jelly melts, pouring out on to the plate once the pudding is cut into.

200g butter
200g dark chocolate (70 per cent cocoa solids)
4 eggs, plus 4 yolks
100g caster sugar
40g plain flour
Sea-salted Caramel Ice Cream (see page 275), to serve

You will also need: 8 stainless steel rings, about 7cm in diameter by 4cm high or ramekins of a similar size

Place the butter and chocolate in a large heatproof bowl and set the bowl over a pan of barely simmering water, making sure the level of water doesn't touch the bottom of the bowl. Melt the butter and chocolate slowly with the heat of the steam, stirring regularly. Once the butter and chocolate have melted completely and are well mixed, place the bowl to one side and allow to cool slightly for about 5 minutes.

In a large mixing bowl, whisk the whole eggs, egg yolks and sugar until light and fluffy. Fold the chocolate and butter mixture into the whisked eggs using a large metal spoon, then sift over the flour. Fold the flour into the mixture gently with the spoon trying not to knock too much air out of the eggs.

Line the inside of each ring with greaseproof paper. Place on to a baking tray lined with a sheet of greaseproof paper (if using rings; there's no need for the paper if you're using ramekins) and pour in the mixture. Leave about 1cm of room at the top of each ring to allow the puddings to rise.

Place the puddings in the fridge to set for at least 30 minutes or until you're ready to bake them. You can make them several hours in advance. Preheat your oven to 180°C/Gas Mark 4.

Bake the puddings for 9 minutes, until cooked on the outside but still gooey in the centre. Once ready, if using rings, place all the puddings, still in their rings, on to serving plates using a flat

broad spatula. Using an oven cloth, so you don't burn your fingers, carefully remove the hot rings, then peel off the greaseproof paper. If using ramekins, simply place them on the plates. Serve with sea-salted caramel ice cream. If you don't want to go to the effort of making the sea-salted caramel ice cream, try it with shop-bought vanilla ice cream, clotted cream or even crème fraîche.

Jelly and Ice Cream

I thought it important to pay homage to this great institution. It's the dessert that was most often served at home when I was a child, and it has become commonplace on the menu at Roast in various combinations. Have a bit of fun with the jelly moulds; there are so many different shapes available online these days. You can either make individual jellies or one large jelly to present at the table. If you decide on making a large jelly you may need to increase the number of gelatine leaves you use to ensure it won't collapse. As a rule, for large jellies I use 1 leaf (2g) of gelatine per 100ml of liquid. Larger jellies should always be set overnight, just to be sure!

If you're a keen home cook and like to dabble in desserts, then spoiling yourself by buying an electric ice-cream machine is a must. There is nothing more sensual in food than spooning rich velvety ice cream straight from the churn into your mouth. This simple pleasure should be on everyone's bucket list. However, if you don't have the luxury of an ice-cream machine, don't let that hold you back. You can churn ice cream by hand if you have time and patience on your side. Simply place the finished custard into a bowl in the freezer and come back to it every hour or so, giving it a good whisk. About 3–4 trips to the freezer should suffice. The idea is to incorporate a little air into your ice cream, making it light and smooth and free from large ice crystals.

Once you've become confident in the processes of making jelly and ice cream, the possibilities and flavour combinations are endless.

Blood orange jelly with
Jaffa ripple ice cream makes 4 jellies

You can use standard orange juice in this recipe but visually it's much more impressive with blood oranges.

To suspend some orange segments inside the jelly follow the same method as for the Elderflower and Summer Berry Jelly on page 270.

12g or 6 leaves of gelatine
100ml water
100g caster sugar
500g blood orange juice
Jaffa Ripple Ice Cream (see page 274),
    to serve

You will also need: four 150ml jelly moulds

Soak the gelatine leaves in cold water for 5 minutes, until soft.

Bring the water and sugar to the boil in a saucepan, then remove from the heat. Drain the gelatine well, giving it a squeeze to rid it of any excess water, then add it to the hot syrup. Stir gently until the gelatine has completely dissolved; it will only take a few seconds. Add the blood orange juice, then pass the mixture through a fine-mesh sieve. Pour into the moulds and leave to set in the fridge. Allow 3–4 hours' setting time.

To turn out your jellies for serving, dip the mould briefly in a bowl of boiling water to release it. Serve with Jaffa ripple ice cream.

Sloe gin jelly with clotted cream ice cream makes 4 jellies

It's so easy to go out and buy your sloe gin for this recipe, but the satisfaction of making your own, and the three months of painful anticipation while you wait for it to steep can be very rewarding. So much so, that I suggest you make it in larger batches, as the novelty of having it ready takes a while to wear off, and it doesn't seem to last very long! The recipe below makes approximately 1 litre but you could scale it up as necessary.

12g or 6 leaves of gelatine
350ml water
100g caster sugar
250ml Sloe Gin (see below)
Clotted Cream Ice Cream (see page 273),
  to serve

For the sloe gin
500g sloes
500g caster sugar
600ml gin

You will also need: four 150ml jelly moulds

To make the sloe gin, wash the sloes then spread them out on kitchen paper to dry. Once dry, prick each sloe a few times with a needle and divide evenly between two clean sterilised wine bottles.

Using a dry funnel, pour half the caster sugar slowly down the neck of each bottle. Follow the sugar with 300ml of gin for each. Cork the bottles and give them a good shake.

Store the sloe gin in a cool dark place for three months returning once a week for a shake.

For the jelly, soak the gelatine leaves in cold water for 5 minutes, until soft.

Bring the water and sugar to the boil in a saucepan, then remove from the heat. Drain the gelatine well, giving it a squeeze to rid it of any excess water, then add it to the hot syrup. Stir gently until the gelatine has completely dissolved; it will only take a few seconds. Add the sloe gin and pass the mixture through a fine-mesh sieve. Pour into the moulds and leave to set in the fridge. Allow 3–4 hours' setting time.

To turn out your jelly for serving, dip the mould briefly into a bowl of boiling water to release it. Serve with the clotted cream ice cream.

Elderflower and summer berry jelly with vanilla ice cream makes 4 jellies

Elderflower is one of my absolute favourite flavours and it is intrinsically British. When I made elderflower cordial for the first time a few years ago, I was blown away by the flavour obtained from a flower that doesn't actually have a very powerful scent. I definitely recommend making the cordial yourself. The recipe is great, and one I look forward to making at the beginning of every summer. The recipe for the cordial makes about 4½ litres, which is much more than you need for the jelly, but it will keep for about 2–3 weeks in the fridge and is ready to drink straight away.

12g or 6 leaves of gelatine
700ml Elderflower Cordial (see below)
about 40 individual elderflowers (optional)
4 small strawberries, hulled and quartered
4 raspberries
4 blackberries, sliced
8 blueberries
8 redcurrants
Vanilla Ice Cream (see page 276), to serve

For the elderflower cordial
16 large elderflower heads
4 litres water
450g caster sugar
3 tbsp white wine vinegar
2 lemons

You will also need: four 150ml jelly moulds

Start by making the elderflower cordial. Shake any insects from the elderflowers. Don't make the mistake of washing them with water or you will lose much of their flavour. Remove most of the stem with a pair of scissors. Place the elderflowers in a clean plastic bucket or a large bowl. Add the water, sugar, and vinegar.

Peel the rind from the lemon with a vegetable peeler. Try not to peel too deeply as you want to avoid the bitter white pith. Add the rind and the juice from both lemons. Stir the cordial until the sugar has completely dissolved. Cover and allow it to infuse for 24 hours. Strain the cordial through a muslin cloth, then bottle it. I just use washed out sterilised wine bottles.

For the jelly, soak the gelatine leaves in cold water for 5 minutes, until soft.

Bring 100ml of the elderflower cordial to the boil, then remove from the heat. Drain the gelatine well, giving it a squeeze to rid it of any excess water, and add it to the hot cordial. Stir gently until the gelatine has completely dissolved – it will only take a few seconds. Add the rest of the cordial, then pass the mixture through a fine-mesh sieve.

Suspending the berries and elderflowers evenly throughout the jelly takes patience, but the pretty, visual effect is well worth the effort. You must work in layers. Start by pouring 1cm of liquid jelly into each 150ml mould and place in the fridge for approximately 10–15 minutes to set. Add a couple of berries and a few flowers, then a little more liquid jelly and return to the fridge to set. Continue this process until all the berries and flowers are finished and your mould is full.

To turn out your jellies for serving, dip the mould briefly in a bowl of boiling water to release it. Serve with vanilla ice cream.

Pimm's Jelly with mint choc chip ice cream makes 4 jellies

A nice refreshing Pimm's on the lawn epitomises British summertime. The beverage is almost as much a tradition as the cup of tea, and the gin-based drink is downed by the pitcherful during the summer months. I'm sure you all have your own recipes for the perfect Pimm's, so the garnish for this jelly is a loose guideline – to be adapted to personal preference.

500ml lemonade
12g or 6 leaves of gelatine
200ml Pimm's
1 small orange
50g cucumber, deseeded and diced into ½cm cubes
4 small strawberries, hulled and quartered
4 mint leaves, central vein removed and sliced very finely
4 borage leaves and flowers (optional)
Mint Choc Chip Ice Cream (see page 277), to serve

You will also need: four 150ml jelly moulds

Soak the gelatine leaves in cold water for 5 minutes, until soft.

Bring 100ml of the lemonade to the boil, then remove it from the heat. Drain the gelatine well, giving it a squeeze to rid it of any excess water, and add it to the hot lemonade. Stir gently until the gelatine has completely dissolved – it will only take a few seconds. Add the rest of the lemonade and then the Pimm's. Pass the mixture through a fine-mesh sieve.

To segment the orange, using a small sharp knife, cut both ends off the orange down to the flesh. Sit the orange on its flat end, and in a curved motion, cut off the skin all the way down to the flesh, removing all of the bitter white pith. Holding the orange in the palm of your hand, carefully cut out each segment removing them one at a time and liberating them of any pips. Cut each segment in half so they are a suitable size to suspend in the jelly.

To suspend the fruit, leaves and flowers throughout the jelly you must work in layers. Start by pouring 1cm of liquid jelly into each mould and place in the fridge for approximately 10–15 minutes to set.

Add a piece of orange, a couple of cucumber cubes, some strawberry, a little mint and a borage flower, if using, to each mould then pour over a little more liquid jelly and return to the fridge to set for another 10–15 minutes. Continue this process until all of the garnish is finished and your mould is full.

To turn out your jellies for serving, dip each mould briefly in a bowl of boiling water to release it. Serve with mint choc chip ice cream.

Bay leaf ice cream

makes approximately 1.5 litres

500ml whole milk
500ml double cream
5 bay leaves
250g caster sugar
12 egg yolks

In a heavy-based saucepan, gently heat the milk, cream, bay leaves and half the sugar until it almost reaches boiling point. Stir occasionally to ensure it doesn't catch on the bottom of the pan. Remove from the heat and allow the bay leaves to infuse for 30 minutes.

In a clean, dry mixing bowl, whisk the egg yolks and remaining sugar until the yolks start to lighten in colour. Once the bay leaves have had their time to infuse, slowly pour the mixture over the yolks, whisking as you do so, then return the whole mixture to the saucepan.

Fill a large bowl with iced water and have another slightly smaller bowl and a fine-mesh sieve to hand.

Place the ice cream mixture over a very low heat and cook the custard, stirring constantly with a wooden spoon, until it starts to thicken slightly and coats the back of the spoon. Be patient; don't be tempted to raise the temperature as you will run the risk of scrambling the custard.

When ready, pour the custard through the sieve into the empty bowl. Place the bowl carefully into the ice bath to cool. Cover the custard directly with a disc of baking parchment so a skin doesn't form and cool completely before churning in an ice-cream machine.

Clotted cream ice cream

makes approximately 1.5 litres

800ml whole milk
250g caster sugar
12 egg yolks
200g clotted cream

In a heavy-based saucepan gently heat the milk and half the sugar until it almost reaches boiling point. Stir occasionally to ensure it doesn't catch on the bottom of the pan.

In a clean, dry mixing bowl, whisk together the egg yolks and remaining sugar until the yolks start to lighten in colour. Slowly pour the milk mixture over the yolks, whisking quickly so it doesn't scramble, then return the whole mixture to the saucepan.

Fill a large bowl with iced water and have another slightly smaller bowl and a fine-mesh sieve to hand.

Place the ice cream mixture over a very low heat and cook the custard, stirring constantly with a wooden spoon, until it starts to thicken slightly and coats the back of the spoon. Be patient; don't be tempted to raise the temperature as you will run the risk of scrambling the custard. Once the desired consistency is reached, fold in the clotted cream until it is well incorporated.

When ready, pour the custard through the sieve into the empty bowl. Place the bowl carefully into the ice bath to cool. Once the temperature of the custard has dropped to tepid, stir in the clotted cream until well mixed. Cover the custard by putting a disc of baking parchment directly on the surface so that a skin doesn't form and cool completely before churning in an ice- cream machine.

Jaffa ripple ice cream

makes approximately 1.7 litres

I use jam sugar in the recipe for the orange ripple as it contains pectin, which thickens it to a jammy consistency and stops the ripple from freezing too hard.

500ml whole milk
500ml double cream
grated zest of 2 oranges
250g caster sugar
12 egg yolks
200g dark chocolate buttons

For the orange ripple
3 oranges
80g jam sugar

In a heavy-based saucepan gently heat the milk, cream, orange zest and half the sugar until it almost reaches boiling point. Stir occasionally to ensure it doesn't catch on the bottom of the pan. Set the saucepan to one side and allow the zest to infuse for 15 minutes.

In a clean, dry mixing bowl, whisk the egg yolks and remaining sugar until the yolks start to lighten in colour. Slowly pour the infused milk mixture over the yolks, whisking quickly so it doesn't scramble, then return the whole mixture to the saucepan.

Fill a large bowl with iced water and have another slightly smaller bowl and a fine-mesh sieve to hand.

Place the ice cream mixture over a very low heat, add the chocolate and cook the custard, stirring constantly with a wooden spoon, until it starts to thicken slightly and coats the back of the spoon. Be patient; don't be tempted to raise the temperature as you will run the risk of scrambling the custard.

When ready, pour the custard through the sieve into the empty bowl. Place the bowl carefully into the ice bath to cool. Cover the custard by putting a disc of baking parchment directly on the surface so that a skin doesn't form and cool completely before churning in an ice-cream machine.

For the orange ripple, peel the oranges with a sharp knife, leaving no pith. Using a small knife, cut each individual segment from the orange, leaving them clean and free of any of the tough membrane that encases them.

Place the segments into a small saucepan along with any juice you manage to squeeze from the waste. Add the jam sugar and cook on a low heat until the segments break down and the liquids have reduced down to a concentrated syrup. Transfer to a bowl and store in the fridge until required.

When the ice cream is ready, spoon it into your storage container lacing it with thin, haphazard layers of orange ripple so that when serving balls you achieve the rippled effect.

Sea-salted caramel ice cream

makes approximately 1.5 litres

350g caster sugar
50ml water
600ml double cream
400ml whole milk
1 tsp sea salt
12 egg yolks

Place 250g of the sugar in a heavy based saucepan and mix in the water so all the sugar is wet. Heat the pan over a medium-high heat to melt the sugar and bring it to the boil. Have a pastry brush and a glass of water to hand to brush down the sides of the pan should any sugar crystals start to form. Once the sugar has reached a dark caramel, switch off the heat source, and gently stir in the cream slowly using a whisk. Be careful, as the cream will boil rapidly on contact with the very hot caramel. Once all the cream has been added, add the milk and the sea salt and place the pan back on a medium heat, removing it just before it boils.

In a clean, dry mixing bowl, whisk the egg yolks and remaining sugar until the yolks start to lighten in colour. Slowly pour the caramel mixture into the yolks, whisking quickly so they don't scramble, and then return the whole mixture to the pan.

Fill a large bowl with iced water and have another slightly smaller bowl and a fine-mesh sieve close to hand.

Place the ice cream base over a very low heat and, stirring constantly with a wooden spoon, cook the custard until it starts to thicken slightly and coats the back of the spoon. Be patient. Don't be tempted to raise the temperature as you will run the risk of scrambling the custard.

When ready, pour the custard through the sieve into the empty bowl. Place the bowl carefully into the ice bath to cool. Cover the custard by putting a disc of baking parchment directly on the surface so that a skin doesn't form as it cools. Churn when required, either in an ice-cream machine, according to the manufacturer's instructions, or by hand, following the method described on page 267.

White chocolate ice cream

makes approximately 1.7 litres

500ml whole milk
500ml double cream
180g caster sugar
12 egg yolks
200g white chocolate buttons

In a heavy-based saucepan gently heat the milk, cream and half the sugar until it almost reaches boiling point. Stir occasionally to ensure it doesn't catch on the bottom of the pan.

In a clean, dry mixing bowl, whisk the egg yolks and remaining sugar until the yolks start to lighten in colour. Slowly pour the hot milk and cream mixture over the yolks, whisking quickly so it doesn't scramble, then return the whole mixture to the saucepan.

Fill a large bowl with iced water and have another slightly smaller bowl and a fine-mesh sieve to hand.

Place the ice cream mixture over a very low heat, add the white chocolate and cook the custard, stirring constantly with a wooden spoon, until it starts to thicken slightly and coats the back of the spoon. Be patient; don't be tempted to raise the temperature as you will run the risk of scrambling the custard.

When ready, pour the custard through the sieve into the empty bowl. Place the bowl carefully into the ice bath to cool. Cover the custard by putting a disc of baking parchment directly on the surface so that a skin doesn't form and cool completely before churning in an ice-cream machine.

Vanilla ice cream

makes approximately 1.5 litres

500ml whole milk
500ml double cream
1 vanilla pod, split in half, seeds
  scraped
250g caster sugar
12 egg yolks

In a heavy-based saucepan gently heat the milk, cream, vanilla pod and seeds and half the sugar until it almost reaches boiling point. Stir occasionally to ensure it doesn't catch on the bottom of the pan.

In a clean, dry mixing bowl, whisk the egg yolks and remaining sugar until the yolks start to lighten in colour. Slowly pour the hot milk and cream mixture over the yolks, whisking quickly so it doesn't scramble, then return the whole mixture to the saucepan.

Fill a large bowl with iced water and have another slightly smaller bowl and a fine-mesh sieve to hand.

Place the ice cream mixture over a very low heat and cook the custard, stirring constantly with a wooden spoon, until it starts to thicken slightly and coats the back of the spoon. Be patient; don't be tempted to raise the temperature as you will run the risk of scrambling the custard.

When ready, pour the custard through the sieve into the empty bowl. Place the bowl carefully into the ice bath to cool. Cover the custard by putting a disc of baking parchment directly on the surface so that a skin doesn't form and cool completely before churning in an ice-cream machine.

Mint choc chip ice cream

makes approximately 1.5 litres

500ml whole milk
500ml double cream
250g caster sugar
12 egg yolks
50g mint leaves, bruised with the back
of a ladle
50ml crème de menthe liqueur
200g dark chocolate chips

In a heavy-based sauce gently heat the milk, cream and half the sugar until it almost reaches boiling point. Stir occasionally to ensure it doesn't catch on the bottom of the pan.

In a clean, dry mixing bowl, whisk the egg yolks and remaining sugar until the yolks start to lighten in colour. Slowly pour the hot milk and cream mixture over the yolks, whisking as you do so, then return the whole mixture to the saucepan.

Place the ice cream mixture over a very low heat and cook the custard, stirring constantly with a wooden spoon, until it starts to thicken slightly and coats the back of the spoon. Be patient; don't be tempted to raise the temperature as you will run the risk of scrambling the custard.

When ready, pour the custard into an empty bowl and stir in the bruised mint leaves. Allow the mint to infuse for 1 hour, stirring occasionally as the custard cools slowly. Once infused, strain the custard through a fine-mesh sieve, add the crème de menthe and refrigerate until completely chilled. A little alcohol is a welcome addition to an ice cream base as it keeps the ice cream soft in the freezer. Don't overdo it though, or your ice cream won't set. Churn in an ice- cream machine, adding the chocolate chips just before the ice cream is ready to be removed from the churn, or churn by hand, following the method described on page 267, in which case add the chips the fourth time you churn the mixture.

basics

Bashed neeps serves 8

This is the traditional accompaniment for haggis. There are many variations but the core ingredient is always swede. In the Orkney Isles they make a version called clapshot in which they add potato and chives. At Roast we add carrot for a little sweetness and colour.

1 large swede, peeled and cut
into 2½ cm cubes
4 carrots, peeled and chopped
into 2½ cm pieces
100g softened butter
sea salt and freshly milled black pepper

Bring a large saucepan of lightly salted water to the boil. Add the swede and boil for 15 minutes. The swede takes longer to cook than the carrot so this is added first. After the swede has cooked for 15 minutes, add the carrot. Cook for a further 15 minutes then check them – both vegetables should be cooked until quite soft so they can be mashed with a potato masher. Once the vegetables are soft, strain them in a colander and allow them to steam for a few minutes to release some of the moisture before you mash them vigorously. Try to leave the neeps with a little texture; you don't want to end up with a smooth lifeless purée. Once you're happy that your mash is the right consistency fold in the butter and season with salt and pepper.

Creamed sweetcorn serves 8

Sweetcorn is one of my all time favourite vegetables. Between the ages of 14 and 17 I had a mouth full of braces in an attempt to sort out my smile. Besides stripping me of my dignity and any chance I may have had with the girls, the braces also hugely limited what I could eat. When I finally had them removed, the first thing I had to eat was corn on the cob and I can still remember how good it tasted. If you have a teenager with braces, cheer them up with this recipe – it's easier to eat than corn on the cob and is great with all kinds of poultry.

8 ears of corn, husks removed
50g butter
2 small banana shallots, finely diced
4 sprigs of thyme, leaves only, chopped
500ml double cream
sea salt and freshly milled black pepper

Stand each ear of cob on one end, holding it at the other, and run a sharp knife down the cob, slicing off the kernels. Work your way around each ear of corn removing all the kernels. Scrape out all the juices and any pulp left in the cob carefully using the sharp edge of the knife and set aside.

Melt the butter in a large saucepan over a medium heat, then add the shallots and thyme. Cook gently, stirring regularly until the shallots are soft and translucent. This should take about 3–4 minutes.

Add the corn, including the scraped juices, and continue to cook for another 3–4 minutes, stirring regularly. Pour in the cream, and keeping the heat at medium, gently bring it to a simmer. Cook the corn in the cream for a further 4–5 minutes continuing to stir regularly until the cream has reduced to a coating consistency and the corn is cooked through. Season to your liking with salt and pepper before serving.

Sage-roasted heritage squash with smoked bacon

serves 8

Thanks to heritage seed banks there are countless varieties of squash available throughout autumn and into winter. From the common butternut to Turk's turban, spaghetti, harlequin, acorn, onion or hubbard, they come in such a huge variety of colours, shapes and sizes that when roasted with the skins left on they look spectacular on any table setting. This recipe is particularly good with Roast Chicken (see page 102).

3kg heritage squash (of different varieties, see above)
8 rashers of rindless smoked streaky bacon, cut in half
8 large garlic cloves, unpeeled
8 sprigs of sage
150ml extra virgin rapeseed oil
sea salt and freshly milled black pepper

Preheat your oven to 200°C/Gas Mark 6.

Using a large sharp knife, cut each squash in half and scoop out the seeds with a spoon. Cut the squash into large chunks, trying to keep their natural shape, and place them into a large mixing bowl. Add the bacon. Prick each clove of garlic a few times with a small pointed knife, so that as they cook they release their flavour into the oil. Add the garlic and sage to the bowl and drizzle in the rapeseed oil. Season liberally with salt and pepper and toss all the ingredients together until well coated with the oil and seasoning.

Spread the mixture out on two oven trays and roast in the oven for 40 minutes. Use large trays so the squash isn't too crowded. Turn the squash over halfway so they caramelise evenly.

Mashed potato serves 4

A wise woman once said: 'Let them be entirely free from lumps, for nothing can be more indicative of carelessness or want of skill on the part of the cook, than mashed potatoes sent to table full of these.' *Eliza Acton, 1858*

Different varieties of potato are available throughout the year and each variety has its speciality (for more on this, see page 282). This being the case, nothing is more frustrating than when buying potatoes at some supermarkets, you encounter bags labelled 'white' or 'red' potatoes. Whose idea was this? As with roast potatoes and chips, for mashing I go for a good all-rounder, such as Maris Piper, King Edward or Desiree. Try to avoid large starchy baking varieties or you'll end up with a sticky, gluey mess.

For the best results use a potato ricer rather than a masher. By using a ricer, you will not overwork the potatoes as you do with a hand-held masher as you try to rid the mash of lumps. Make sure the potatoes are hot when they're mashed and this also goes for the cream, milk and butter when added. If the ingredients are cold they won't combine as effectively as when hot.

1kg floury potatoes (Maris Piper, King Edward or Desiree)
75ml milk
75ml double cream
80g butter
sea salt

Peel the potatoes and cut them into quarters. Place them in a saucepan and cover with cold water. Add a little salt and bring the potatoes to the boil. After about 15–20 minutes, once the potatoes are soft, drain them in a colander. Allow the potatoes to stand for a few minutes so they release some steam and dry out. While they're drying out, bring the milk, cream and butter to the boil in a small saucepan, then remove from the heat. Once the potatoes have rested but are still hot, press them through the ricer back into the pan. Fold in the hot milk, cream and butter using a plastic spatula, a little at a time, until you reach the desired consistency. If you like your mash looser, add a little more hot milk. Season with salt and serve immediately.

Roast potatoes

For any roast dinner, the roast potatoes must be shown the same care and attention given to the joint itself. The customers at Roast are more particular about their roast potatoes than anything else. As I always tell the team in the kitchen, 'It's the simple things we do that we will be judged on.'

First of all you need to select the correct variety of potato. At Roast, we predominantly use Maris Piper, which is a great all-rounder. The potatoes have a good flavour and dry floury texture making smooth creamy mash, great fluffy roasties and crispy chips. If for some reason you can't find Maris Piper, readily available alternative roasting varieties include King Edward or Desiree.

At the restaurant we roast all of our potatoes in beef dripping. Not only is the practice of roasting in dripping very British but the flavour is fantastic. However, when I'm at home, the fat I choose for the potatoes depends on what they are accompanying. For roast beef, the obvious option is beef dripping. For duck or goose, I'd use duck or goose fat, and for chicken or pork, vegetable oil would be my choice. The only time I ever add any different flavours to my roasties is to accompany roast lamb. For this I use olive oil, garlic cloves, lemon wedges and rosemary. If you want to try these ingredients, add them for the last 10 minutes of the cooking time, otherwise due to the moisture they add, the potatoes won't crisp up.

The fat you choose should be of your personal preference, not just for flavour, but also health reasons. If you're worried about your cholesterol, don't be afraid to use goose fat. The lowest incidence of heart-related illness in France is in the very region where 90 per cent of their

geese are reared. No matter which fat you've chosen, for perfect roasties the basic cooking technique is always the same. Don't make the common mistake of scattering the potatoes around the joint to roast. The potatoes need a dry environment in order for them to crisp up. You should use a large heavy roasting tin to give the potatoes space between each other for air to circulate.

floury potatoes (Maris Piper,
    King Edward or Desiree)
fat of your choice (beef dripping,
    vegetable oil, duck or goose fat)
sea salt

Preheat your oven to 200°C/Gas Mark 6. If you are roasting the potatoes in the same oven as your joint of meat, cook them above the joint on the temperature specified for the meat and adjust the cooking time accordingly.

Peel the potatoes and depending on their size, cut them into halves or quarters. Place the potatoes into a saucepan and cover with lightly salted cold water. Bring the potatoes to the boil and par-boil them until the edges of the potatoes just begin to crack – this should take about 5 minutes from boiling point. Test them with a knife: they should still feel slightly hard in the centre, but the outside should be cooked. Drain the potatoes in a colander and leave them to steam for 10-15 minutes. While the potatoes are resting, add whichever fat you've chosen to a large roasting dish. Don't be shy with the amount of fat you use. The fat should be at a depth of about 1cm in the dish.

Place the roasting dish in the oven for 7–10 minutes, until the fat is very hot. Toss the potatoes gently in the colander to fluff up the edges. This fluffing creates

surface area, allowing the fat to be absorbed by the outside of the potato, crisping it up as it roasts. Carefully add the potatoes to the hot fat. When the potatoes are added, the fat should be hot enough so that it bubbles on contact, otherwise you risk the potatoes sticking to the dish. Once the potatoes are in the dish, season them with sea salt and space them evenly, turning them individually so they are completely coated in fat. Place in the oven for 20 minutes, then turn them so they cook evenly. Continue roasting for a further 15–20 minutes until the potatoes are golden and crispy. Drain off the fat and transfer the potatoes to kitchen paper to rest for a minute. Season with a little more sea salt if required before serving immediately.

Thrice-cooked chips serves 10 (depending on appetite)

There are so many different varieties of potato available these days, and all have specific qualities. At Roast we predominantly use Maris Pipers (see the introduction for Roast Potatoes on the opposite page for more on our potato choices). Any good roasting variety can be used for chipping though as the principles are the same the outcome for both should be a crunchy outer casing that stays crisp and a soft centre.

You could try King Edward, Desiree or Yukon Gold but don't bother with large baking varieties as they tend to be a bit sweet and caramelise too quickly in the fryer. At Roast we cook our chips in three stages in order to get a chip that stays crispy for longer. For an authentic chip-shop flavour, you could fry your chips in beef dripping instead of oil using the same method.

2kg large Maris Piper potatoes, peeled and cut into chunky chips
vegetable oil, for deep-frying
sea salt

Set your deep-fat fryer to 120°C. If you don't have a fryer, place the oil into a large, deep saucepan, leaving enough room at the top to allow for rapid boiling when the chips are added. Place the oil over a high heat but be very careful that it doesn't get too hot. If you have a cooking thermometer, use it so you can regulate the temperature. If not, test the heat by dropping a cube of bread into the oil; it should bubble on entry and start to brown after about 15 seconds.

Run the cut chips under cold water for 5 minutes to remove some of the starch content.

Blanch the chips in lightly salted boiling water until the edges just begin to crack, but the middle is still slightly undercooked. Doing this increases the surface area for the oil to penetrate and turn crispy. It's the same principal as fluffing up par-cooked potatoes before roasting.

Remove the chips from the boiling water and lay them out on a tray for a few minutes to allow some of the steam to escape. Fry the chips at 120°C until they are cooked through but without colouring – this shouldn't take any longer than 2 minutes. Lift the chips from the fryer and allow them to drain in the fryer basket or in a colander on kitchen paper. Turn the fryer up to 190°C and when you are ready to serve, fry the chips until golden and crispy. Note: the first two steps in this recipe can be done well in advance and the final frying at 190°C just before serving. If you decide on this, store the par-cooked chips in the fridge until you need them. They will be good for two days.

Scrumpy-battered onion rings serves 4

A few years ago I had a coeliac friend over for dinner. I wanted to prepare steak with battered onion rings so I tried making the batter with Doves Farm gluten- and wheat-free self-raising flour. I couldn't believe how long the batter held its crunch! I had made far too many onion rings that evening, and we sat around the table munching on them long after we had finished our steaks.

At work the following week, I made two batches of batter, one using the gluten-free self-raising flour and the other with standard self-raising flour. I tested them with two pieces of haddock. The standard batter was soggy after about 3–4 minutes, but the gluten-free batter stayed crisp even once the fish had completely cooled. Since then I have never looked back. It's such a pleasure to offer our coeliac guests at Roast something they'd never usually be able to eat.

For battered fish, just substitute the scrumpy for beer.

300g Doves Farm gluten- and wheat-free self-raising flour (available in the 'free from' aisle of most supermarkets), plus extra for rolling
500–600ml scrumpy (at Roast we use Scrumpy Jack)
2 litres vegetable oil, for deep-frying
4 large onions, peeled, centres removed and cut into 1cm thick rings
sea salt

Make the batter by placing the flour in a large mixing bowl. Add the cider and mix it with the flour using a balloon whisk to form a thick batter. Leave the batter to rest for 30 minutes.

Set your deep-fat fryer to 190°C. If you don't have a fryer, place the oil into a large, deep saucepan, leaving enough room at the top to allow for rapid boiling when the onion rings are added. Place the oil over a high heat but be very careful that it doesn't get too hot. If you have a cooking thermometer, use it so you can regulate the temperature. If not, test the heat by dropping a cube of bread into the oil; it should bubble on entry and start to brown after about 15 seconds.

Have to hand some kitchen paper and a slotted spoon to remove the onion rings from the hot oil. (Don't try to use spring-loaded tongs; this can be very dangerous for obvious reasons.)

To test the batter, place some more gluten-free self-raising flour in a bowl and add one onion ring, coating it with flour so the batter has something to stick to. Dip the ring in the batter then gently lower it into the oil. It will float to the top and will need turning over halfway through, in order to cook the other side. If the onion emerges with a good covering of crispy batter that is not too thick, then start frying the rest of the rings in small batches, being careful not to overload the fryer. If the batter doesn't coat the test ring, add a little more flour, or if it is too thick, add some more scrumpy. Fry the onions until golden brown and drain on kitchen paper. Season with salt and serve hot.

Boxty pancakes makes about eight 10cm pancakes

Boxty is a traditional Irish pancake made, surprisingly enough, from potatoes. Recipes vary from region to region, but I like this one, as the addition of the whipped egg whites lightens the mixture, and the pancakes soufflé slightly as they cook.

They are traditionally served with bacon as a breakfast staple, but they are very versatile. I've suggested serving them as an accompaniment to the Pan-fried Lamb's Kidneys with Bacon and Girolles (see page 144).

100g potatoes (Maris Piper or
    King Edward are best), peeled
200g mashed potato (dry mash,
    without cream, milk or butter)
150g self-raising flour

1/2 tsp bicarbonate of soda
2 eggs, separated
200ml buttermilk (or regular milk)
1 tsp sea salt
60g butter

Grate the raw potatoes, wrap them in a clean tea towel and squeeze out any excess water and starch. Place the grated potato into a large mixing bowl and add the dry mashed potato.

Sift the flour and bicarbonate of soda into the bowl and make a well in the middle for the wet ingredients. Add the egg yolks to the bowl along with the buttermilk. Mix all the ingredients together thoroughly using a sturdy whisk, to form a thick batter.

In a separate bowl, whisk the egg whites until soft peaks form, then gently fold them into the batter being careful not to knock out too much air. Season the batter with the salt.

Heat a large non-stick frying pan over a medium heat and add a knob of the butter. Spoon the mixture into the pan to form pancakes of about 10cm in diameter. Fry for 3–4 minutes or so on each side until golden and crispy. Don't cook over too high a heat or the outside will be golden before the centre is ready. Add a fresh knob of butter to the pan for each batch.

Savoury pancakes makes about 8 large crêpes

This is the recipe for the pancakes required to prepare the Venison Wellington on page 203. However, they also make a wonderful light breakfast.

240ml milk
20g butter, plus a little extra for frying
100g plain flour
2 eggs
1 tbsp chopped flat-leaf parsley

Heat the milk and butter gently in a small saucepan until the butter has melted, then allow to cool.

Sift the flour into a mixing bowl and make a well in the centre. Crack the eggs into the well and mix thoroughly with a whisk. Add the milk and melted butter mixture and continue to whisk until you have a smooth thin batter. Pass the batter through a fine-mesh sieve and add the parsley.

To cook the crêpes, heat a non-stick frying pan over a medium heat. Melt a small knob of butter in the pan then add a small ladleful of batter - the pancakes are meant to be very thin. Tilt the pan, spreading the batter all the way to the pan's edges. After about a minute the crêpe will have set on the surface; at this point, turn it carefully with a spatula and cook on the other side for about 30 seconds.

Whipped peas

This simple purée can be served with the Salt Beef Croquettes on page 170, but it's also good with pan-fried scallops, lamb's sweetbreads or even fish fingers.

Be careful not to overcook the peas or the purée will lose its freshness and vibrant colour.

500g frozen peas, defrosted
50g softened butter
sea salt and freshly milled black pepper

Bring a large saucepan of lightly salted water to the boil. Add the peas and bring back to the boil. Strain immediately and transfer the peas to a blender. Add the butter and blend to a smooth purée. Add a little warm water if required to achieve the desired consistency. Season with salt and pepper. Either serve immediately or spread on to a tray and cool quickly in the fridge so it retains its colour.

Pickled red cabbage (the traditional accompaniment for Lancashire hotpot) serves 8

300ml red wine vinegar
3 dried allspice berries
1 bay leaf
1 tbsp caster sugar
1 tsp sea salt
$\frac{1}{4}$ tsp freshly milled black pepper
$\frac{1}{2}$ red cabbage, cored and finely shredded

Bring the vinegar to the boil in a saucepan with the allspice, bay leaf, sugar, salt and pepper. Once boiled remove from the heat and allow to cool.

Place the shredded cabbage into a large sterilised pickling jar and pour over enough infused vinegar to cover. Cover with a lid.

Allow the cabbage to pickle for at least 24 hours (at room temperature or in the fridge) before use. The pickled cabbage will keep in the fridge for six months and will only improve in that time.

Yorkshire puddings makes 10–12 large puddings

There are many rules to follow when making Yorkshire puddings and sometimes, even if all are followed to the letter, they still may not come out as you had hoped. They're temperamental. The rules at Roast are as follows:

• Have designated Yorkshire pudding baking trays (see below). Use the same ones each time and do not wash them. Just wipe them clean with kitchen paper. If they're washed the puddings tend to stick.

• The mix must be made the previous day and left to rest in the fridge overnight.

• The beef dripping must be very hot before the batter is poured into the moulds.

• Once in the oven, under no circumstances can the door be opened.

• Allow the puddings to rest in the trays for 2–3 minutes before attempting to release them.

If you follow these guidelines you should be okay but I can't make any promises. Good luck!

6 eggs
200g plain flour, sifted
200ml milk
500g beef dripping
1 tsp sea salt

To make large Yorkshire puddings you will need a shallow muffin tin with moulds that each hold about 80ml of batter.

In a large mixing bowl beat the eggs with a whisk. Add the sifted flour and mix well to form a thick batter. Pour in the milk in stages, mixing well after each addition until all the milk is added. Whisk the batter until it's completely smooth. Do not add the salt at this stage as it affects the stability of the eggs. Cover with clingfilm and rest in the fridge overnight.

The next day, preheat your oven to 180°C/Gas Mark 4.

Half fill each mould in the baking tray with beef dripping and place the tray in another larger flat tray or roasting tin. The reason for this is that when you add the batter the beef dripping will overflow requiring something underneath to catch the drips. Place the trays into the oven.

While the dripping is heating up, stir the salt into the batter and check the consistency. It tends to thicken in the fridge as it rests. The batter should not be too thick - it should only just lightly coat the back of a spoon. Add more milk if required, to reach this consistency.

After the dripping has been in the oven for about 10 minutes, it should be sufficiently hot. Pull the tray from the oven and carefully pour the batter into each mould right to the rim. Place the puddings back into the oven and set the timer for 20–25 minutes. Under no circumstances should the oven door be opened otherwise the puddings will drop and not rise to their full potential.

When the timer goes off, pull the trays out of the oven and leave the puddings to rest for a couple of minutes before releasing them from the tray. You can also make the puddings an hour or two in advance and just put them back in the hot oven for a couple of minutes before serving.

Suet pastry makes about 750g

There are important rules to follow when making suet pastry. Your suet, butter and water must be cold so that when you mix them with the flour the suet and butter don't soften too much and lose their form – the shreds should be flecked evenly through the final dough.

The second important rule is when bringing the dough together into a ball with your hands, be careful not to overwork it or the pastry will shrink during cooking and the texture will be tough rather than flaky. This is suitable for a pie crust or steamed pudding.

100g butter, chilled then coarsely grated
140g shredded beef suet, chilled
375g self-raising flour
1½ tsp salt
approximately 130ml cold water
 (from the fridge)

Place the chilled butter and suet into a large mixing bowl. Add the self-raising flour and salt and using the blade of a butter knife or palette knife, mix the ingredients together. Once the dry ingredients are well mixed and each individual shred of butter and suet is coated, slowly add the water a little at a time, continuing to mix with folding motions of the knife. The reason you use the blade of a knife is that the metal blade is cold and its shape works the pastry less than if you were using a wooden spoon or your hands.

Continue to add water until the dough starts to come together. Adding the water is not an exact science, you may need a few more drops if it seems too dry. Finish bringing the dough together with your hands to form a ball, until the sides of the bowl are clean. Do not overwork the dough or the pastry will be tough. The final product should be an elastic ball of dough flecked with shreds of suet and butter. Wrap the dough in clingfilm and allow to rest in the fridge for 30 minutes before use.

Preserved lemons

8 unwaxed lemons, plus extra lemon
 juice
a 2½ cm piece of cinnamon stick
2 star anise
100g caster sugar
150g sea salt

If you can't manage to find unwaxed lemons just give them a good scrub.

Make a criss-cross cut into the top of each lemon to a depth of about halfway though.

Crush the cinnamon stick and star anise in a pestle and mortar and mix with the sugar and salt. Stuff the mixture into the cuts in the lemons and place the lemons in a sterilised jar large enough to hold them. Add the remaining curing mixture and just cover with cold water. Screw the lid on tightly and store in a cool dark place for 2–3 months. The curing mixture will draw the juice out of the lemons creating a brine as it mixes with the salt and sugar. Give the jar a good shake once a week or so but make sure the lemons stay submerged or they may develop a white mould, which doesn't look great but is harmless.

Bramley apple sauce makes about 300ml

In 1809 a young girl by the name of Mary Ann Brailsford planted some apple pips in her back garden in Southwell, Nottinghamshire. Thirty-seven years later, her cottage was bought by Matthew Bramley, a local butcher. A local nurseryman, Henry Merryweather, asked if he could take cuttings from the tree and start to sell the apples. Bramley agreed, but insisted the apple should bear his name, so Merryweather named it 'Bramley's Seedling'. Over the years, 'Bramley's Seedling' won great acclaim as the UK's favourite cooking apple. But disaster struck in 1900 when the original Bramley tree was blown down in a violent storm. However, the tree somehow survived and is still bearing fruit to this day. To cut a long story short, those few pips planted by a little girl in her garden in Nottinghamshire over 200 years ago are responsible for what is today a £50 million industry, with commercial growers across Kent, East Anglia and the West Midlands.

40g butter
4 large Bramley apples, peeled, cored and roughly diced
1 tsp lemon juice
50g caster sugar

Melt the butter on a medium heat in a saucepan. Add the diced apple, lemon juice and sugar. Cook the apples down, stirring regularly, until they are completely soft. This should only take 8–10 minutes. Once they're soft, give the sauce a thorough whisk until it's nice and smooth.

Taste the sauce and add more sugar if you find it too tart, but remember the whole marriage between roasted pork and Bramley apple sauce is based on the tartness of the apples cutting through the fat and crackling of the pork. It is truly a partnership of perfection.

Bread sauce makes just over 1 litre

This very simple creamy sauce is ideal with roasted birds other than duck or goose. Duck and geese have a high fat content and are better served with a more acidic sauce to cut through that fat. Bread sauce is too rich for this.

1 onion
1 bay leaf
3 cloves
1 litre milk
8 thick slices of white bread, crusts removed
30g butter
sea salt and freshly milled black pepper

Peel the onion, leaving it whole. Lay the bay leaf across the onion and pin it in place with the cloves, using them as studs to hold it in place. Place the studded onion into a small saucepan and cover it with the milk. Over a medium heat, bring the milk to the boil gradually, being careful as it comes up not to let it boil over. Set aside and allow the infusion to cool down to room temperature giving the onion, bay leaf and cloves enough time to impart their flavour.

While the milk is infusing, pulse the bread in a food processor leaving the breadcrumbs course so that the resulting sauce isn't too smooth.

Once the milk infusion has cooled pour two thirds of it into a fresh saucepan, leaving the studded onion behind. Bring the infusion up to a gentle simmer and slowly whisk in two thirds of the breadcrumbs. Turn the heat down to very low and continue to stir – as the milk is absorbed by the breadcrumbs, the sauce will thicken. The correct consistency should resemble a loose porridge. Add more milk infusion or more breadcrumbs until the desired consistency is reached and then whisk in the butter and season with salt and pepper. Serve immediately – if allowed to stand for too long the sauce may set.

Mum's mint relish makes enough to fill two 500ml jars

When I was a child, we always had a few jars of this fantastic mint relish ready to be served with barbecued lamb chops or roast leg of lamb on a Sunday. It even works well as a dressing for a crisp bean salad. My mother used to make it in batches as it keeps indefinitely stored in a cool dark corner of the pantry.

300g ripe tomatoes
5 shallots, finely chopped
50g raisins, roughly chopped
100g mint leaves, chopped
300g Granny Smith apples, grated
375ml good-quality cider vinegar
1 tsp wholegrain mustard
250g clear honey
1 tsp sea salt

To blanch the tomatoes in order to make them easy to peel, bring a large pan of water to the boil. Have to hand a large bowl of iced water and a slotted spoon. With a small paring knife, remove the core of the tomatoes and at the opposite end make a small, shallow cross cut. Plunge the tomatoes into the boiling water and leave until the skin begins to come away from the flesh at the cross cut. This will only take a few seconds, especially if the tomatoes are very ripe. Remove from the boiling water with the slotted spoon and refresh briefly in the iced water. Carefully peel the tomatoes, cut them into quarters, then deseed and dice them finely, then mix with the shallots, raisins, mint and apple together in a large bowl.

In a saucepan, bring the vinegar, mustard, honey and salt to the boil, then pour over the rest of the ingredients. The final consistency will be a chunky relish in a loose liquid. If you wish to preserve the mint relish, decant into hot sterilised jars while the mixture is still hot and seal with the lids straight away. Otherwise keep refrigerated and it will be good for about 3 months

Mayonnaise makes almost 1 litre

6 egg yolks
20g English mustard
40g Dijon mustard
35ml white wine vinegar
500ml vegetable oil
250ml olive oil
juice of 1/2 lemon or to taste
sea salt and freshly milled black pepper

Mayonnaise is made easily by using an electric mixer with a whisk attachment, but if you don't have one it's still very simple by hand.

In a large rounded bowl whisk the egg yolks, mustards and vinegar until well combined. Slowly drizzle in the oils, whisking continuously, until the mixture is thick and emulsified. Don't rush this stage or the oils won't incorporate with

the egg yolks and your mayonnaise will split. If you don't have a spare set of hands around to hold the bowl steady, try resting it on a folded oven cloth to free up your hands. Add enough lemon juice and season with salt and pepper to your taste. If the mayonnaise is too thick for your liking, add a touch of warm water. The mayonnaise will keep for up to 2 weeks in the fridge.

Tartare sauce makes 250ml

1 gherkin, finely diced
2 tbsp capers, roughly chopped
200g Mayonnaise (see page 290)
½ small red onion, finely diced
a few sprigs of parsley, leaves only,
  chopped
a few drops of lemon juice
sea salt and freshly milled black pepper

Squeeze the pickling juices out of the diced gherkins and chopped capers and mix them through the mayonnaise along with the red onion and parsley. Add the lemon juice and season with salt and pepper to taste.

Horseradish cream makes 200g

We go through vast quantities of horseradish cream in the restaurant and have to make it in large batches. It's not the most pleasant job in the kitchen as the fumes given off while grating the horseradish are enough to reduce the whole brigade to tears.

Adjust the quantities in this simple recipe to suit your own palate.

100g fresh horseradish, peeled and
  finely grated
100g crème fraîche
sea salt

Mix the grated horseradish and crème fraîche together in a mixing bowl and season with the salt. Check the use-by date on your crème fraîche: the horseradish cream will keep in the fridge until the same date.

Lemon and rapeseed oil dressing makes 500ml

We use this dressing for so many different dishes at Roast and I always have a bottle in the fridge at home as it's really versatile. Use it to dress a light salad of delicate leaves or crisp summer vegetables. It's also good drizzled over grilled fish.

2 garlic cloves
a few sprigs of tarragon
80ml good cider vinegar
juice of 1 lemon
400ml extra virgin rapeseed oil
sea salt and freshly milled black pepper

Crush the garlic with the flat side of a knife and bruise the tarragon with the back of a spoon to release their flavours. Whisk all the ingredients together and allow to infuse in the fridge overnight. Strain and decant into a bottle so you can give it a good shake before using.

Vinaigrette makes 350ml

This recipe uses the Lemon and Rapeseed Oil Dressing, above, as its base. This is then whisked into Dijon mustard to emulsify it.

300ml Lemon and Rapeseed Oil
Dressing (see page 292)
1 tbsp Dijon mustard
iced water

Shake the lemon and rapeseed oil dressing well before measuring out the 300ml to ensure you achieve the correct ratio of oil to acid. Place the Dijon mustard in a bowl and slowly drizzle in the lemon and rapeseed oil dressing, whisking quickly to emulsify. As it thickens add a teaspoon or two of iced water to loosen. Store in a bottle in the fridge. If the vinaigrette separates, it's not a disaster; just give it a good shake before you use it to re-emulsify it.

Blood orange, honey and mustard dressing

500ml blood orange juice (plain orange juice will give the same flavour but without the vibrant colour)
100ml red wine vinegar
3 tbsp clear honey
3 tbsp wholegrain mustard
600ml rapeseed oil
sea salt and freshly milled black pepper

In a saucepan, bring the orange juice and vinegar to the boil and reduce until you're left with approximately 150ml. Remove from the heat and refrigerate to cool. Once the orange juice and vinegar mixture is cold, place into a large rounded bowl with the honey and mustard. Slowly drizzle in the rapeseed oil, whisking quickly to emulsify the dressing. Store in a bottle or jar in the fridge. If the dressing separates, it's not a disaster. Just give it a good shake before you use it to bring it back.

Rowan berry jelly

The bright red fruit of the rowan (or mountain ash) tree generally come into season towards the end of July. However, unlike their sweet summer berry brethren, such as strawberries and raspberries, rowan berries have high levels of parasorbic acid which makes intensely bitter and can also lead to a fairly nasty stomach ache. To neutralise the parasorbic acid, the berries must be frozen before preparing the jelly.

Crab apples are very high in pectin – the property that sets jelly. The pectin is highly concentrated in the seeds, so you must use the whole fruit – core and all – for the best results.

If you have trouble finding crab apples, a good substitute is to use the same weight of Bramley apple cores.

300g rowan berries, stalks removed
300g crab apples
jam sugar (the quantity may vary, as explained in the method)

You will also need: a muslin cloth and 2–4 jam jars, depending on size

Wash the rowanberries in cold water, then dry them thoroughly and freeze overnight to in order to neutralise the parasorbic acid in the fruit.

The following day thaw the fruit. Wash the whole crab apples, removing any bruised parts and cut each in half. Place the crab apples and rowan berries in a large heavy-based saucepan, adding just enough water to cover them. Bring to the boil then reduce to a simmer and cook for 25 minutes or so, until tender. Strain the mixture through a muslin cloth hanging over a bowl to catch the liquid (this will take up to 5 hours) but do not squeeze, otherwise the jelly will become cloudy.

Measure the volume of liquid you have (discard the berries) and add 450g of jam sugar per 600ml of liquid. Return the juice to a clean heavy-based pan and add the jam sugar, stirring until fully dissolved. Bring to the boil and cook rapidly for about 15 minutes, until the 'setting point' is reached. Test for this point by placing a teaspoon of the mixture on a plate in the fridge. Allow for it to cool for 5 minutes or so and then if a skin forms when you push the mixture with your fingernail it's ready to be put into jars. If you don't get a skin continue boiling for a further 10 minutes and test again.

When ready, skim the surface, allow to cool for about 7–8 minutes then pour into warmed, sterilised jars.

Gravy

When making gravy, in essence you are trying to capture all the concentrated flavour from the roasted meat left behind in the bottom of the roasting dish. I find one of the best ways to achieve this is to cook your joint on a rack set over roughly chopped onions, carrots, celery and leeks. As the joint roasts, the escaping juices drip down into the slowly roasting vegetables and mingle with them. The vegetables' natural sugars caramelise with the juices, creating a sweet sticky concentrated base to produce a sauce to complement any roast.

Deglazing your roasting dish is the next vital step. There is so much flavour to be harnessed in those dark, caramelised morsels stuck to the bottom of the dish. So whether it be with wine, beer, cider or stock, pour in your chosen liquid, boil it to help loosen and scrape off every last one.

The following recipes all use the same fundamental principles with slight variations to complement the meat you're roasting. The recipes make fairly large quantities but anything left over can be frozen in batches to be conveniently pulled out when serving a smaller joint such as the rack of lamb on page 140.

Gravy for roast beef makes approximately 1.5 litres

Use the Roast Fore Rib of Beef recipe on page 169 as the basis of your gravy, then follow the instructions below.

300ml red wine
4 tbsp plain flour
1 bay leaf
4 sprigs of thyme
1.2 litres hot Beef Stock (see page 297)
sea salt and freshly milled black pepper

Transfer all the roasted vegetables to a saucepan using a slotted spoon. Drain off all the fat left in the roasting tray. Place the roasting tray on to a medium heat and pour in the red wine to deglaze the tray. As the wine boils it will start to loosen all the flavoursome caramelised morsels, but it's a good idea to help in this process by also scraping with a wooden spoon.

Place the saucepan containing the vegetables over a medium heat and add the flour. Cook the flour gently, stirring regularly, for 2 minutes. Add the red wine and deglazed roasting juices from the roasting dish and cook for a further 2 minutes or so to evaporate any remaining alcohol. Stir well so the wine mixes with the flour and thickens. Add the bay leaf and thyme and gradually pour in the hot beef stock, stirring to avoid any lumps forming.

Bring the gravy to the boil, giving it a thorough skim with a ladle to remove any fat that collects on the surface. Turn the heat down to a simmer and reduce the liquid, skimming regularly, until you have reached a desirable gravy consistency – this should only take a few minutes. Taste the gravy to check the seasoning and adjust accordingly. Strain the gravy through a fine-mesh sieve and serve at the table.

Gravy for roast chicken makes approximately 600ml

Use the Roast Chicken recipe on page
102 as the basis of your gravy, then
follow the instructions below.

2 tbsp flour
100ml white wine
  (optional; if not using add an extra
  100ml chicken stock)
1 bay leaf
2 sprigs of thyme
600ml hot Chicken Stock (see page 298)
sea salt and freshly milled black pepper

Transfer all the roasted vegetables,
chopped wings and giblets, if using, to
a small saucepan using a slotted spoon.
Place the pan over a medium heat and
add the flour. Cook the flour gently,
stirring regularly, for 2 minutes. Add the
white wine, if using, and cook for a
further minute or so to evaporate the
alcohol. Stir well so the wine mixes with
the flour and thickens. Add the bay leaf
and thyme and gradually pour in the hot
chicken stock, stirring to avoid any
lumps forming. Bring the gravy to the
boil, giving it a thorough skim with a
ladle to remove any fat that collects on
the surface. Turn the heat down to a
simmer and reduce the sauce, skimming
regularly, until you have reached a
desirable gravy consistency. Taste the
gravy to check the seasoning and adjust
accordingly. Strain the gravy through a
fine-mesh sieve and keep warm until
ready to serve.

Gravy for game makes approximately 600ml

500g chopped game bones
1 carrot, peeled and roughly chopped
1 celery stick, roughly chopped
½ leek, roughly chopped
1 onion, peeled and roughly chopped
2 garlic cloves, unpeeled
250ml red wine
3 tbsp plain flour
3 juniper berries, crushed
1 tbsp redcurrant jelly
1 bay leaf
2 sprigs of thyme
300ml hot Chicken Stock (see page 298)
300ml hot Beef Stock (see page 297)
sea salt and freshly milled black pepper

Preheat your oven to 200°C/Gas Mark 6.

Place the game bones, carrot, celery,
leek, onion and garlic in a roasting tin
with a little vegetable oil to coat and
roast in the oven for 30 minutes, stirring
occasionally, until the vegetables are soft
and the bones nicely caramelised.
Remove from the tin and transfer to a
saucepan. Place the roasting tray on to a
medium heat and pour in the red wine to
deglaze the tray. As the wine boils it will
start to loosen all the flavoursome
caramelised morsels, but it's a good idea
to help in this process by also scraping
with a wooden spoon.

Place the saucepan containing the bones
and vegetables over a medium heat and
add the flour. Cook the flour gently,
stirring regularly, for 2 minutes. Add the
red wine and deglazed roasting juices
from the roasting tin and cook for a
further 2 minutes or so to evaporate any
remaining alcohol. Stir well so the wine
mixes with the flour and thickens.
Add the juniper berries, redcurrant jelly,
bay leaf and thyme and gradually pour in
the hot chicken and beef stocks, stirring
to avoid any lumps forming. Bring the
gravy to the boil, giving it a thorough
skim with a ladle to remove any fat that
collects on the surface. Turn the heat
down to a simmer and reduce the liquid,
skimming regularly, until you have
reached a desirable gravy consistency –
it will take about 5–10 minutes. Taste the
gravy to check the seasoning and adjust
accordingly. Strain the gravy through a
fine-mesh sieve and serve at the table.

Gravy for roast lamb makes approximately 600ml

Use the Slow-roast Shoulder of Lamb recipe on see page 135 as the basis of your gravy, then follow the instructions below.

150ml red wine
2 tbsp plain flour
1 tsp tomato purée
1 bay leaf
4 sprigs of thyme
500ml hot Lamb Stock (see page 298)
sea salt and freshly milled black pepper

Transfer all the roasted vegetables to a saucepan using a slotted spoon. Skim off all the fat left in the roasting dish but leave behind any meat juices. Place the roasting tray on to a medium heat and pour in the red wine to deglaze the tray. As the wine boils it will start to loosen all the flavoursome caramelised morsels, but it's a good idea to help in this process by also scraping with a wooden spoon.

Place the saucepan containing the vegetables over a medium heat and add the flour and tomato purée. Cook gently, stirring regularly, for 2 minutes. Add the red wine and roasting juices from the roasting dish and cook for a further 2 minutes or so to evaporate any remaining alcohol. Stir well so the wine mixes with the flour and thickens. Add the bay leaf and thyme and gradually pour in the hot lamb stock, stirring to avoid any lumps forming. Bring the gravy to the boil, giving it a thorough skim with a ladle to remove any fat that collects on the surface as it comes up. Turn the heat down to a simmer and reduce the liquid, skimming regularly, until you have reached a light gravy consistency. Taste the gravy to check the seasoning and adjust accordingly. Strain the gravy through a fine-mesh sieve and serve at the table.

Gravy for roast pork makes approximately 800ml

Use the Slow-roasted Pork Belly recipe on page 151 as the basis of your gravy, then follow the instructions below.

200ml dry cider
2 tbsp flour
1 bay leaf
2 sprigs of thyme
400ml hot Chicken Stock (see page 298)
400ml hot Beef Stock (see page 297)
sea salt and freshly milled black pepper

Transfer all the roasted vegetables from the roasting tray to a saucepan using a slotted spoon. Skim off all the fat left in the roasting dish but leave behind any meat juices. Place the roasting tray on to a medium heat and pour in the cider to deglaze the tray. As the cider boils it will start to loosen all the flavoursome caramelised morsels, but it's a good idea to help in this process by also scraping with a wooden spoon.

Place the saucepan containing the vegetables over a medium heat and add the flour. Cook the flour gently, stirring regularly, for 2 minutes. Add the cider and deglazed roasting juices from the roasting dish and cook for a further 2 minutes or so to evaporate any remaining alcohol. Stir well so the cider mixes with the flour and thickens. Add the bay leaf and thyme and gradually pour in the hot chicken and beef stocks, stirring to avoid any lumps forming. Bring the gravy to the boil, giving it a thorough skim with a ladle to remove any fat that collects on the surface. Turn the heat down to a simmer and reduce the sauce, skimming regularly, until you have reached a desirable gravy consistency. Taste the gravy to check the seasoning and adjust accordingly. Strain the gravy through a fine-mesh sieve and serve at the table.

Beef or veal stock makes 2–3 litres

At Roast we go through over 100kg of veal bones every day just to create enough stock to produce the amount of gravy we use on a daily basis. We use large knee joints that our butcher halves on a bandsaw to open the bones and allow more access to the natural gelatin inside. The pots of stock are ticking over in batches all day and all night and this is one of the most important processes in the kitchen. Whatever the stock is being used for, whether it be a soup, braise or sauce, the quality of the final product will depend entirely on the quality of stock used.

To cut down the cooking time and so it's more manageable in your kitchen at home, ask your butcher to cut the bones down into smaller pieces so they will fit more comfortably in your stock pot. Knee joints could prove difficult to obtain so ask for chopped spinal bones.

3kg chopped beef or veal bones
1 onion, peeled and cut into quarters
1 leek, white part only, cut into 4 pieces
3 celery sticks, halved
3 carrots, peeled and halved
3 garlic cloves, crushed
1 tbsp concentrated tomato purée
a few sprigs of thyme
1 bay leaf
10 black peppercorns

Preheat your oven to 200°C/Gas Mark 6.

Place the bones in a deep roasting tin and roast them for 30 minutes. Turn the bones over and roast for a further 15–20 minutes until they're well browned. Using a pair of strong tongs, place the bones into a large stockpot, leaving behind all the fat that has collected in the bottom of the roasting tin, and add enough cold water just to cover them. Bring the stock up to the boil, then turn the heat down to a gentle simmer. While the stock is coming to the boil, scatter the onion, leek, celery and carrot into the roasting tin and stir, coating them with the fat that has rendered out of the bones. Roast the vegetables for 20–30 minutes, until golden and caramelised, stirring them halfway so they cook evenly.

Once the vegetables have caramelised, add the garlic and stir in the tomato purée. Place the tray of vegetables back into the oven for a further 10 minutes to cook the tomato purée.

Once the vegetables and tomato purée are cooked, stir them into the simmering stock. Add the herbs and peppercorns and allow the stock to simmer gently for 3 hours. A helpful tip is to place the pan just slightly to one side of the hob. All the fat and impurities that rise to the surface as it simmers will collect on the cooler side of the pan and can be skimmed off easily with a ladle. Top up with a little cold water from time to time, just enough to keep the bones covered.

After 3 hours, turn off the heat and allow the stock to rest for about 20 minutes. Strain the stock gently through a fine-mesh sieve and discard the bones. Allow to cool before refrigerating. As the stock chills, any fat that is left will solidify on the surface. This can be lifted off easily and you should be left with 2–3 litres of gelatinous stock. The stock will keep in the fridge for a week but can be batch frozen for later use – use within 3 months if frozen.

more **roast**
Scan the QR code to see
Marcus making gravy for roast pork.
http://roastcookbook.com/making-pork-gravy/

Chicken stock makes 750ml–1 litre

Roast chicken is one of the meals my wife Masha and I have regularly. Once any remaining meat has been picked off the carcass for sandwiches, we make this delicious versatile stock. We use it for soups and light braises, but more often than not it's used as a base for the gravy when we have our next roast chicken.

1 roast chicken carcass, chopped into
    large pieces
1/2 onion, peeled and roughly chopped
1/4 leek, white part only, roughly
    chopped
1 celery stick, roughly chopped
1 carrot, peeled and roughly chopped
1 garlic clove, crushed

a few sprigs of thyme
1 bay leaf
10 black peppercorns
1 tsp sea salt

Place all the ingredients into a saucepan and pour in enough cold water just to cover – if you add too much water you will dilute the stock.

Bring the stock to the boil and then turn the heat down to a gentle simmer. Simmer the stock for 1 hour, skimming the surface regularly and topping up with a little cold water from time to time, just enough to keep the bones covered. A helpful tip is to place the pan just slightly to one side of the hob. All the fat and impurities that rise to the surface as it simmers will collect on the cooler side of the pan and can be skimmed off easily with a ladle.

After 1 hour, turn off the heat and allow the stock to rest for about 20 minutes so any impurities will drop to the bottom of the pan. Strain the stock gently through a fine-mesh sieve and discard the bones. Allow to cool before refrigerating. As the stock chills, any fat that is left will solidify on the surface. This can be lifted off easily and you should be left with 750ml–1 litre of gelatinous stock. The stock will keep in the fridge for 5–6 days but can be batch frozen for later use – use within 3 months if frozen.

Lamb stock makes 1.5–2 litres

This recipe makes a white lamb stock that is ideal for Lancashire Hotpot (see page 138). For a brown stock for braising lamb shanks, just roast the bones and the vegetables as you would for beef stock (see page 297).

3kg lamb spinal bones, chopped into
    pieces
1 onion, peeled and roughly chopped
1/2 leek, white part only, roughly chopped
3 celery sticks, roughly chopped
2 carrots, peeled and roughly chopped
3 garlic cloves, crushed
1 sprig of rosemary
1 bay leaf
10 black peppercorns
1 tsp sea salt

Place all the ingredients into a saucepan and pour in enough cold water just to cover – if you add too much water you will dilute the stock.

Bring the stock to the boil and then turn the heat down to a gentle simmer. Simmer the stock for 2 hours, skimming the surface regularly and topping up with a little cold water from time to time, just enough to keep the bones covered. A helpful tip is to place the pan just slightly to one side of the hob. All the fat and impurities that rise to the surface as it simmers will collect on the cooler side of the pan and can be skimmed off easily with a ladle.

After 2 hours, turn off the heat and allow the stock to rest for about 20 minutes so any impurities will drop to the bottom of the pan. Strain the stock gently through a fine-mesh sieve and discard the bones. Allow to cool before refrigerating. As the stock chills, any fat that is left will solidify on the surface. This can be lifted off easily and you should be left with 1½–2 litres of flavoursome stock. The stock will keep in the fridge for 5–6 days but can be batch frozen for later use – use within 3 months if frozen.

Fish stock makes 1.5–2 litres

When purchasing fish bones for fish stock from your fishmonger, avoid bones from oily fish such as salmon, tuna, trout, mackerel, sea bream or even sea bass. The best bones are from white flat fish, such as sole, brill or turbot. At Roast we try to use halibut bones as these large fish bones produce a flavoursome, high-yielding, gelatinous stock, good for soups and sauces.

2kg fresh white fish heads and bones
1 onion, peeled and roughly chopped
½ leek, white part only, roughly chopped
2 celery sticks, roughly chopped
½ fennel bulb, roughly chopped (optional)
1 bay leaf
a few sprigs of thyme
10 black peppercorns
1 tsp sea salt
juice of ½ lemon
a few sprigs of parsley

Using a pair of robust kitchen scissors, remove the gills underneath the flap behind each fish head and discard them. The gills are the first part of the fish to go off and will reduce the shelf life of the stock and give it an unpleasant flavour. Chop through the spinal bones with the heel of a heavy knife, or if the bones are small enough continue to use the kitchen scissors. There is a vein of blood running the length of the spine. Chopping through the spinal bones opens this vein allowing the blood to be flushed out when washed. The blood, if left, will cloud the stock and leave a bitter taste in your mouth. Place the prepared bones and heads into a bowl and run them under cold water for 10 minutes to wash them.

Place the washed bones and heads into a large saucepan and add all the ingredients except the lemon and parsley. Add cold water just to cover the bones – if you add too much water you will dilute the stock.

Bring the stock to the boil and then turn the heat down to a gentle simmer. Simmer the stock gently for 20–30 minutes skimming regularly. A helpful tip is to place the pan just slightly to one side of the hob. All the scum that rises to the surface as it simmers will collect on the cooler side of the pan and can be skimmed off easily with a ladle. After this time, add the lemon juice and parsley. Turn off the heat and allow the stock to rest for about 30 minutes so any impurities will drop to the bottom of the pan.

Strain the stock gently, ladle by ladle, through a fine-mesh sieve, trying your best not to disturb the sediment resting at the bottom of the pan. Allow the stock to cool before refrigerating. You should be left with about 1.5–2 litres of stock. The stock will keep in the fridge for 3–4 days but can be batch frozen for later use – use within 3 months if frozen.

cocktails
and wine

Spring flavours

Shard sour

50ml Hakushu 12-year-old whisky
25ml maraschino cherry syrup
  (from a jar of maraschino cherries)
20ml fresh lemon juice
5ml sugar syrup
1 egg white
lemon twist and maraschino cherries
  on a cocktail stick, to garnish

Put all the ingredients into a cocktail shaker filled with ice. Shake well, then strain into a chilled short tumbler or old-fashioned glass with an ice cube and garnish.

The twinkle stars

50ml gin
25ml Don PX sherry
10ml fresh lemon juice

Put all the ingredients into a mixing glass with some ice. Stir until cold then pour into a short tumbler filled with crushed ice and garnish. In the bar, we garnish with little lemon stars cut from lemon rind but this might be a little fiddly to do at home.

Banoffee tini

35ml your favourite rum
15ml banana liqueur
1/2 banana, roughly chopped then
  mashed
20ml cold milk
10ml double cream
5ml maple syrup
slice of unpeeled banana, to garnish

Put all the ingredients into a cocktail shaker filled with ice. Shake well, then strain into a chilled martini glass and garnish with the banana slice.

Eternal happiness

35ml gin
20ml apricot brandy
50ml lychee juice
15ml goji berry liqueur
8 mint leaves, plus a mint sprig to
  garnish

Put all the ingredients into a cocktail shaker filled with ice. Shake well, then strain into a chilled short tumbler filled with ice cubes and garnish with the mint sprig.

Summer flavours

SW19

40ml gin
20ml cointreau
20ml cucumber celery purée
10ml elderflower cordial
15ml lemon juice
strawberry slice, to garnish

To make the cucumber celery purée for this cocktail, simply blend a celery stick with two cucumbers until very smooth. And for the finishing touch we serve this cocktail with ice cubes made from lime cordial. Simply freeze undiluted cordial in an icc-cube tray. Put all the ingredients into a cocktail shaker filled with ice. Shake well, then strain into a chilled old-fashioned glass with an ice cube made with lime cordial and garnish.

Kings and queens julep

3 fresh cucumber slices
6 mint leaves
50ml cucumber gin
50ml lager
25ml honey
10ml fresh lemon juice
long, thin cucumber slice, to garnish
mint sprig, to garnish

To make this cocktail you will need to infuse your gin with cucumber first.

Simply place a third of a whole cucumber in a bottle of gin and let it sit for three days, then decant the gin into a fresh bottle or carafe, without the cucumber. Place the cucumber and mint in a cocktail tin and crush gently using a pestle to release their flavours. Add the rest of the ingredients, then some crushed ice. Mix well with a spoon, garnish with the cucumber and mint and serve in the tin.

Royalty bliss

6 fresh strawberries
25ml Dubonnet red vermouth
30ml gin
5ml rose liqueur
70ml ginger ale
1 strawberry, to garnish

Put the strawberries into a shaker and smash them gently with the help of a spoon. Add the Dubonnet, gin and the rose liqueur and shake for 15 seconds, then pour into a tumbler filled with ice cubes. Pour over the ginger ale, then stir the drink. Garnish with the strawberry and serve with a straw.

Raspberry cheesecake martini

8 raspberries
15ml raspberry Chambord liqueur
1 lemon twist
50ml vanilla vodka
15ml vanilla syrup
25ml double cream
5 tsp mascarpone cheese
1 raspberry, to garnish

Crush the raspberries with the Chambord liqueur in a chilled martini glass. Put all the remaining ingredients into a cocktail shaker filled with ice. Shake well, then strain into the glass and garnish with the raspberry.

Autumn flavours

Angel's wings

50ml Somerset apple brandy infused
  with fresh figs
10ml sugar syrup
10ml myrtille (blueberry) liqueur
2 drops of Angostura bitters
1 fresh fig, sliced
50ml soda water
fresh fig segment, to garnish

To make this cocktail you will need to infuse the apple brandy with figs first. Cut five figs into quarters, add to the brandy and leave to infuse for five days. Decant the brandy into a clean bottle or carafe, removing the figs first. Put all the ingredients into a cocktail shaker filled with ice. Shake well, then strain into a small tumbler and top up with soda water before garnishing with the fig segment.

Pumpkin bite

35ml pumpkin purée
50ml spiced rum
50ml cranberry juice
25ml ginger liqueur
6 gooseberries, to garnish

To make the pumpkin purée for this cocktail, simply peel, deseed and roughly chop half a pumpkin or butternut squash. Place in a preheated oven set at 200°C/Gas Mark 6, cover with foil and roast for about 45 minutes or until very soft. Transfer to a blender and blend until you have a smooth purée. Put all the ingredients into a cocktail shaker filled with ice. Shake well, then strain into an old-fashioned glass containing an ice cube and garnish with the gooseberries.

Ladies and gentlemen tipple

8 fresh mint leaves
50ml Cognac
35ml fresh apple juice
15ml sugar syrup
10ml fresh lemon juice
1 tsp marmalade
apple fan, to garnish
mint sprig, to garnish

Put all the ingredients into a cocktail shaker. Shake well, then pour into a long glass filled with crushed ice and garnish with apple fan and mint sprig.

Stinger II

50ml vodka
25ml white mint liqueur
25ml white chocolate liqueur
  (I use Mozart)
mint sprig, to garnish
4 squares dark chocolate, to serve

Put all the ingredients into a cocktail shaker. Shake well, then pour into an old-fashioned glass filled with crushed ice and garnish with the mint sprig. Serve with the chocolate, which you should eat while sipping the cocktail.

Winter flavours

Jingle bell

1 sugar cube
5ml mandarin juice
25ml Mandarine Napoleon Imperial
   Reserve liqueur
1 hibiscus flower
sparkling wine

Place the sugar cube in a champagne flute, then add the remaining ingredients in the order in which they're listed.

Sumptuous old-fashioned

50ml whisky infused with cinnamon
   and orange twist
1 sugar cube
5ml chocolate bitters
1 cocktail cherry
1 orange slice, cut from half an orange
orange twist, to garnish
1 cocktail cherry, to garnish
3 squares dark chocolate, to serve

To make this cocktail you will need to infuse the whisky first. Place four cinnamon sticks and six orange twists in a bottle of whisky and leave to infuse for two days. Decant the whisky into a clean bottle or carafe, removing the cinnamon and orange first. Place the sugar cube in an old-fashioned glass. Add the chocolate bitters to dampen it, then add the cherry and orange slice and crush together to release the fruit oils. Add plenty of ice cubes, pour in half the whisky and stir until a few ice cubes have melted, then add the rest of the whisky. Stir again until the glass is very cold, then garnish with the orange twist and cherry and enjoy the chocolate while sipping the cocktail.

Buckthorn elixir

15ml Aperol
35ml Penderyn Port Wood Finish
   whisky
15ml sea buckthorn juice
15ml grenadine
10ml fresh lemon juice
1 physalis, to garnish

Put all the ingredients into a cocktail shaker filled with ice. Shake well, then strain into a chilled old-fashioned glass containing an ice cube and garnish with the physalis.

Trifle

1 orange slice
3 cocktail cherries
25ml double cream
35ml Finlandia cranberry vodka
15ml Chambord raspberry liqueur
35ml Drambuie
mint sprig, to garnish
cocktail cherry, to garnish
orange slice, to garnish

Crush the orange slice and cocktail cherries with the double cream in an old-fashioned glass, then add crushed ice to the glass. Shake the rest of the ingredients over ice, then strain into the glass. Garnish with the mint, cherry and orange and serve with a spoon.

Unusual

Snappy bull dog

2 tsp parsnip purée
10ml sugar syrup
10ml fresh lemon juice
25ml apple juice
10ml rose liqueur
50ml cucumber gin (see page 305)
apple slice, to garnish
mint sprig, to garnish

To prepare the parsnip purée for this cocktail, simply peel one parsnip, steam until softened, then blend with 150ml apple juice. Put all the ingredients into a cocktail shaker. Shake well, then pour into an old-fashioned glass containing an ice cube and garnish with the apple and mint.

Market up beet

2 tsp beetroot purée
freshly ground black pepper, for the
    glass's rim
15ml maraschino liqueur
15ml tequila
10ml triple sec
pinch of ground cumin
5ml lime juice
100ml rosé sparkling wine
lime slice, to garnish

To prepare the beetroot purée for this cocktail, blend 50g ready-cooked beetroot with 20ml sugar syrup. Grind about a tablespoon of black pepper on to a small plate. Dampen the rim of a chilled champagne flute, then dip it in the pepper. Put all the ingredients except the sparkling wine into a cocktail shaker. Shake well, then strain into the champagne flute and top up with the sparkling wine, then garnish with the lime slice.

Whitechapel walk

35ml tequila
10ml smoked whisky
35ml tomato juice
15ml fresh orange juice
10ml fresh lemon juice
5ml British cassis
5ml ketchup
3 drops Tabasco green pepper sauce
rasher crispy bacon, to garnish
1/2 celery stick, to garnish

Put all the ingredients into a cocktail shaker. Shake well, then strain into a chilled martini or coupette glass and garnish with the bacon and celery.

Jingle bell, page 309

A note on our wines by Sergei Gubars General Manager, Roast

The fact that Roast's best selling white is English explains a great deal about our approach to wine. Made from a grape variety called Bacchus which creates crisp, citrus- and elderflower-scented wines not unlike a Sauvignon Blanc, the appeal is obvious – but it seemed a brave decision at the time putting our name on an English wine

Grapes have been grown across the southern half of the United Kingdom since Roman times but it's in the last 20 years that the English wine industry has really come on in leaps and bounds. There are now some 400 wineries dotted over the south of the country from Cornwall to Kent though there are vineyards as far north as Leeds and Lancashire.

But the big success story has been sparkling wine. The soil and climate in the south of England is very similar to that of the Champagne region in northern France so growers have by and large planted the same varieties – Pinot Noir, Pinot Meunier and Chardonnay that have had such success there. The results have been impressive. For sceptics who doubt that English sparkling wine can reach the heights of its French counterpart we made a video which showed that our customers marginally preferred our own Roast Chapter Two made for the restaurant by the Kent-based Chapel Down to champagne when they tasted it blind!

The style of English whites has changed too. Where the market was once dominated by dull-ish medium-dry whites made from obscure German grape varieties winemakers have turned to more fashionable crisp dry styles but still with appealingly low levels of alcohol. We even – goodness knows how in this weather – make appealingly soft fruity reds. The Union red we list in the restaurant is again a product of the enterprising Chapel Down with whom we have a long-standing relationship.

This 'locavore' approach to wine fits in with our philosophy of sourcing British ingredients, entirely appropriate for a restaurant situated inside London's most famous food market. The list, which has picked up an AA 'notable wine list' award, changes from season to season. In the spring and summer the focus is more on whites and lighter reds, in the autumn and winter, more on heartier ones.

Obviously it's not just British wines that are featured, however. The 411 bins are divided by grape variety and country, encompassing so called 'New World' wine producing countries such as Australia, California, New Zealand and South Africa as well as the classic wine producing areas of Europe. You can drink Croatian chardonnay as well as white burgundy, for instance (a tip – it's always worth going for the lesser known wines on a restaurant list. They'll be there on the grounds of exceptional quality not just their famous name) or Vidal ice wine from Canada as an alternative to Sauternes.

Surprisingly too it's not Cabernet or Pinot Noir but the lesser known Malbec grape that has been the most popular red especially since we launched our own-label Malbec which is made by the Argentinian winery Ruca Malen. Well, maybe not so surprising, given its generous, full-bodied character which fits in with all kinds of meat dishes. (Another tip – rare meat tames tannins which is why full-bodied reds are so good with beef and lamb). So enthusiastic has the Malbec following become that we celebrated a Malbec Week in spring 2013 including a dinner attended by the Argentinian ambassador.

Italy has been another great passion of mine and the Roast wine-buying team. The restaurant stocks a wide range of food-friendly Italian whites as well as great Italian reds such as Brunello and Barbaresco and always-in-demand Supertuscans There's also a selection of biodynamic wines made from vines cultivated without chemicals, treated with special composts and pruned and harvested following the phases of the moon – 'a supercharged system of organic farming' as I describe it on the list. Sounds crazy but it works!

When it comes to picking a wine to go with the recipes in the book it's worth choosing ones that reflect the time of year and the ingredients you're using, taking advice from a local wine merchant if you're lucky enough to have one nearby, just as you would from a local butcher or cheese shop.

It also helps to look at the way the dish is cooked rather than the base ingredient. The old rule of white wine with fish and red wine with meat is less useful than basing your choice on the temperature of the dish and way it's cooked. So cold dishes like salads or raw shellfish for example suit lighter wines (usually whites, admittedly, but you could serve a chilled red or rosé) while hot, roast or grilled foods need a more robust bottle with maybe a lick of oak. Accompaniments like sauces and flavourful vegetable side dishes will also make a dish richer and call for a more full-bodied wine – white or red.

Take one ingredient, lamb: if you were making the classic slow-roasted shoulder of Laverstock lamb with rosemary root vegetables (page 135), for example, that's a wine-friendly dish that would suit almost any medium to full-bodied oak-aged red like a Bordeaux whereas the barbecued fillet of lamb neck with a spelt, lemon and herb salad and cucumber yoghurt (page 132) would be better suited to a fresher fruitier red such as a young Syrah or even, given the preserved lemon and yoghurt, a crisp white like a Sauvignon Blanc.

Crumbed lambs' brains with a broad bean and caper salad (page 143) on the other hand would be better with an English sparkling wine (fizz is always great with fried food) while the warming Lancashire hotpot and pickled red cabbage (page 286) would be best matched by a pale ale. (It's always worth thinking about what would be drunk in the area the dish comes from.)

Speaking of beer, in keeping with our philosophy of sourcing British drinks, we also commissioned our own craft beers from Whitstable Brewery including an oyster stout that pairs fantastically well with oysters, a wheat beer (also great with seafood) and a hoppy East India Pale Ale – and our own whiskies, a 22 year old Bablair and a rare 26 y.o. Caperdonich Speyside single malt.

When you come to think about it – the occasional glass of vin rouge or vino apart – there's no reason not to drink British....

Index

Thank you

Firstly, enormous thanks go to my Mum for her support and enthusiasm for this project. I sent her every recipe, all of which she pre-edited and some of them she tested in her own kitchen at home on the Sunshine Coast in Australia.

Also to my second mother, Sharron for instilling in me a great respect for and interest in food. I don't think I would be cooking if it weren't for her.

To my beautiful wife Masha for her constant love and belief in me. She is my world and brings out the best in me.

For the support and encouragement from rest of my family: my dad and his wife Maggie, my brothers and sisters who also happen to be my best friends in the world – Scott, Jo, Nicky, Suny, Shahan and Jan.

To Iqbal Wahhab to whom I am greatly indebted to for the many doors he has opened for me and for his endless guidance and support. Much gratitude Iqbal.

Sergei Gubars, our tireless manager who does the work of at least three, and has been there beside me all the way since I started at Roast.

To Calum Franklin (Senior Sous Chef) and the rest of the kitchen team, for guiding the ship in my absence while I have been travelling and writing, and for your support in testing the recipes.

To the Roast front of house team. Thanks for your enthusiasm and thirst for knowledge.

To my previous head chefs and mentors, Dean Clure, Paul and Nicky Cogman, Bill Marchetti, Tim Hughes, Mark Hix and Kevin Gratton, for sharing your knowledge and skill.

Thanks to Jon Croft and Matt Inwood of Absolute Press for convincing me that I can actually write as well as cook!

Massive thanks to Lara Holmes, whose photography brings the book to life. Lara, it has been a great adventure and an absolute pleasure working with you.

To Adam Alexander and Roger Huyton for producing the short films linked to the book. Thanks for your patience and thank god for editing, the cutting room floor must look like a bombsite!

To Imogen Fortes for the mammoth task of editing my writing. Thanks so much for your patience and understanding.

As a theme running through the book, I wanted to emphasise the important relationship we have at Roast with our suppliers.

Ben and Silvy Weatherall. Ben, thanks for risking life and limb in putting a shotgun in my hands and for allowing me to realise my dream of shooting a grouse. Silvy, thanks for your wonderful hospitality and for your understanding after I had made such a mess of your beautiful kitchen.

To Guy and Juliet Grieve and their boys – a beautiful family in a beautiful part of the world! I'm in awe of your passion for your scallops and for the environment in which you dive for them.

To Fergus Howie of Wicks Manor. Thanks for a great day with your inquisitive pigs and for the quality and consistency of your products. Breakfast at Roast wouldn't be the same without them.

To Reg Johnson, your poultry is second to none. Here's to another 10 years of supply!

To Jody Sheckter and Stuart Busby of Laverstoke Park Farm. Thanks for the ' insightful tour of your unique farm and for great-tasting lamb and phenomenal British-produced buffalo mozzarella.

To Miles Irving. Thanks for opening my eyes to the forgotten bounty of wild produce we have all around us and for stoking the hunter-gatherer fire inside me.

To Simon Smith and Master Butcher Bob Spring of Aubrey Allen, for the educational tour of your facilities and supplying us with the best beef the UK has to offer.

And a huge thanks to all our other suppliers at Roast, in particular, Steve Grover, Darren North, Tony Booth, Steve Machon, Tim Croft, Charles Ashbridge and all at Neal's Yard we couldn't do what we do without you.